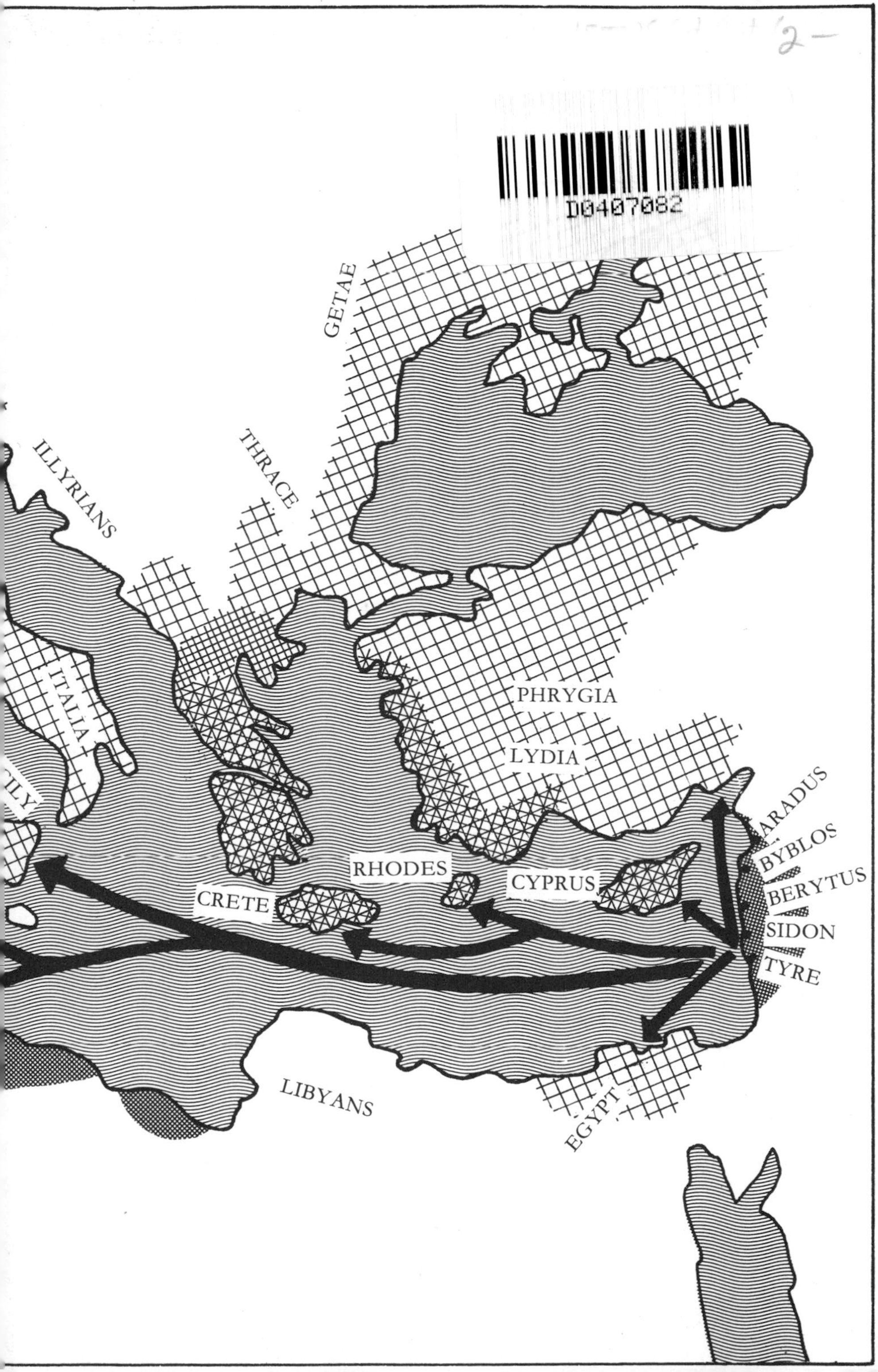

GETAE

ILLYRIANS

THRACE

ITALIA

PHRYGIA

LYDIA

RHODES

CRETE

CYPRUS

ARADUS

BYBLOS

BERYTUS

SIDON

TYRE

LIBYANS

EGYPT

The Phoenicians

THE PHOENICIANS

THE PURPLE EMPIRE
OF THE ANCIENT WORLD

GERHARD HERM

TRANSLATED BY
CAROLINE HILLIER

William Morrow and Company, Inc.
New York   1975

Library of Congress Catalog Card Number 75-10554

ISBN 0-688-02908-6

Printed in the United States of America.
1   2   3   4   5   79   78   77   76   75

Dedicated to my wife Christina

CONTENTS

ILLUSTRATIONS

Acknowledgments are due to the following for permission to reproduce photographs in this book: Bavaria Verlag, Gauting; Hirmer Fotoarchiv; Staatsbibliothek Berlin. Thirteen photographs have been taken from *Tyre through the Ages* by kind permission of the publishers, Dar el Machrey, Beirut, Lebanon.

The Phoenicians

CHAPTER I

The Bedouins of the Sea

THE DEATH SENTENCE was nobly spoken—in the form of a riddle.

A mole, Alexander the Great told his disconcerted generals, would show the inhabitants of Tyre 'that they too belonged to the mainland'. Then he added that this information had been given to him by the gods, in a dream.

But this last statement was merely part of the usual trappings, a precautionary measure. The young king did not want to risk being called mad by the honest swordsmen gathered in his tent. His announcement was the result of tortuous deliberation and of a complex train of events, but also threatened to present the army with a task which would demand little heroism and much sweat—and soldiers are known to prefer shedding blood to sweat.

However, Alexander finally convinced his officers. Whether they fully understood him, even then, is open to doubt. They may have agreed simply because they were in an angry mood. The Phoenician town of Tyre had affronted the King and his victorious army in the most shameful way, and the insult had to be avenged.

The events leading up to this curious general staff briefing were as follows:

The Macedonians, who had just beaten the Persian army at Issus, were preparing to march down the Syro-Lebanese coast from Eastern Anatolia to Egypt. Their route lay through the rich Phoenician city-states of Aradus, Byblos, Berytus, Sidon and Tyre. Each of these places had been asked, politely but firmly, to co-operate in a friendly way with the advancing army, the smaller towns with more firmness than politeness, the larger ones with extreme politeness, and Tyre most politely of all. Alexander's messengers had explained that he had no desire to take the town by storm, and that the King begged only that he might be allowed to make a sacrifice to their god Melqart in the chief temple. No one could deny that this was a modest request, particularly as the Greeks equated Melqart with their Heracles, and Heracles was held to be the mythical founder of the Macedonian dynasty. Alexander wanted to pay his respects to his ancestors, as it were.

It was hardly surprising that he should feel affronted at the reply of the Tyrian city elders. The latter had informed him coldly that they regretted they were not in a position to receive him within their city walls. If, however, he still wished to pay homage to Melqart, he could do so at an altar which they would gladly build for him on the coast.

It was a message of seemingly crashing arrogance and indescribable stupidity. One could dismiss a tiresome petitioner in this way, but not the leader of the most powerful army in the world at that time. One might also ask—and this first gave Alexander cause to ponder—why the Tyrians had considered it necessary to react in this way. Was it really only stupidity? The Macedonian couldn't believe so, because the Phoenicians were considered, even by the Greeks, as almost proverbially shrewd and cunning. Arrogance then? That seemed more likely, because they were also notorious for their pride. But that couldn't be the real explanation either, because even arrogant behaviour, if it wasn't founded in sheer stupidity, must have some other motivating factor.

Alexander, who had given proof more than once of a clear-sightedness compounded of intuition and intelligence, thought he could guess what the Tyrians' real motives were.

On the one hand, he had to assume that they didn't want to be drawn into the Persian-Macedonian conflict until it was clear which side would finally emerge victorious; a merchant-like over-cautiousness. On the other hand, however, and this lay at the root of their arrogance, they simply didn't believe that the King and his army constituted any real danger to them. The main part of Tyre lay on a heavily fortified island, which was separated from the outlying districts on the mainland by a channel roughly six hundred metres wide. On the shores of this giant divide Nebuchadnezzar II of Babylon had already had to admit in impotent rage that he was indeed in a position to storm strong citadels such as Jerusalem, but was unable to gain control of this comparatively small merchants' eyrie.

This is what must have led the Tyrians to reply to Alexander as they did. To base their actions on this past event must have seemed logical to them, since Nebuchadnezzar's army had been far larger than the Macedonian's. Yet it was not a fair comparison. Nebuchadnezzar had ruled by the grace of his armies; when they failed, he failed too. Whereas Alexander stood as the very personification of the power at his command, which meant that it was not his army which the Tyrians had to fear, but him himself. And he had seen through them.

The Phoenicians had always seemed rather uncanny and mysterious to the Mediterranean peoples, particularly to the Greeks. The Hellenes could not understand how this tiny race had succeeded in building up an empire which spread over almost the entire area between Gibraltar and the Lebanese coast, and it was all the more difficult to understand because their empire was so elusive. It was founded less on strong cities and great tracts of land than on a dense network of trading routes, whose only visible trace was the wake left by a fleet of fragile ships. There were, it was true, strongholds which served as staging-posts on some of these routes—unobtrusive, walled settlements, usually round a sheltered bay. One could see storehouses, barracks and watchtowers as one sailed past, the larger building where the commander of the town lived, and possibly a temple, but nothing which was at all comparable to a Greek trading city—no marble façades, pillars, or brightly painted statues of the gods.

In spite of this there was more treasure heaped in the storerooms of these drab trading headquarters than in the coffers of many a royal palace—or so the Greeks believed.

The inhabitants or owners of these bases were themselves a familiar sight. They could be seen in any port, and their oriental gestures and volubility and their thin, aquiline features were well known. But they were only known as types, which meant that hardly anything was in fact known about them. All that seemed certain was that they belonged to a different world from the Greeks. They were orientals, but within this wider category clearly made up a small, seemingly exclusive group, which operated according to its own obscure rules. The Phoenicians gave little away. They arrived, did their business, and disappeared again. They offered wares which could only be found in the holds of their ships, and sometimes let it be seen that they had travelled to lands where no Greek had yet set foot.

Their all-pervasiveness was particularly disconcerting. The cry of many a Greek captain upon sighting a new-found shore died on his lips, on discovering a Tyrian or Sidonian trading base hidden behind a rocky promontory. The Phoenicians had footholds on the Bosphorus, in Italy, in Sicily, on the Spanish and North African coasts. Their agents stood as counsellors behind the thrones of Egyptian rulers and whispered advice into the ears of Assyrian, Babylonian and Persian kings. They even had dealings with the equally foreign-seeming Etruscans. Wherever one went, it seemed impossible to shake them off. And finally the Greeks accepted the idea that they were involved in every conspiracy against them, no matter by whom it was hatched. Naturally they hated them for this reason, and worked off their hate in contemptuous mockery. But they feared them still more, because they could not understand them.

Probably even Alexander, with all his genius for intuitive insight, did not give himself time to understand them properly. But he saw through them—at least in one respect. He realized what it was which helped above all to give them their self-confidence and the conviction that they were different from others: their closeness to the sea.

Wherever they settled, even in the most prosperous and powerful towns on the Levant coast, the Phoenicians lived on the sea rather than on dry land. Their cities faced the sea and were sea-oriented. The land served merely as a base from which they could launch themselves into their true element. It seemed almost as if they mistrusted the firmness and finiteness of the earth, as if they did not believe in permanence and immutability. The changeableness of the sea, its dangers and its infiniteness, seemed to suit their concept of life better than the security the land offered them.

This attitude may have been instinctive to them, or may have stemmed from a mixture of wisdom and scepticism. It was certainly a sign of weakness, because men are not amphibians but creatures of the earth. Their existence is rooted in the ground, not in the sea. Anyone who tries to evade this truth is indulging in escapism.

This was exactly what Alexander perceived. On the sea and

in alliance with her the Tyrians were invincible—at any rate by the means he had at his command. But on *terra firma* they would be at a hopeless disadvantage. It was therefore a matter of normalizing the situation in which they had taken refuge and confronting them with reality, or as the King put it himself, reminding the city elders 'that they too belonged to the mainland'. Tyre must be robbed of its island character—by a causeway.

It was, as has already been noted, a complicated thought process, but it was logical and was followed by appropriate commands. Grumble as the army might, the mole was built. It still links Tyre to the Lebanese coast today.

Alexander's soldiers worked for seven months on its construction, then they threw aside their picks and took up their swords once more. In one of the most brutal attacks they had ever undertaken, the desperate resistance of the citizens was broken. The Tyrians made them pay for every square yard of ground with streams of blood, but the King's hunch paid off. Away from the water his opponents were like birds with their wings torn off, or magicians bereft of their magic hats. Now they had only the ordinary strength of ordinary men—and it was not enough.

But Alexander was not only taking a town, he was also destroying a myth and must have been fully conscious of the fact. Whereas he usually treated his prisoners fairly humanely, he made a hideous example of Tyre. Crosses were hewn for two thousand male citizens and set up along the shores of the island. Thirty thousand women, children and older people were sold into slavery. It was an act of vengeance, but it was also a calculated act. The world would learn that the Phoenician lords of the sea had been vanquished by him, the lord of the earth, and that there were no other demi-gods but the demi-god Alexander of Macedonia.

With the crucified Tyrians died the belief in the special nature of this race, which had been too small and too weak to realize its conception of itself on land and had therefore chosen the vast expanse of the sea as its living-quarters. Yet the myth which this people had thus started was nearly a thousand years old in 332 BC. The crucified men were paying for the realization of a dream conceived by a handful of Bedouins generations earlier. They—the Phoenicians—had come from the wilderness.

The origin of the seafaring people whom Alexander wiped from the pages of history may explain to a great extent why they later seemed outsiders amongst the Mediterranean peoples. When they originally settled in fixed towns the Phoenicians still behaved as if they were wandering nomads. Ships took the place of pack-animals, and trading bases in hidden bays became their new pasturing grounds. Even their mistrust of the rigidly ordered life of great cities was reminiscent of the anxiety felt by wandering herdsmen as they hurried past the settlements of more stable communities. Thus there is a parallel between their close connection with the sea and the life-style developed by their ancestors in the desert.

The desert, like the sea, is a world in which nothing can be regarded as permanent. Water-holes where cattle drank the autumn before may have completely dried up by the following spring. Sand-drifts fill whole valleys, rocks crumble away, and even mountains do not keep their shape for long. Only the sky is always there. By day the giant, eternally blue dome with its small fleck of molten brass emitting burning rays; by night the flickering compass points from whose course one can count the hours.

Nomads—as history has confirmed from time to time—adjust quite well to life at sea, once they have taken the decision to leave dry land. But before they do so, it is usually necessary for something to happen which completely destroys their pleasure in a land-based life. This applied to the people whom the Greeks later called *Phoinikes*. If their ancestors had been born water-rats, they could have taken the leap into the watery element from their old homeland. The waves of the Red Sea broke on the shores where they pastured their goats. But they remained on land.

The Phoenicians, or more exactly, the most important of the three peoples which later came to make up the Phoenician race, came, as far as we know, and we do not know very much, from Sinai. Their ancestors had perched amongst the clefts and crevices of the rocky peninsula between the Gulf of Suez and the Gulf of Aqaba. They were a poor, bedraggled lot, who often had nothing to be thankful for but the fact that they had got through another day without dying of hunger or thirst.

The descendants of this early people still live there, under much the same conditions. I visited one of them. He was called Salem.

Salem lives about eighty kilometres from the 'End of the World'. This is a bar in Eilat, the Israeli port on the Gulf of Aqaba. To see Salem, you need a guide and interpreter. Mine was called Alfonso Nussgruber and came from Zürich-Wollishofen.

As we set out, the dawn was only a glowing streak on the horizon. But a little later the great white ball of the sun burst through, and dispelled the blue night sky almost instantly. The light blazed in blinding cascades against the windscreen of our Land Rover. By this time we were already in the heart of the mountains. Alfonso was driving through a fantastic browny violet landscape.

The Sinai desert is not a desert in the classic sense of the word. There are no rolling sands as in the Sahara or endless stony slopes as in the Rub 'al Khali. Compared to them it seems almost idyllic: a plateau, with rifts running across it, surrounded by hills. The wadis are freshly green here and there, and there are even springs in the heart of steep valleys.

The journey to find Salem took about five hours. We finally drove round a hillock and there he sat: a bundle of rags, a friendly dark brown face, topped by a piece of torn white cloth which, if one was being polite, could be called a turban or head-dress. He was squatting in the shade of a pistachio tree by a smouldering fire, over which hung a tin can of tea. Nothing else—a man in an empty landscape.

But this first impression was deceptive. A wretched construction nearby, made of two or three sheets of corrugated iron, a few twigs, branches and stones, turned out to be his house. At first sight the shelter looked like a part of the landscape, or a pile of rubbish.

Our arrival didn't seem to surprise Salem in the least. He behaved as if people dropped by to drink tea with him every day. And he drank tea almost without a break. During the short time I was there, the can, which must have held four litres, was twice refilled. The water was kept in a beautiful unglazed pottery jug.

We began our conversation with the usual polite platitudes:

weather, health, the state of the route we had come by. Then I began asking him questions. I discovered that he had a wife and two children. Girls, alas! They were busy working at the moment. His wife was fetching water from a distant spring. His daughters were herding his fifteen goats. Salem himself had better things to do. He sat there, let the flies walk over his face and talked to his visitors. He was a stone-carver.

With little more than two strong carpenter's nails he made beautifully shaped hashish pipe bowls and other carved objects, from small pieces of limestone. His artistic skill had already won him a certain local fame—one day he will be discovered as a primitive artist. I had in fact come to see him because of his sculpture, but I only managed to lead the conversation round to it after three cups of tea. Salem lifted a corner of the piece of torn cloth on which he was sitting and drew out three of his works. They were remarkable pieces. The first was an idol, barely two inches high, with thick lips, great heavy-lidded eyes and pointed ears. It squatted with its knees drawn up to its chin and stared at me with an expression of calm disdain which I couldn't forget for a long time. The second was a car, or at least something which from a distance looked like a car. It had five wheels on the left and three on the right. The bodywork was elongated and almost stream-lined, with a boot half as long as the whole machine. The third of Salem's works I found the most moving: a ship, a simple boat shape with a high prow and stern, with a Bedouin in it, or rather the head of a Bedouin with a correctly shaped head-dress and an expression like that of the idol. He stared out indifferently and even a little scornfully from the prow of the boat, across a sea which Salem—I later learnt—had only seen once, when he had gone as far as the Gulf.

After the sixth or seventh cup of tea I bought the seafarer from him. He wanted five Israeli pounds for it, which was then about the equivalent of sixty pence and seemed very cheap to me. Alfonso said I'd been swindled, and that Salem and his family could live for nearly a week on five pounds; but it had probably taken him almost as long, with his primitive tools, to finish this small work of art.

When we took our leave, the Bedouin stood up for the first time, and I saw that he was quite short. He only just came up to my chin. The flies were still swarming over his face, which had kept its friendly expression all the time we were talking. He didn't seem to notice them. The hand he held out to me was hard and dry, but lay with a strange limpness in mine. There were two joints missing from his index finger. I thought Salem must be about forty to forty-five. When I said so to Alfonso, he laughed and replied that at forty-five the little Bedouin would be walking with a stick, and that he was thirty at the most, and probably even younger.

As we left I waved to Salem, and he returned the greeting with a suggestion of a bow. My last impression of him was: a man in an empty landscape, nothing else. A monument to unspeakable loneliness.

As we reached the head of the pass above the Gulf, the blue bowl of the night sky closed over us again; above us flickered those great lights, which we call stars.

Salem is only one of about five thousand Bedouins who live in Sinai today, all under more or less the same conditions. Their family groups seldom number more than fifteen. They do have a kind of tribal order, meet occasionally on feast days and festivals, and care for each other in an emergency, but as a rule they live for themselves, one in one corner of their vast land and one in another, and have done so for centuries.

How they see the world, what they hope, fear and believe, no one outside their circle can tell for certain. Officially they are Mohammedans. In fact they seem to follow a kind of nature religion which is older than Islam. The facial expression of Salem's idol can also be seen on African or Indian religious figures: it reflects a primeval fear and the desire to overcome it—and is thus a testimony to immense courage.

We have no yardstick by which to measure the standard of living of the Sinai Bedouins. Salem certainly lives well below what we would call the poverty line. His few goats provide him with milk and occasionally meat, the pistachio trees with nuts. For three of his pipes he gets the equivalent of a pound of meal, but on the other hand if one or more water-holes dry up it can prove fatal to him. In spite of this he does not seem to consider himself poor, and at least he is free. He has no passport, pays no taxes, does not have to do military service, is not bothered about Egyptians or Israelis and is not tied to any one place or confined by borders. Life as he lives it has its own quality, which cannot be compared with any other kind of existence. If he none the less dreams of heavenly pastures which are always green and fertile, where springs babble and sweet fruit grows on the trees, it is all part of the picture and must not be taken to mean that he is unhappy with his lot.

All this must have applied equally to the forebears of the Phoenicians. They were not the proud type of Bedouin which one meets in children's adventure stories; they did not live in tents hung with fine carpets, or travel from one oasis to another with great herds and mounted warriors. They were, like Salem, nomads herding small livestock, and did not have horses, which here in the Near East were only introduced as domestic animals during the second millennium BC, or camels, which were domesticated at about the same time. In the fourth millennium, the period to which one can trace back their history, there were neither. But quite apart from that they lived in total isolation, untouched by the events which were beginning to change the world at the time.

One thousand five hundred kilometres east of Sinai, in this same fourth millennium, the miracle occurred to which we owe practically the whole basis of our culture. Human civilization evolved on the hard ground of Lower Mesopotamia. Sturdy tillers of the soil, the so-called Ubaid peoples settled in the flat territory between the Tigris and the Euphrates, their round huts being in the main made from mud and straw.

Yet these were town-like communities, protected by fences and ramparts; and therefore, in a world in which such habitations were probably unknown, a sight to awaken fear and envy. They must have particularly struck the Semitic nomads of the southern desert lands as being places where life differed favourably in more than one respect from theirs. And thus it was that they were almost irresistibly drawn to the Ubaid culture, coming by night as marauding robbers, but also by day as peaceful trading partners. The result was a gradual reciprocal intermingling of two races and two ways of life, and this led to a new, more productive era.

The foundation stone of mankind's first real civilization was, it is true, only laid later, around the year 3,500 BC. At that time a new people migrated from Central Asia to Southern Mesopotamia—the round-headed Sumerians, who some historians believe to have come from India. Following the customs already instituted by the Ubaid people, these immigrants developed communities which only differed in detail from states as we know them today. From a stable religious order a political system developed, from small officials with their staffs of office a massive bureaucracy, from the early democratic institutions a temporary and then a permanent monarchy. A division of labour, the basis of all political economy, began to assert itself and small hamlets grew into vast towns, in the centre of which gigantic stepped temples, the so-called ziggurats, towered towards the sky.

The name of one of these great colonies is given in the Bible—it is 'Ur of the Chaldees', where Abraham was born. Ur is near Basra on the Persian Gulf. In the early 'twenties it was excavated by Sir Leonard Woolley, and was revealed as having been built on a magnificent scale. The richer inhabitants of Ur lived in solidly built villas of thirteen or fourteen rooms. They walked on broad, well-paved streets, divided up the day into twenty-four hours of sixty minutes or 3,600 seconds, could read and write, had trouble with their tax returns, could extract square or cubic roots and were concerned with literature.

For nearly two hundred years Ur was the capital of a commonwealth which could be called the Sumerian Empire. Then it had to cede its place to the newly arisen, westerly-lying Akkad, whose ruler, Sargon I, one of the most notable figures of the ancient world, was not a Sumerian but a Semite. He was typical of the desert people who from the earliest times had tried to infiltrate into the man-made paradise between the Tigris and the Euphrates.

The Empire which rose to power under Sargon dwindled in importance again after his death in 2,300 BC. The Semites, however, with their hunger for better living conditions, remained one of the most important factors in the evolution of all the states which developed in the territory opened up by the Sumerians.

Much the same can be said of the other great cultural centre of the ancient world which flowered in the Nile Valley. The Egyptian state was founded under much more favourable conditions than

the Sumerian. Its wealth lay in the fertile mud which was thrown
up onto the fields by regularly recurring floods. In the Old
Stone Age there had already been tillers of the soil here, of a kind
similar to the Ubaid peoples, who had developed their primitive
cultures, known in the history books as Badarian, Merimdean
and Naqada. But a state evolved from these at approximately
the same time as the Sumerian Empire, in about 3,000 BC—the
Old Kingdom. The various stages of its development were
almost identical to those of the Sumerian state: from mud-hut
villages to towns, from an assembly of the people to a kingdom
and bureaucracy, from illiteracy to hieroglyph script, from diverse
religious cults to a single religion, with a Sun god at its centre.

The capital of the Old Kingdom was Men-Nefer which the
Greeks called Memphis. It lay on the left bank of the Nile,
above present-day Cairo, and presented a living contrast to the
greatest necropolis the world has seen, the pyramids of Gizeh,
Abusir, Saqqara and Dahshur. Like Ur and Agade, Memphis
was a glittering city of untold splendour, an unrivalled centre of
civilization; although it had the disadvantage, like Sumeria and
Akkad, of lying in the midst of lands which could hardly have
been more ill-disposed or envious. To the west of the Nile
Valley stretched the vast Libyan desert full of marauding tribes,
to the east a no less unfriendly plateau and, adjoining that, the
Sinai peninsula with its wandering nomads.

To counter this ever-present threat, it was necessary for the
Egyptians to extend military operations far beyond the line now
marked by the Suez canal, and this they did not fail to do. They
safeguarded the Isthmus of Suez itself by means of the Wall of
the Prince, one of the world's first iron curtains, of which a
priest wrote in about 2,650 BC: 'The Wall of the Prince is being
built, to keep the Asians out of Egypt.' Beyond this fortification
were Egyptian outposts which commanded the whole Red Sea
coast of the Sinai peninsula, and in particular the southern tip
with its rich copper and jewel mines. And the pharaohs had
also extended their influence over a large part of Palestine and
the Lebanon. But for the Bedouins this was an obstacle which
the strongest of the tribes could overcome at any time.

The Semites were, and remained, just as much of a threat to
the Nile kingdom as they were to the states of Lower Mesopotamia.

Who in fact were the Semites? History, which is not a very exact science, simplifies matters considerably. It lumps together under this collective name all the major races which from 3,500 BC onwards emigrated from the deserts of Arabia towards the flourishing civilizations of the Nile and Euphrates. Thus the Akkadians who occupied Sumeria are called Semites, and also the later founders of the Assyrian and Babylonian empires. But the Aramaeans who settled in Syria were also Semites, as were the Jews, who would cling so stubbornly to Palestine, and of course their present-day enemies the Arabs.

What seems to have distinguished these peoples as a single group was not so much particular racial characteristics (such as a hooked nose) as their speech—a language rich in guttural and palatal sounds which was common to most of them. But even this cannot be proved with any certainty, as the early nomad tribes did not leave any written evidence in corroboration.

So there remains the vague category, a name taken from the Pentateuch, or table of the nations. There all the tribes known to the authors were traced back to three forefathers, Noah's sons.

Shem, the eldest, was promoted in eighteenth-century Europe as the founder of the Semites; Ham, the second son, was said to be the father of the Hamites, and Japheth was held responsible for the Japhetic race, the peoples of Asia Minor. It was a fairly arbitrary ruling, which has no logical foundation, as the following point illustrates: Canaan and Sidon, two symbolical figures connected with Phoenicia, were held to be descendants of Ham. But the Phoenicians, according to the above, were not Hamites but Semites.

It follows that the concept of a Semitic race was quite unknown to the inhabitants of the Nile Valley and the Mesopotamian states. They probably did not even realize that the attacks from all these desert tribes represented an historical process which we today regard as one of many migrations of peoples. For them the Bedouins must have been simply underprivileged hordes who pushed on eagerly towards the places where there was the greatest concentration of wealth, lured on by rumours of the 'fleshpots of Egypt'. They were driven to do so by the pressure of population in their own land.

Strangely, deserts seem to make good incubators for the human race. The great migratory movements have always sprung from corners of the earth which seemed to be far too unfriendly to life to produce a population overspill. The Mongols came from the Gobi Desert, the Germanic race—probably— from the marshes of Central Russia, and the Semites from the arid area between Sinai and the highland rim of the south coast of Arabia. And they came, seemingly, not because they were tired of their life of freedom in the wilderness, but simply because there was no longer enough room for them in these apparently limitless spaces to live their life in their accustomed manner.

Admittedly there is a certain logic in this process. An area with little pastureland is used up more quickly than great stretches of fertile country, and few water-holes are emptied more quickly than abundant streams and rivers. In the desert a comparatively small increase in the number of people to feed can affect the normal balance of supply and demand of foodstuffs so drastically, that whole groups and tribes are threatened with starvation. If this happens, however, and the population has grown during previous peaceful years, then—one might almost say according to the usual cycle of stagnation and growth—there is a fight for the surplus land in the course of which weaker groups are pushed out or strong, enterprising ones decide to seek their luck elsewhere, and consequently emigrate.

The Bible, which describes migrations of this sort made by the Bedouin tribes, gives a brief but vivid account of the circumstances in which they took place.

The Jews, when they were still weak, made a covenant with Abimelech, King of Gerar in the Negev, which allowed them to dig a well at Beer-Sheba where their cattle could drink in peace. But later, when they came down as a united nation from the mountains of Jordan, they rarely attempted to make covenants, and slew the inhabitants 'with the edge of the sword, utterly destroying them'. The biographer of their leader Joshua became enthusiastic about this description and repeated it again and again as an almost identical refrain.

Both methods—covenants when they were weak and brutal attacks when they were strong—are typical of the advance of the desert tribes into the areas of the so-called Fertile Crescent, the lands on the eastern shores of the Mediterranean and in the Tigris-Euphrates basin. In the course of two thousand years they gave this area its Semitic character, which it still has today.

The most important event in this continual migratory process was the 'Amorite Invasion', which took place some time between 2,300 and 2,000 BC. The name Amurite or Amorite is Babylonian in origin. It is derived from '*Amurru*', western land, which suggests that the races of this name moved in from the Mediterranean coast to Mesopotamia.

In about the year 2,000 they conquered or infiltrated Sargon I's Akkadian Empire and founded successive dynasties, from one of which sprang the Hammurabi who founded modern law with the Codex named after him, and who made the small town of Bab-ili, the 'Gate of God', one of the most famous the world has known. Bab-ili became Babylon.

But the Amorites had not only swept into Mesopotamia. A small number of them had stayed behind during the long migration and had made a home for themselves on the Mediterranean coast, in Palestine and what was to become Phoenicia. They were the Canaanites. The word means either the low, that is to say the lowland, people, or if it comes from the Akkadian word *kinahhu*—purple—the red people. If the latter is the case these, newcomers must have been called by the name under which they later became famous from a very early date. The Greek word *Phoinikes* can also be translated as 'the people from the purple land' or more simply 'the red people'. At all events the Phoenicians themselves usually called themselves Canaanites—even at the time when Alexander took Tyre.

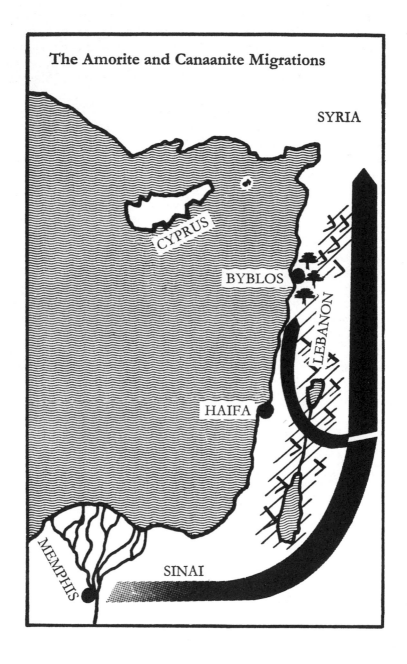

The Amorite and Canaanite Migrations

SYRIA

CYPRUS

BYBLOS

LEBANON

HAIFA

MEMPHIS

SINAI

CHAPTER II

The City in the Cedar Grove

MODERN HISTORICAL RESEARCH only discovered the Phoenicians at a fairly late date. The credit for putting historians on the right track belongs to Napoleon III, who instigated research during one of his military campaigns.

In 1860, the Druzes, the members of an obscure Mohammedan sect, perpetrated a massacre in the then Turkish Syria, killing thirty thousand of their Christian compatriots, the Maronites. Europe was outraged when the news reached the headlines. The Sultan in Constantinople despatched an army unit, with orders to make the embattled religious factions see sense, and Napoleon thought he saw an opportunity of shaking off the shadow of his famous uncle by launching a campaign in the style of the great Bonaparte. He too sent an expeditionary force to the crisis area. But he needed more than soldiers to carry out his grandiose plan. Had not the Corsican also taken a great staff of scholars with him on the Nile Campaign, whose findings and research had later opened up the scientific study of Egyptian culture and history? So his nephew decided to do the same for the history of Phoenicia. He instructed the orientalist Ernest Renan to accompany the expedition.

Renan, who later won world-wide acclaim for his biography of Christ, *Vie de Jésus*, was then, although he was already forty-seven, only at the beginning of his career. He had written a comparative study of Semitic languages and was working on a history of early Christianity. He was especially interested in one town in Phoenicia—Byblos.

It is easy to see why he made this choice. Bublos or Byblos was not only the name of a great Phoenician community, *byblos* was also the Greek word for papyrus, or writing material. From it came the later word *biblion,* book, and thus our name for the greatest book of all, with which Renan was so preoccupied. Byblos was also mentioned by its Semitic name of Gebal in the Old Testament (for example in Ezekiel 27:9). So the Frenchman probably hoped to unearth material there that would help him in his current work.

The hope was not justified. What he found was at first disappointing. Forty-one kilometres north of Beirut, on the spot where Byblos had once flourished, was a wretched Arab dump called Gebeil. Above it towered the ruins of a mighty crusader's castle, and it had a fine oval harbour, but otherwise nothing to show that it had once been a Phoenician trading centre.

Renan, who was allowed free access by the French and Turkish soldiers, was not discouraged. He combed every square yard of the fields, gardens and backyards—a laborious task. The khamsin arrived, the meteorological convector which carries the heat of Arabia to the Mediterranean several times a year. The inhabitants of Gebeil proved to be suspicious, anxious and far from helpful. But finally his work did bear fruit. Granite columns were found in the crusader's castle. Stone slabs with Egyptian hieroglyphs cut in them were embedded in the walls of houses. The most important find he made was the bas-relief of a goddess, with cow's horns and the sun disc on her head. The Frenchman thought she was the Egyptian goddess Hathor, but he was wrong. Today we know that this is the image of Baalat-Gebal, the Phoenician queen of heaven or earth-mother. She is to be seen in the Louvre.

Apart from this one object Renan did not discover much of value in Gebeil, nor did he find anything in the neighbourhood very relevant to his study of the Bible. This was in the main because the old Byblos lay buried under modern Gebeil. But also because the inhabitants had not hesitated to use the ancient ruins as quarries. If they needed lime, they threw marble columns into their kilns—there were enough of them lying around. And if they found some antique pieces while sinking a well or tank, there was usually an antique dealer at hand to buy them cheaply on the quiet and flog them elsewhere. The scholar could only sigh: 'One seldom sees more clearly than here how the limited curiosity of the amateur archaeologist can work against the wider curiosity of a scientific scholar.' Then—the Druze revolt had in the meantime been bloodily suppressed—he returned to Paris.

There he collated the results of his research in a small work, thus helping to give Napoleon III, under whose patronage the discoveries had been made, the credit for having opened up the practical study of Phoenician history.

Renan's work was only continued more than fifty years after the massacre of the Maronites—once again by a Frenchman.

In 1919 the Egyptologist Pierre Montet came to Gebeil and was amazed to find a great number of the hieroglyphic tablets which Renan had described in his account *Mission de Phénicie* still there. In 1921 he returned a second time to look more carefully into this phenomenon. And Byblos was now attacked with spades.

For three years Montet's assistants and workers burrowed through every bit of open ground between the Gebeilites' houses. They found, among other things, a series of alabaster fragments with the engraved seals of pharaohs from various Egyptian dynasties, which seemed to indicate that there had been close trading and cultural links between Byblos and the Nile Kingdom.

But the rediscovery of the ancient trading centre had only just begun. The French owed the find which would turn the small town into an archaeological sensation of the first order, to luck rather than archaeological flair. On a spring day in 1922 they were woken from sleep by excited Arab workers and taken to the cliffs south of the port of Gebeil, where rain during the night had caused a landslide. A large piece of ground had slipped twelve metres downwards. In the declivity thus revealed there was a small cave, which looked very much as if it had been made by human hands rather than by nature, a burial chamber.

However, what really threw the archaeologists into ecstasies was the fact that the chamber was not empty. It contained a vast stone sarcophagus and a large number of funerary offerings, which lay strewn on the ground round it. Moreover, it opened on to further, similar burial chambers. Montet and his assistants discovered nine large tombs altogether in the course of the next few weeks, two of which were linked by an underground passage. All gave evidence of the same methods of construction. Steep shafts, full of earth and ashes, led vertically downwards, then broadened out sideways in each case to form a hollow space in which the sarcophagus could be placed.

It was a discovery which made the experts all over the world

sit up, and the princes' sarcophagi are still of outstanding importance today.

Naturally this necropolis had not been left undisturbed. Four
of the graves had already been discovered and robbed in the
distant past. In the fifth was a piece of paper with English words
scribbled on it, which bore the date 1851. Yet the searchers could
congratulate themselves. They unearthed treasure of incalculable
value: obsidian vases set with gold, silver sandals and silver
vessels, which, because of their shape, they called 'teapots', a
silver looking-glass, a gold breastplate engraved with a flying
falcon and the figures of two seated pharaohs. Also bronze and
pottery jugs, copper tridents and bones.

The most significant of all the objects they found was, however,
one of the three sarcophagi from grave number five. It was
different from the others in both size and shape. Most of these
containers for royal corpses were just simple caskets of polished
limestone, but this one had skilfully executed reliefs on all four
sides, showing walking and sitting figures with decorative
borders of a Lotus-flower pattern above and projecting lions'
heads at the four lower corners.

And then it began to speak. When its lid had been cleared of
earth and dirt, a one-line inscription could be seen on the side,
in Phoenician alphabetic script. It gave the name of the man who
lay in the coffin. 'This coffin,' they deciphered, 'was made by
Ithobaal, the son of Ahiram, King of Byblos, as the eternal
resting place for his father. If any ruler or governor or general
attacks Byblos and touches this coffin, his sceptre will be broken,
his throne will be overthrown and peace will forsake Byblos.
And as for himself: may vandals look upon his epigraph.'

Under the Egyptian rubble the Phoenicians, whom they had
hoped to find at Byblos, had made a sudden and unexpected
appearance. It was an entrance in the grand, almost imperial
manner. These were no petty magistrates speaking, but mighty,
confident rulers.

Now that they were hot on the scent of the Phoenicians, excavations in Byblos were energetically pursued during the years
which followed. In 1930 the French mandatory powers in the
Lebanon bought up all the houses which had hindered the
progress of the archaeologists and had them pulled down.

Large-scale searches could then be made over an extensive area. M. Dunand, Montet's successor, made full use of the opportunity. He dug down through various historical levels to Bronze Age remains and in so doing also unearthed evidence that the place which was later called Byblos and Gebeil had already been occupied in the Old Stone Age, which made it one of the oldest permanently occupied settlements in the world.

The Lebanese tourist industry—which is extremely active—has altered this to *the* oldest town in the world, and loses no opportunity of drawing attention to its historical traditions. It can only be proved that in about 4,500 BC something like a large village arose in a spot situated above the present-day port of Gebeil. It consisted of primitive huts made of branches, the walls and roofs daubed with mud and the floors covered with limestone grit.

A thousand years later the houses were already a bit more solidly constructed. They had strong walls and a roof-ridge. Their owners used bronze implements in place of the old flint adzes and knew how to use a potter's wheel. And in about 2,900 stone buildings replaced the wooden ones. Byblos had become a town. It was not particularly small and by no means insignificant. A wall with two entrances, the land and sea gateways, surrounded the whole community. The streets ran concentrically to the centre of the town. A canal system carried rain and drainage water away. These amenities and the rich funerary offerings from the period indicate that the inhabitants of Byblos of the day were quite well-to-do, prosperous in fact, and prepared to defend their possessions if the need should arise.

In about 2,300 such a catastrophe seems to have occurred. In the temple of Baalat, which Dunand also excavated, there are signs that the building was destroyed by force or burnt. It is not difficult to guess who was responsible for the disaster. Some time between 2,300 and 2,100 the Canaanites descended on the land at the foot of Mount Lebanon. The nomad hordes from the Sinai desert were pressing forward, to win themselves a new home by fire and sword. One can imagine that they were not too squeamish as to the methods they used. Byblos can hardly have been in a better state to withstand them than the almost equally old Jericho was to withstand the Israelite invasion from the wilderness under Joshua about a thousand years later.

The taking of Byblos links two chains of events which until then had developed simultaneously along separate courses. Semitic Bedouins, a people with no history, but who had nevertheless seen several thousand years of development, joined up with the Giblites—as the inhabitants of the old Byblos were called—who could also look back on a long history and who had fashioned their own culture from fragments of the civilizations of other races. Now the two together formed a new race, and historians today are still uncertain whether these were the Phoenicians, whether their history began some time between 2,300 and 2,100 with the burning of a town and a temple.

Opinions on this differ widely, and have done since a very early date. The Greeks Herodotus and Strabo, the Romans Pliny and Justin all seem to have been more or less convinced that the Phoenicians came from the desert as a complete people, so to speak, with their own way of life and civilization, and established themselves on the Mediterranean coast in order to continue living there in the way they had always done. More recently historians such as Otto Eissfeldt and Georges Contenau have disputed the origins of this race at length, but have also to a greater or lesser extent based their theories on the fact that tribes with their own individual character left their homeland one day to settle elsewhere, as the Goths and Turks did later.

But all these theories are not only impossible to prove, they are also, in the light of new discoveries, so inconclusive that Sabatino Moscati, the present pontiff of Phoenician studies, can dismiss them with a wave of the hand. 'The formation of the Phoenician nation . . .' he writes, '. . . seems to result from an historical evolution in the Syro-Palestinian area, and not a migration of people from outside.' In other words: the Phoenicians did not come from somewhere else to settle down here, as an old race in a new country; they developed their identity here.

Byblos and the narrow strip of land at the foot of Mount Lebanon were a melting-pot in which, after several greater and lesser migratory influxes, the strange race of traders which later so fascinated the Greeks was shaped. In this centuries-long process, then, the Amorite-Canaanite migration is only of particular significance because it brought more than the average number of immigrants into the country and therefore accentuated the general process of formation.

Most probably the Giblites as a race were not distinguished by any great individuality either, but equally the product of miscegenation. In any case the first migration into their territory of which there is archaeological proof occurs in the year 3,500 BC, and these people, who introduced them to bronze, were certainly not the first with whom they had had to deal, nor were the Canaanites the last. Taking a more general view, this eternal migration from the wilderness is still going on today. It can be studied as a living phenomenon.

You can see nomad camps on the outskirts of any large town in the Near East, from Jerusalem and Amman to Baghdad. The inhabitants stand silent and humble in the shade of their black woollen tents amidst the derisive bleating of their goats. But at some point the first of them takes a step into the new world, hires himself out as a porter, messenger, or well-cleaner and the next man follows in his footsteps. He himself still dies in the squalor of a tin hut, but his son will possibly have a small business, and his grandson will be an accepted citizen. The Jordanians describe this silent infiltration with the neat phrase: from house servant to house steward to house owner.

In old Byblos, which was then still called Gubal, Gebal or Gabal—it was written *Kpny*—they may have used a similar phrase for the process. At any rate this kind of infiltration must have been common enough.

Byblos lay at the end of a coastal strip which it is comparatively easy to cross (both an advantage and a disadvantage) beginning in the south just behind Acre in modern Israel and running along the foot of the mountains. By the mouth of the Nahr al-Kalb, about fifteen kilometres north of Beirut, a massive rock formation blocks the way for the first time. But this obstacle is not insuperable and then the way is reasonably free again as far as Byblos. On the other side of the port the mountains come right down to the sea again, which was why the immigrants from the south mostly halted there or settled down exhausted. Byblos was an end point for many of the wanderers. More powerful bands, like the Canaanites, occupied it straight away.

Whether the history of the Phoenicians really began with this invasion remains a question over which opinions still differ, because, as has already been pointed out, further immigration occurred, and the transformation process did not end there. It is just as possible to answer the question with a 'no' as with a 'yes'. Admittedly a 'yes' would simplify the whole matter. So let us say at least that the early history of this people began with the Amorite-Canaanitish migratory influx. There were no Phoenicians in the second millennium before Christ, but there may have been Proto-Phoenicians.

So there they were, the tough, hungry, goatherd sons of the desert from Sinai. The surroundings in which they found themselves could hardly have seemed stranger. Instead of the usual bare plateau were steep slopes abundantly covered with firs, cypresses and cedars, with snow-covered two- to three-thousand-metre peaks towering beyond. Instead of the dry wadis, racing mountain streams; instead of the bare land, fertile fields and gardens in which figs and olives grew. And a climate in which corn ripened by May, together with an abundance of game to hunt, from panther and bear to wild sheep. It must have made an impact on them that was both confusing and overpowering.

They did not know then that it was just this combination of sea and wood that would shape their future history in their new land, but they soon came to realize it. Byblos was a lumber camp. In one of the earliest written documents pertaining to its history, called the 'Palermo Stone', there is mention of its timber trade. At a date between 2,650 and 2,600 BC Senefru of Egypt had an account written on a piece of diorite that was found in Egypt and is now in the Sicilian capital, of how he had 'forty shiploads of cedar wood' carried 'from the town at Mount Lebanon', and three ships made from it, an '*Adoration of the Two Lands* ship and from *meru*-wood two ships'. Besides which he had the 'doors of the royal palace made from cedarwood'.

The Lebanon was called the 'Plateau of Cedars' by the Egyptians, and its people lived mainly from the export of the great trees which grew on their doorstep. It was a gilt-edged industry, because wood, particularly building timber, was already at that date a distinctly scarce commodity in the sparsely wooded Near East. Even in the well-irrigated Egypt there were mostly only acacia trees and oil palms, and nothing from which to cut long beams, for example, for the roof-trees of large houses. It was hardly surprising therefore that long before the foundation of the

Old Kingdom the inhabitants of the Nile banks had sent expeditions
to the Sudan, where there was gold, and to the Sinai peninsula,
whose mountains were rich in copper and turquoise, but particularly to the Lebanon with its vast woods. They found the cedars
there especially to their liking. Which was also hardly surprising.

The cedar, or more exactly, the particular species of the
Pinaceae conifer family (*Cedrus libani*) which grows only on some
of the coastal mountains round the Mediterranean, is not only
a useful but also a very spectacular tree. In open country it can
grow to forty metres in height and four metres in width. Its
branches tend to twist in a grotesque way, but grow outwards
to form a flat, often almost symmetrical, pagoda roof. The
Lebanese Republic shows them thus in outline on its flag. If
you climb a cedar tree, you are lost in a small universe of tangled
twigs and shadows. On hot days an almost stupefying bitter-
sweet smell blows round you there; this fragrance was another
factor which made the tree so valuable to the Egyptians. As well
as building-timber from its fine wood they also got a thick,
balmy oil, which was light-brown in colour; cloths soaked in
this were used to bind the bodies of their mummified kings.

Because of this practice the Lebanese trade became more than
an exchange of raw materials and took on the quality of a cult.
Expeditions to the mountainous country were half business
undertakings, half pilgrimages. Besides going there to make
money, they came as messengers from their own gods to the
oil-dispensing Baalat of Byblos—which greatly enhanced the
town's importance. On top of this, in the first instance contacts
were in general made with the temple rather than with the commercial and state institutions. Every worldly action was the
manifestation of a divine disposition. In such cases there is
thus beyond the exchange of material goods an exchange of
immaterial things, representing a mutual interchange of ideas
which breaks through all barriers. In this respect there is little
doubt that the Giblites, at least in the early days, received more
than they gave. They wore Egyptian dress, adorned themselves
with Egyptian jewels, used the hieroglyph script which had
been developed on the Nile, and gave their Baalat the outward
appearance of the Egyptian Hathor-Isis, which was why Renan
made an incorrect interpretation of the relief he found.

An account dating back to the Egyptian Middle Kingdom, which arose in about 2,052 BC as the Old Kingdom disintegrated, illustrates this close relationship between Canaan and the Nile country in an attractive literary text: the *Tale of Sinuhe*.

The hero of this story was a high-ranking official in the entourage of the Princess Nefru at the court of Thebes, in about 1,971 BC; a courtier, like many another, well dressed and living in luxury. But the path he trod was a slippery one, and led to his downfall. When Nefru's father, Amenemhet I, died, there was evidently a series of intrigues as to the succession, in which he was involved. He obviously backed the wrong horse, because when Sesostris I came to the throne he felt his position to be so precarious that he decided the only way to save his skin was to flee.

He stole away from the royal palace in darkness, and slipped across the 'iron curtain' of the Egyptian kingdom, the Wall of the Prince, to Sinai. 'I ducked down behind a bush, because I feared the sentries on guard could see me,' he writes. It was not until evening that he succeeded in passing the barrier and staggering across into the sandy no-man's-land. 'My throat was burning, and I said to myself: "This is how death tastes."'

But he was lucky. He met a wandering tribe of Bedouins. 'Their leader, who had been in Egypt, recognized me. He gave me water and warm milk to drink.' The courtier Sinuhe was saved for the time being, but still far from safe. Most of Sinai was controlled by Egyptian troops.

He therefore continued his flight northwards as soon as possible. 'I passed from one country to another,' he wrote. 'Finally I came to Byblos.' He had chosen the route which all the refugees from the south took, along the coast of Palestine to the mountains. When they reached Byblos they went no farther.

Sinuhe, a well-educated member of the upper classes, probably knew the trading port well. He could not stay in a place teeming with Egyptians any more than he could remain at Thebes; but he did succeed in making a useful contact there. 'I went,' he continues in his account, 'to Qedem and remained there for a year and a half. Then Ammi-enshi, the chief of the upper Retenu, took me in. He said, "You will be safe here with me; we even speak your language." He said that because he knew who I was. Egyptians who had passed through had told him about me.'

Sinuhe's description becomes a little vague here. Qedem is simply a Semitic term for the east, and the Egyptians used the name upper Retenu for the whole of the Lebanese-Palestinian uplands. However, as he had gone from Byblos towards the east, one can take it that he reached the El-Bika valley, the vast basin between Mount Lebanon and the Anti-Lebanon mountains, and that he joined up with one of the immigrant tribes of Semites who had become farmers rather than townsmen and traders. At all events, he called the specific area where he now lived Yaa, and describes it as a miniature paradise: 'There were figs and grapes and more wine than water. There was an abundance of honey, and oil. All kinds of fruit grew on the trees. There was wheat and barley and many herds of cattle.'

Ammi-enshi, who probably attributed a higher political market-value to Sinuhe than the nervous refugee did himself, treated him like a royal guest. 'He made me the leader of a tribe in the best part of his country. I had my fill of bread, and cooked meat, roast geese and wild game, which they caught for me in snares.' Finally the prince also gave him his eldest daughter in marriage. 'Thus I spent many years there, and my children became strong men, respected by all.'

But as his spirits revived, Sinuhe once more became pre-occupied with his old ideas. He made tentative contacts with Thebes and sought to make his name known there again. 'The messenger, who was on his way from Egypt to the north, stayed with me; I made everyone welcome.'

His cautious approach gradually bore fruit. Sesostris I was prepared to forget the past and received him graciously. 'It is not right,' he wrote to him, 'that you should die in a foreign country, that Asiatics should bury you and that you should be wrapped in sheepskins.' Which was exactly what Sinuhe had hoped to hear.

Accompanied by the warriors of his tribe, the émigré returned to the Egyptian border fortress. Shortly afterwards he was received in the capital like a long-lost son. With back-slapping joviality he said, '"Greetings, O Queen"—probably Sinuhe's old mistress, following the Egyptian custom, had married her brother—"Behold Sinuhe, who returns in the guise of an Asiatic and has become a Bedouin." She gave a loud cry and the royal children screamed in chorus.'

In a word, the perfect happy ending. The prodigal was made court chamberlain. 'They wiped out the years, which had scored my body. The foreign mud was washed from me and the rough garments of the desert dwellers taken away. I was wrapped in robes of fine linen and anointed with the best oil in the land. I slept in a bed once more.' In addition the Pharaoh had a pyramid built for him and assigned priests to him who would prepare him for death. 'Thus I lived in the king's favour, until the day of my departure came.'

Sinuhe tells his tale from beyond the grave. His account is an adventure story decked out with all the elements of a fairy-tale, and gives no indication as to whether his experiences were true or not. One thing is certain, however; the author was thoroughly acquainted with conditions in the mountain country of Canaan and describes them with the utmost accuracy.

We can therefore deduce from his story that Byblos was indeed an important trading centre on the borders of the Egyptian sphere of influence, that behind it lay rich agricultural land, the inhabitants of which doubtless also brought their produce to sell in its markets, and that it was a territory that held, for the Egyptians, a fascination similar to that of the Western frontier country for nineteenth-century Americans. You could do well out there, have adventures and prove yourself a man, but all this meant nothing unless you returned one day as the rich uncle from overseas, to enjoy your fame and riches in the civilized home country.

Sinuhe's story was an out-and-out bestseller. It was copied many times and possibly even influenced the Bible. In the Fifth Book of Moses the land of Canaan is described in the same terms as in this early yarn of the wild west about a man who went out to conquer his fear.

CHAPTER III

The Coming of the Aryans

IT SEEMS FROM what we know that the links between Egypt and Byblos continued to be close, and profitable to both sides, for about a century and a half. But after that, in about 1,600 BC, the first dark cloud appeared to disturb this sunny relationship. In Thebes, the capital of the Middle Kingdom, the timber suppliers of the Lebanon were execrated. In the most literal sense of the word.

The Egyptian diplomats, who otherwise used methods very similar to those of present-day foreign ministers, occasionally thought that they ought to use magic to further their ends. For this their preferred technique was one which is still surreptitiously practised in civilized society—black magic. It is a simple process: you make an image of the person you want to be harmed, and pierce it with pins, in the hope that the distant victim will grow sick in the appropriate places. The Egyptian practice was as follows: a small terracotta figure which represented the enemy was given his name, then smashed in a solemn ceremony, and thrown away. The intention was clear: the one thus cursed was to be broken and to disappear like his image. Whether it worked, is not recounted.

We only know that the magic formula failed in one case at least: when it was used against Byblos. Towards the end of the Middle Kingdom, Egyptian priests destroyed a statue, which had previously been given the name of the wood-trading town, but the terracotta fragments imprinted with the sign of *Kpny* slumbered for three and a half millennia in the sand of Egypt without causing any greater havoc than the excitement felt by the archaeologists who finally found them.

One naturally wonders why the pharaohs suddenly felt obliged to harm their wood purveyors in such an underhand way. The fragments of the figure gave no clue to the reason, and one can only guess at it. It may have been because Byblos had simply become too rich and too powerful to go on existing in its peaceful state of self-sufficiency. It was wooed by other states because of its timber-land and its favourable situation, and was drawn into the network of international politics. Hence trouble with Egypt.

Support for this supposition is offered by cuneiform tablets from the records of the ruler of Mari, which were found in Mesopotamia. They state that Jantin-hamu, Prince of Byblos, has sent costly presents to King Zimri-Lim, an erstwhile ally of Hammurabi of Babylon. Since, however, Jantin-hamu was also listed as a vassal in Egyptian documents under the name of Inten, the Pharaoh's officials may have interpreted this attempt to curry favour with the north as a breach of faith, which ought to be punished. Their most important suppliers of wood should be knocking on their office doors down at the Delta ports, not elsewhere. This particularly applied when the political situation seemed worrying. At the time when the details about Jantin-hamu or Inten were set down, this was the case. The Middle Kingdom was on the brink of a serious internal crisis; its rulers must have feared that hostile nations would take advantage of the situation and attack them. It was very understandable that they should keep good track of their allies and consider anyone a traitor who looked as if he was trying to sneak off in order to avoid being drawn into the forthcoming holocaust. They seem to have suspected Byblos of this intention—which, if it was the case, was hardly surprising. The pillars on which that town had based its trade were about to totter, and they had to look around for a substitute, for which purpose the kings of Mari were as suitable as any other powerful neighbour.

In fact the disaster which had been foreseen in the Lebanon as much as on the Nile speedily came to pass. The Middle Kingdom fell, and the previously unchallenged supremacy of Egypt in the Syro-Palestinian area came to an end for some considerable time.

We do not know for certain how Byblos came out of this situation. How Egypt weathered the storm, is better documented. It had to suffer invasion by an alien race, shook the invaders off, rose to new greatness, was threatened a second time, overcame this danger also and was then prey to an third attack, which it again withstood. It held out valiantly. But in the course of these events, which lasted nearly five hundred years, it lost so much power and authority that the nations over which it held sway won an ever-increasing measure of independence, and finally —and this applied particularly to the Canaanites—were allowed to shape their own fates as independent communities.

If one looks for a common link through all these ups and downs, one finds a race of people who until then had not distinguished themselves by any very spectacular ventures in the Near East: the Aryans. They were responsible for each of the three large invasions into Egyptian territory.

Where the Aryans originally came from is still not known for certain. It is thought that they originated in the Kirghiz steppe, but it is also known that the launching ground for their further migration was the area between western Europe and southern Russia. They had probably penetrated into this territory at some point in their history, and had developed a modest standard of living as cattle breeders and farmers, pressing on farther as their population increased. They moved across present-day Germany, India, Persia and Mesopotamia in the process. They settled in Anatolia and parts of present-day Iraq and Syria, and finally encountered the equally land-hungry Semites, whom they managed in part to displace.

One of the Aryan migrations occurred in the middle of the second millennium BC. They probably came from Armenia to the Tigris-Euphrates plain and altered the whole population structure of the area. One of the many groups thus disrupted was the one the Egyptians called '*hekau-khasut*', 'the rulers of foreign lands'. It would seem they were a band of Semitic warrior kings who commanded outstanding men and also the new weapon, the horse-drawn chariot. The Nile Kingdom, which they reached after crossing the Sinai peninsula, capitulated almost without a fight—which indicates how seriously it must have been weakened by the inner conflicts already mentioned.

The '*hekau-khasut*' or Hyksos, as we call them, were somewhat at a loss as to how to deal with their prey. The Egyptian priest Manetho, who wrote a history of his country in the third century AD, describes them disparagingly as 'herdsman kings' and tyrants, who thought of little but exploitation. His account is probably accurate. The Hyksos left no permanent mark on Egyptian culture and were crippled fairly rapidly by the most dangerous strategy a highly civilized people can use as a defence against barbarian invaders: they were lapped in a cocoon of luxury and riches until they were eventually too weak to be able to defend themselves effectively against revolt. By about 1,570 BC they had reached this state. King Amosis of Upper Egypt drove the Hyksos kings from their capital in the Delta and founded the New Kingdom, which was to last for four centuries.

It was the first of the three Egyptian victories I have mentioned, and probably the most successful. The Nile Kingdom seemed to be stronger after it than ever before. Amosis's successors led victorious expeditions as far as the Euphrates and succeeded where their predecessors of the Old and Middle Kingdoms had failed, in making the Lebanon zone an Egyptian province, and Byblos one of their ports. It is doubtful, in fact very unlikely, that the Canaanites were particularly happy about this promotion. It meant that the Egyptians no longer came as buyers and pilgrims, but as tax collectors. The duties they demanded had to be paid mostly in the form of cedarwood. Tuthmosis III, one of the conqueror pharaohs, stated as much in an official report. 'Every year,' it announces, 'real cedars of Lebanon are felled for me and brought to my court. . . . When my army returns, they bring as tribute the cedars of my victory, which I have won according to the designs of my father [the god Amun-Re], who has entrusted all foreign lands to me. I have left none for the Asiatics, because it is a material which he loves.' The pharaohs' weakness for sweet-smelling wood cost the Canaanites a great deal. Their forests were turned into crown lands, their ships commandeered.

But this state of affairs did not last long either. Under Tuthmosis's followers the fiscal hold was already loosening, and we know for certain that at a later date Egypt had to shell out again. And then finally, in 1,377 BC, Amenophis IV, who was not very interested in trade or foreign affairs, came to the throne. He directed all his energies to getting rid of the Egyptian Olympus and replacing it with a single god called Aten. He later took for himself the name Akh-en-Aten or Ekhnaten, which can be translated as 'it pleases Aten'. His fanaticism had unleashed a religious controversy which split the whole nation and, two

hundred and fifty years after the last crisis, had thrown the
kingdom once more into a state where its very existence was
threatened, when, for the second time, disaster came about
through the intervention of an Aryan people. The Hittites—
the oldest of all the civilized Aryan nations—broke forth from
their Anatolian bastions. They swept across the Egyptian outposts in northern Syria, reached the foothills of Mount Lebanon
and there joined up with the Amorite Habiru, who helped them
press on southwards.

Byblos, which had long since become re-oriented towards
Egypt, lay in the path of this invasion and had to decide once
more which side to take. Was the Nile Kingdom still strong
enough to repay them if they supported her? Or would they do
better to back the strong invaders from the north and ensure
a basis for future friendly relations by a timely co-operation?
Concepts such as loyalty and morality seldom carry much weight
in such deliberations, even if they are later frequently bandied
about by the victors. It is a case of sheer survival. The city elders
of Byblos were thus probably calculating rather than conscien-
tious. Unfortunately they calculated wrongly. They decided this
time—and certainly not for fear of being execrated once more—
to throw in their lot with the Egyptians, but they thus brought
about the personal tragedy of a man who was responsible for
the policy of their town and a few small allied neighbouring
states. His name was Rib-Adi.

We have fairly exact information about this prince and his
story, thanks to a series of letters, which were found in Tell
el-Amarna in Egypt—the same Amarna in which the world-
famous bust of the beautiful Nofretete, Ekhnaten's wife, was
also found.

It was due to a fellah woman that the Amarna letters were discovered. While working on her husband's land, in 1887, she
came across clay tablets, covered with cuneiform signs. She
naturally ran at once to the nearest antique dealer, who—naturally
—bought them at once. Months later the first of these documents
turned up in Europe. They caused feverish archaeological
activity. Excavators rushed to Tell el-Amarna and were led to
the spot. They were incredibly lucky. The tablets found by the
peasant woman were not single pieces but part of the archives

of Amenophis III and his son, the monotheist, who had built his capital Akhetaten there.

In the course of several archaeological searches a total of 377 of the priceless tablets were salvaged and partly evaluated on the spot. They are the most important records of the history of pre-Israelite Palestine that we have. Most of them are written in a demotic Akkadian dialect interspersed with Canaanitisms, the diplomatic language of the day, and must therefore have been written by scribes in the Lebanon and sent to the court of the Pharaoh. Rib-Adi, the governor of Byblos, dictated some of them.

In his first letters he gives a clear picture of the situation caused by the invasion of the Habiru. He warns the Egyptians emphatically about this Amorite people, whose leader Abdi-Ashirta gives out that he is a vassal of Egypt although he has secretly long made common cause with Shuppiluliumash, the King of the Hittites. The traitor is also trying to get Byblos on his side, that is to say his allies' side, but has had—Rib-Adi assures them—no success so far. The governor stresses his unswerving loyalty to the Nile Kingdom and begs the Pharaoh for help against the invaders. 'I bow down at the feet of the King, my lord, seven times and seven times,' he writes; 'Byblos remains a true servant of her King.'

The early letters among the fifty-four he wrote are addressed to Amenophis III, the later ones to Ekhnaten. But gradually the assurances of loyalty become heart-rending cries for help. The position of the letter-writer is growing more desperate month by month. One Canaanite town after another goes over to the Habiru, and Byblos itself is besieged by Abdi-Ashirta. At one point Rib-Adi tries to kill the leader of the rebels, but his attempt fails. Then even his fellow citizens conspire against him. He discovers that 'the gate-keepers have taken money', that guards have been killed. Finally he fears for his life and begs the Pharaoh to be allowed to flee. But Egypt, busy with her internal conflicts, is silent. She sends neither bread nor soldiers. Rib-Adi now turns to an acquaintance at court, General Amanappa, and complains to him about the sovereign's lack of interest. That too is a vain plea. Amanappa merely asks to be sent axes and copper, two products which Byblos specialized in supplying. Rib-Adi is nearly in despair. Meanwhile food has become scarce. In neighbouring towns revolts break out against the pro-Egyptian party, and Rib-Adi's own relatives implore him to give up his rigid stand.

Then a letter from Ekhnaten comes at last. There is a fragile wave of hope. But disappointment soon follows. The god-obsessed ruler does not say a word about the problems of his vassals. He merely asks whether they can send him good cedar-wood, from which to make chests and trunks. Rib-Adi writes back bitterly that he cannot send wood because the main ports are already in the hands of the Habiru and so his ships cannot sail for Egypt. Moreover, the Hittites are now advancing on Byblos itself. The position is untenable. They must at least see to it that the statue of Baalat is saved and taken safely to the Nile. Again there is no reply.

Rib-Adi's next letter no longer comes from Byblos, but from neighbouring Berytus. The governor has fled there to beg help from his colleague, who is also still loyal to Egypt. When he returns, his citizens have shut the gates on him and will not let him into the town again. He is on the verge of hysteria.

'For see,' he writes, 'many people in Byblos love me; only a few have rebelled. If one unit of archers could be sent, and they might hear of it, then the town would turn back to the King, my lord. My lord shall know that I am ready to die for him. When I am in the town again, I will hold it for my lord; my heart hangs on the King, my lord. I will not give the town to the sons of Abdi-Ashirta, although my brother has turned the town from me in order to give it into the hands of the sons of Abdi-Ashirta. Let not the King, my lord, desert the town. Truly, there is much silver and gold therein, and her temple houses great riches.'

It is a testament to human need, a stammer rather than an official report. Rib-Adi begs, entreats and finally offers money. He is at the end of his tether. In his final letter to Ekhnaten he only pleads for help for Berytus. He says that the citizens of Byblos thought he was dead and therefore considered they should now really give the town up to the Habiru. The letter ends with a cry: 'Why has my lord abandoned me?'

But the royal seeker after god in Akhetaten does not reply to this either. The result: the Lebanon falls into the hands of the Habiru and so to the Hittites. Shuppiluliumash forces Aziru, the son of Abdi-Ashirta (who has been killed in the meantime), to swear an oath of allegiance to him, and has thus won a whole province without striking a single blow.

The epoch during which Egypt was so concerned with her own problems that she could not even go to the help of her most faithful allies, came to an end with the death of Ekhnaten. The latter's son-in-law Tutankhamun—known to posterity because of his richly adorned tomb—discontinues the politically disruptive experiment of teaching that there is only one god, seeks reconciliation with the powerful priests and makes contact with the Canaanite province again. He has the message engraved on a stele in the temple at Karnak, that 'His Majesty has had river barges built from new cedarwood from the Lebanon, decorated with gold from the Sudan. They illumine the river.'

Tutankhamun's successors Horemheb, Rameses I and Sethos I then try to win back the territory that the Hittites have taken from the Egyptians. Rameses II finally advances to the north of Damascus, and gives battle to Murshilish II, a successor of Shuppiluliumash, in 1,299 BC at Kadesh, which is later claimed as a victory for their side by both parties. In fact, however, it probably ended in defeat for Rameses.

The pharaohs were never again to have so much control over their northern provinces as they had had before Ekhnaten. They have constantly to send punitive expeditions to Canaan to bring the many small towns which have arisen there to order—punitive expeditions being the somewhat broad circumlocution for a parade-like display of military strength and splendour. This uneasy situation only comes to an end with a peace treaty between Rameses II and Khattushilish III. The Pharaoh takes a daughter of the Hittite king as his wife. From now on the borderline between his kingdom and that of the Aryans is a line which begins on the Mediterranean coast north of Byblos and stretches away into the far distance in the east. The wood-trading town remains just inside the Egyptian territory, and the name Canaan, which until then was used rather loosely for the coastal plain of Syria and Palestine, becomes a precise geographical and political location. From now on Canaan is more or less the strip of land which was later called Phoenicia, and its inhabitants begin to think of themselves as a race in their own right. They finally cut free from the Nile—a process which is illustrated in a fairly drastic way by the last Egyptian document we have concerned with Byblos: the Wen-Amon papyrus.

Some time early in the eleventh century a trade representative called Wen-Amon was sent by Herihor, the high priest of Amun in Thebes, to Byblos, to buy wood. His superior could supply him with all the necessary travel documents and credentials, but had no ship for him. The priest's envoy had to travel in a Syrian vessel.

Four months and twelve days after he had left Thebes, Wen-Amon reached Byblos. The reception which greeted him was shattering. The ruler of the town, a man called Sakarbaal, not only refused to trade with him, but also forbade him to enter the city. Egyptian names seemed to have become rather unpopular in the Lebanon.

For twenty-nine days Wen-Amon had to hang about at the harbour, before he succeeded in approaching a young nobleman, who had entry to the palace and was able to smuggle him in. Sakarbaal received the priest's envoy in an upper room. 'He sat,' the Egyptian reports, 'in front of a window, so that the waves of the great Syrian Sea [the Mediterranean] broke behind his head.' The palace must have stood right at the sea's edge.

Wen-Amon explained to the prince that he had come 'to fetch wood for the great majestic barge of Amun-Re, the king of gods. Your father supplied it, your grandfather supplied it, and you too will do so.' It was an attempt to revive the old colonial-rule methods, but it failed dismally.

'To be sure,' Sakarbaal replied with unexpected sharpness, 'they did so. And if you pay me, I will do so too. Before, when my people had to carry out such an order, the Pharaoh used to send—long may he live, flourish and prosper—six ships full of Egyptian wares, which they unloaded in their warehouses [their own, which they maintained in Byblos]. But you, what do you bring me?'

This reply must have completely staggered Wen-Amon; it was quite unprecedented. Did this man have the effrontery to talk of payment? Where were his manners? On the Nile one never did business, one gave generously that which was due to the gods, and if one or other of their earthly representatives profited thereby, one was tactful enough not to mention it—it was an understood thing.

When Wen-Amon had recovered a little, he tried to steer his interlocutor back on to the path of good manners. He stressed the religious bonds between Byblos and the Nile; he made an appeal to the old code of loyalty. But Sakarbaal remained coldly adamant. He was not a merchant of the old Egyptian but of the new Phoenician kind. Business was business and nothing else. 'Amun,' he said, 'created every land, but firstly he created the land of Egypt, from whence you come, for all [artisan] skill stems from there and was meant to provide for places such as that in which I find myself.'

This was a partial surrender, as Sakarbaal had demoted himself to being a member of an underdeveloped country and had given Egypt the rank of an industrial state in comparison. But the point was still made: no goods without payment. Wen-Amon understood that he must descend to the level of the Canaanites. He about-faced completely and now promised that indeed he would pay, if he could, but that alas all his money had been stolen on the voyage. Sakarbaal replied briskly that in that case he must have more sent to him.

The Egyptian agreed reluctantly. He sent a messenger to this end to Nesbanebded, the King of Lower Egypt, at which Sakarbaal gave his people orders to fell trees again and bring them to the ports.

Weeks later the desired sum did in fact arrive from the Nile Delta. Among other things, Nesbanebded sent four gold vessels, five silver vessels, ten robes of fine linen, five hundred rolls of papyrus, five hundred cowhides and five hundred ropes. The Canaanite was extremely pleased with this offering. He ordered another three hundred men into the forests and had three hundred ox teams made ready to transport the timber.

Then something strange happened. Members of a piratical seafaring people, the Thekel, whom Wen-Amon had already come across on his outward voyage, came into the harbour at Byblos and were taken to Sakarbaal. There was an angry exchange at the palace. It was a case of who should transport the wood to the Nile. The Egyptian had obviously not intended to hire the Thekel for this purpose. Now they wanted to get even with him.

But even stranger than this proposal was the way in which Sakarbaal reacted to it. He did not simply throw the strangers out; he did not even protest at their suggestion, but sidestepped the issue very ungraciously. 'I cannot,' he said, 'take steps against an emissary of Amun. But I will send him away, and if you capture him outside my territory, you may do with him what you will.' It seemed that he was afraid of them.

Wen-Amon himself does not enlarge on this incident in his account. He only notes that he wept with fear, when he heard about it, and that he at once took to flight. But ill luck dogged him. The ship which he took sailed into a storm and was driven off course to Cyprus. How he got back to Egypt from there is not revealed. His notes break off at this point.

All in all the Wen-Amon papyrus is a rather mysterious document. The information it gives about the political situation is outweighed by the many questions it raises. What does the story of the money which was stolen from him mean? Surely he behaved in the beginning as if he could merely command them to supply wood, without paying for it? And, anyway, why was he travelling without any attendants as a passenger on a strange ship? Did the man who sent him, one of the highest officials of the all-powerful Egypt, really not have the means to provide him with an escort and his own ship? Then the Thekel. Who were they? Why did Sakarbaal at once give in when they threatened one of his guests with force? Was he really afraid of them? If so, why? Even the list of goods which Nesbanebded sent to Wen-Amon gives food for thought. Could the people of Byblos at that time not weave fine linen, when only a little later the Phoenicians were to become the leading textile manufacturers in the Mediterranean? Did they not know how to make ropes? And what made five hundred rolls of papyrus so valuable that they were accepted as the price for a considerable amount of expensive cedarwood in a town which itself bore the Greek name for papyrus?

We can answer some of these questions—beginning with the easiest. Papyrus was indeed a dear and sought-after product, and it came exclusively from Egypt. The raw material from which it was made, a type of reed with the scientific name *Cyperus papyrus*, is only found in Africa. It was exploited ingeniously by the Nile people. They cut the pith from the stems of the reeds into thin sheets and pressed two layers of them together. When

these were firmly stuck together by the sap, they could be
polished, levelled off and stuck together to make long webs or
smaller sheets. The end-product of this complicated process was
an ivory-coloured paper which very quickly turned yellow but
which was extraordinarily strong, and highly sought after by
the chancellery clerks in all the bureaucratic states of the ancient
world because it took up less space in their files than the usual
stone or clay tablets. Egypt had a monopoly on its production
and made a handsome profit from it.

The same applied to the ropes. They also were made from the
papyrus plant, but from the stem, not the pith, and, since clearly
there was no binding material then with the same strength, they
also were best-sellers. Homer describes them in the twenty-
first book of the Odyssey as 'rope of Byblos-bast from a curved
ship'. The hero of this epic used it to secure the doors behind
which he slew Penelope's suitors. The material was known
throughout the Mediterranean.

The question thus arises as to why the Greeks, who knew that
the papyrus products came from Egypt, called a Canaanite
town after them. It was for the same reason for which Bremen
could just as well have been called 'coffee'. The town at Mount
Lebanon was simply the main cargo port for the writing material
and ropes from the Nile. Egyptian ships transported both from
the Delta ports to the north and at Byblos loaded them onto
other craft which would sail on to Syria or, if they were Cretan
boats, via Cyprus to Anatolia and the Peloponnese. In this
way the papyrus reached Greece, and from their point of view
it may have seemed to come from Canaan, not the Nile. So if
they said 'paper' in Greece, they could also mean the town on
the Lebanese coast, because they usually thought of it in that
context. This also explains why papyrus and ropes featured so
prominently in the Wen-Amon list. Both were important merchandise for Sakarbaal.

And the same applied equally to the fine linen which Nesbanebded also sent. It was again not a material which any skilful
weaver could produce, but byssus, a featherlight mixture of
flax, silk and silky filaments from molluscs which the Egyptians
specialized in making. The Canaanites only learnt the art of
making fine materials a few generations later. At the time of
Wen-Amon's journey the future prestige product of the Phoe-

nicians, their purple cloth, was only made in northerly Ugarit, a trading centre which was inhabited by Hurrians as well as Canaanites. The secret of its production only reached the south as a sequel to the events in which Herihor's envoy was involved in such a tragi-comic way.

With this we come to the Thekel, who are the subject matter of the end of this chapter and the beginning of the next. The Thekel were Aryans, a splinter group remaining from the third of the invasionary forces which attacked Egypt in the half-millennium between 1,700 BC and 1,200 BC. Their existence explains why at the time of Wen-Amon's journey Egypt was no longer in a position to protect her emissaries and give them the authority that would have enabled them to demand the cedarwood as an offering to their gods. It also explains why Sakarbaal feared the threats of a handful of tough blackmailers more than a possible counterblast from the high priest of Thebes. The high priest was a long way off, but the Thekel were on his doorstep, and they could not only threaten but also strike if necessary. Their ships had control of the whole of the eastern Mediterranean, and they allowed no other ships to sail besides theirs. Neither the Egyptians nor the Canaanites could measure up to them in points of seamanship and sea warfare. They were the best, the fastest and the bravest. And they were pretty ruthless.

They did not play a very major role on land, but the sea belonged to them. So the whole group of which they were a part were called the Sea Peoples. In the history of Egypt their arrival on the scene marked the end of an era in which the Nile State had had world-power status. In the history of Canaan they symbolized the beginning of an amazing advance. For it was the Sea Peoples who first made the strip of land in the Lebanon into Phoenicia.

But who in fact were they, and where did they come from?

CHAPTER IV

Odysseus and Achilles—
Ancestors of the Phoenicians

THERE ARE MANY qualities which can be described as typically
Phoenician. Shrewdness is one, their skill as merchants another,
and technical inventiveness might well be called a third. Yet
today we see them not so much as prototypes of the merchant
or engineer, as simply the great seafarers of antiquity. That they
were nautical men *par excellence* is the character that history has
attributed to them. It is probably a fair assessment.

The question of how this nomad people from the desert took
to the sea is usually answered with a tailor-made cliché. 'The
Phoinikier' (that is, the immigrant nomads from Sinai), as the
historian Philipp Hiltebrandt wrote in about 1953, 'united with
the original inhabitants (of the Levant coast) and adopted their
seafaring character. A pre-condition was wood suitable for
building ships, which was lacking along almost the entire Anterior
Asian and African coasts, but was amply provided by the abundant cedars of Lebanon.' A simple process therefore: they came,
they conquered, and from 'nomads of the steppes' became
'nomads of the sea'.

If this over-simplified formula were only approximately
accurate, there would be no problem as to when the history of
the Phoenicians begins, for it would be manifestly clear that
it began with the Amorite-Canaanitish migration in about
2,300 BC. The invaders took over Byblos, and in the same
campaign took over the sea. They then gradually developed from
the small beginnings of primitive coastal navigation the navigational techniques which later enabled them to extend their
empire from the Lebanon as far as Spain and even across the
Red Sea to the east coast of Africa.

As I said, that is a widely held and generally accepted theory, but it has one or two flaws; the most important being that it does not quite coincide with what actually happened on the Lebanon coast between 2,300 BC and 1,200 BC. Certainly, the immigrant Canaanites fairly speedily realized that it was simpler to transport the valuable cedarwood to Egypt across the sea than by land, and also learnt in the shipyards of Byblos how to construct the necessary vessels. But that does not mean to say this change-over from ox-carts to ships automatically made them seafarers, and proverbially good ones at that.

Coastal navigation in the Lebanon, even in the heyday of trading between Egypt and Byblos, was hardly more than an advanced form of rafting. It is true that Senefru of the Old Kingdom, in his much-quoted account, speaks of the *Adoration of the Two Lands* ships, with which he fetched wood from the mountains of Canaan, and also mentions that each of them was a hundred cubits long—about forty-five metres. But if one compares these measurements with Egyptian drawings of the same period, it is clear that even such vessels can hardly have been more than outsize canoes. Developed from the square barges which were used as pleasure craft on the Nile, and flat-bottomed, they glided over the water. You could navigate close to the shore (there was no rudder as yet), but had to pull in to land if even the suspicion of a breeze arose. Certainly navigation on the high seas would have been as impossible in them as in a flat-bottomed Chinese junk.

In the period before the eleventh century BC the Canaanites had not progressed beyond this state of development—coastal navigation with short daily runs and night stops on dry land— any more than had their Egyptian colleagues, who always had a very ambivalent relationship with the sea. When they wanted to send papyrus, ropes or any of their other staple exports to distant parts from the Nile State, they had to hire Cretan, or later Mycenaean merchantmen. These Greeks were the only ones who sailed on the open seas at that time, and who possibly had keeled ships.

And then suddenly, you could almost say overnight, the Canaanites had such boats too. From the eleventh century onwards they sailed to lands which until then had been out of their reach. They left Cyprus behind in the east; before them lay

Crete, and the world of Aegean islands was open to them; the Peloponnesian coast rose on the horizon, and beyond it Sicily, Sardinia and Spain.

What had happened?

The search for an answer to this question took me to one of the finest universities in the world, the American College in Beirut. There it was answered by Dimitri Baramki, the curator of the university archaeological museum, one of the leaders of Phoenician research in the Lebanon. We spoke in the shade of palm trees. The voices of the lecturers drifted from the open windows of the lecture-halls. Far below us glowed the Mediterranean, as blue as on the cover of a package-tour brochure. Baramki, a Jordanian, instructed me with visible satisfaction, his sharply-chiselled Bedouin head hunched owl-like into his shoulders, a characteristic posture of his.

It was true, he pointed out, that the Canaanite Proto-Phoenicians had been a people who possessed all the qualities necessary to open up the Mediterranean to navigation and trade. They were good merchants and passable organizers; they possessed the daring of their Bedouin ancestors and also possessed (which is important in this context) an unusual religious strength; but—Baramki wagged his index finger at me—one thing was almost entirely missing: the fund of nautical and technical knowledge, without which ocean-going voyages were out of the question.

It was just this, however—he stabbed the air with his finger—which the mysterious invaders who in about 1,200 BC swept over the lands of the Near East—the Sea Peoples—undoubtedly possessed at that time.

And now Baramki came to the crux of his argument. Since, he said, at precisely this date, i.e. in the eleventh century before Christ, the spectacular metamorphosis took place which changed the Canaanites from coastal navigators into the rulers of the high seas, it seemed almost overwhelmingly logical to draw the conclusion that the Sea Peoples, who also ravaged part of the Lebanon, later joined with the Canaanites and let themselves be absorbed by them. And in this process of fusion, during which the former introduced their maritime skills, the Phoenician nation—Baramki used the word race—was created. Among other things, he continued, this also becomes clear from the fact that, from this particular century onwards, the literature of neighbouring countries refers less and less to the inhabitants of individual *towns* in the Lebanon; instead it begins to refer to a sharply defined, closed group, the Phoenicians, calling them Tyrians or Sidonians.

Baramki's theory offers an amazingly simple explanation for a seemingly puzzling process. The Phoenicians did not develop from coastal sailors to ocean navigators of their own accord; it was through their fusion with foreign invaders that they found themselves in a position to move out from their former territory towards new and wider horizons. The Lebanese professor enjoys talking about this theory, and even admits that he is a little in love with his own argument. It cannot, he then adds, be definitively proved, but it does have the great advantage of making sense. Someone merely had to put two and two together.

Well, that is exactly what he did; and many of his colleagues agree with him or have meanwhile developed similar theories themselves. For Sabatino Moscati too, the formula 'Canaanites plus Sea Peoples equals Phoenicians', is not something to argue about. It is an accepted fact.

This means, however, that the irruption of the Sea Peoples is the second main pivotal point, after the Canaanitish migration, in the history of the people of the Lebanon. The Aryans from the far north mingled with the original inhabitants and the Sinai-nomads who had integrated with them and gave their development an entirely new direction.

In the records of the old Anterior Asian historians the Sea Peoples and the other splinter groups derived from them appear under many different names. Besides the Thekel, the Egyptians mention the Shekelesh, the Weshesh and the Peleset. The latter are called Philistines in the Bible, but besides them there were also, as a kind of foreign legion or Swiss Guard within King David's palace guard, the Cherethites and Pelethites, whom Luther introduced into the German cultural heritage as 'Krethi and Plethi'.

Only one of these names has stuck in general usage: the Philistines—although Krethi and Plethi has become a German popular phrase for 'Tom, Dick and Harry'. As regards the Philistines, we know that they were a tough breed of tall men, whom the Jews even regarded as giants. Samson, Saul and

David grappled with them. The strip of land in which they lived is still called after them, as the word Palestine is derived from the Greek Philistaia. With Goliath, David's opponent, the Sea People become flesh and blood, so to speak, but the phrase 'Krethi and Plethi' tells part of the secret of their origin in a nutshell. The Kerethi or Cherethites were Cretans, the Pelethi or Pelethites, Philistines. If the Kerethi came from the island of Crete, as their name suggests, it seems logical to suppose that the Pelethi came from somewhere nearby. In fact archaeologists have proved that this is the case.

During excavations in Gaza, Ashdod, Ashkelon, Gath and Ekron, the chief towns of the Philistine league, they found pottery vessels which seemed strangely familiar to them. Where had they seen this fawn colour, these geometrical patterns in black and red, these stylized bird designs before? It probably did not take them long to remember, but considerably longer to believe. Pottery vessels of similar, in fact almost exactly the same, shape and design had been discovered in Mycenaean tombs in Greece. The kings and warriors who sacked Troy, the historical prototypes of Homer's heroes, drank out of them and traded with them. From this it appeared conclusive that the Philistines were at least in close contact with the Achaeans, as Homer calls them. But then further tombs were discovered and other discoveries made, which not only confirmed this theory but outstripped it. Weapons were found near the pottery vessels which were made from the most expensive metal of the time, iron. This also pointed to the Achaeans. The Hittites were virtually the only people who had iron at that time, the end of the Bronze Age, and these Anatolian warriors were close trading partners of the Mycenaean Greeks, and their kingdom was later conquered and taken over by them.

The pieces of the puzzle gradually took shape to show the following pattern: some of the Philistines had not only had close contacts with the Achaeans, but in fact stemmed directly from them. Goliath, who challenged David wearing Mycenaean armour, could have been a descendant of Menelaus, Achilles, Odysseus, Helen or Penelope, if—another possibility—he wasn't a Dane. Thus here in the Gaza strip the last act of a drama was played out which had begun in Crete about two hundred and fifty years before. It could well be called 'Kerethi and Pelethi'.

The prelude to the Cretan-Mycenaean action proper has been described thus by Oswald Spengler: 'In the middle of the second millennium BC there are two opposing worlds in the Aegean Sea, one which quietly grows towards the future, in dim unconsciousness, heavy with hope and drunk with pain and glory: the Mycenaean—and another which rests happily, sated with the riches of an old culture, gracious and light, all major problems long since overcome: the Minoan on Crete.' It is difficult to put it better or more vividly: on one hand the blossoming island, inhabited by men who have succeeded, mainly through peaceful endeavours, in creating a culture in which all the wishes, at least of the well-to-do, can be fulfilled in a civilized way; on the other the peasant warriors of the wooded Peloponnese, brooding by their hearths, wrapped in leather and coarse linen. Here, spacious villa complexes, adjoining palaces without heavy dividing walls; there the Cyclopean walls of gigantic castles. Here, women who display their breasts above *peplos* and girdle; there shrouded females, who sit spinning wool in their laps. Here religious ceremonies celebrated with graceful agility in the bull-games; there a mist of faces and figures, which only gradually take shape to form a heavenly order. Here joyfulness and frivolity; there statuesque earnestness and dignified attitudes. Here Kerethi, there Pelethi.

This was the picture that historians had of the Cretan-Mycenaean world for about sixty years. Doubts as to its veracity have now been voiced. In 1972 the German geologist H. G. Wunderlich put forward the theory that it was quite otherwise, and that the palace of Knossos which Sir Arthur Evans discovered, excavated and partly reconstructed towards the turn of the century was not a palace but a citadel of the dead, that the lightly clad women were not society ladies but mourning women, the whole city complex a single graveyard, whose dead inhabitants were buried in the huge clay jars which until then were thought to have been storage containers. The evidence with which Wunderlich supports his surprising theory is not based on archaeological but on scientific methods. The rooms decorated with alabaster, he says, which were thought hitherto to be bathrooms, could not have been used for this purpose, because alabaster cannot stand up to damp or water for any length of time; the double-headed axes which have been found are too

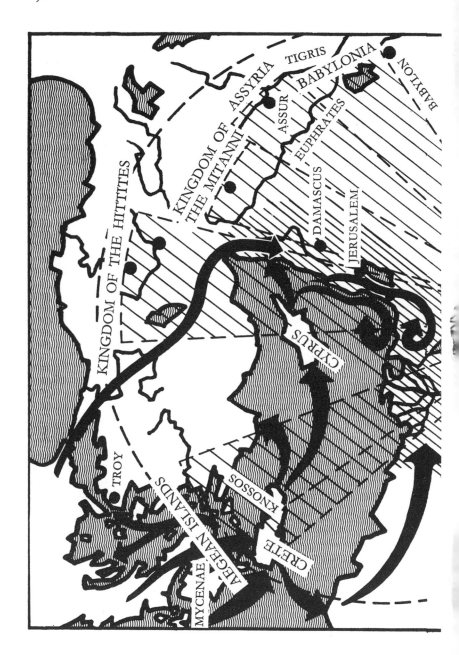

TIGRIS
KINGDOM OF ASSYRIA
BABYLONIA
BABYLON
ASSUR
EUPHRATES
KINGDOM OF THE MITANNI
DAMASCUS
JERUSALEM
KINGDOM OF THE HITTITES
CYPRUS
TROY
KNOSSOS
CRETE
AEGEAN ISLANDS
MYCENAE

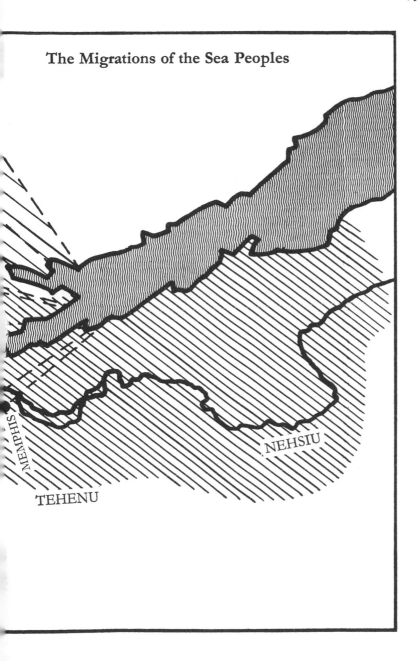

The Migrations of the Sea Peoples

MEMPHIS

TEHENU

NEHSIU

thin for actual use and therefore were only symbolical grave gifts, the lack of means of defence being explained by the fact that there is no need to defend graveyards.

The Stuttgart professor's theory seems at first glance to be hard to refute, but is not entirely satisfactory, because if all the remains of the Minoan world which have been found to date were merely memorials to the dead, where did the living live? Did they invest all their skill and riches in plaster dummies and themselves live in caves or huts? Did they look after their corpses better than themselves? Were there no real prototypes of the imitation axes?

Even if Wunderlich is right and Minoan society devoted a large part of its creative energy to an unprecedented cult of the dead—a suggestion which, by the way, Spengler had already put forward—the foundations of Knossos and Phaistos remain witnesses to an advanced civilization which at the time described by the author of *The Decline of the West* had already reached a stage which one can compare with German rococo or with the culture of the present era. It was all flirtation and gossip, and life was one long party. The Egyptian style, which had also influenced Crete, had yielded to the lascivious and was fostered under the safe protection of a fleet which commanded the whole of the eastern Mediterranean. They had long been living on the interest of a capital that was itself expended.

But then—Act One—the representatives of the other world, the Achaeans from Mycenae, enter this silken idyll with clumping tread. Theseus, brought as a concessionary slave to Crete, kills the Minotaur, the fabulous creature with a bull's head and a man's body that played so important a part in the Minoan religion, and makes off with the Princess Ariadne. In other words, if one translates from the mythological into the historical, the State of the island dwellers who had grown slack through luxurious living was taken over by their robust neighbours from the mainland. Pelethi slew Kerethi, but then themselves took over palaces, slaves and customs, were influenced by the more highly developed culture of the vanquished and adopted the latter's maritime heritage. The Thalassocracy, the absolute naval supremacy of the Cretans, fell to the Achaeans, and remained theirs until approximately 1,150 BC—for close on 250 years.

Then—Act Two—as a new variation on the old theme of

kill or be killed, there appear other, possibly blond, blue-eyed barbarians, who advance both from the sea and by land into the Mycenaean sphere of power, and inflict upon them the same fate that the Mycenaeans themselves had inflicted upon the Minoans. The last warriors of the Bronze Age are vanquished by these hordes with their clattering iron weapons—they too possessed the grey metal—are integrated into their number and driven onwards with them. For the invaders did not remain in Crete for very long. The impetus of their onrush carried them farther to more easterly shores.

The Achaeans of the mainland, however, subjected to the same fate, pile—Act Three—onto the ox-carts which they use, cross the Bosphorus together with the newcomers and attack the Hittite empire, which is unable to withstand the force of these migrant bands. They sweep across Anatolia, possibly improving their forging techniques as a result of Hittite methods, enter Syria, destroy among other places the towns of Carchemish, and Ugarit of the purple-producing Hurrians (apparently by-passing Byblos, though not sparing Tyre and Sidon) and finally reach the Nile Delta, where Rameses III awaits them with hurriedly enlisted troops.

At the same time those who chose the sea route reach Cyprus, an island which already partly belonged to the Kerethi. For them too the next step onwards is the Lebanon with its ports which they know well, and the Nile Kingdom, which was probably also familiar to them. The pincers of both movements close in, with Canaan and Egypt caught within their grasp. But— as will be seen in the Fourth Act—King Rameses was a match for the invaders.

At Pelusium, a port at the most easterly point of the mouth of the Nile, two battles of great historical significance took place. In 525 BC the Persian King Cambyses defeated King Psammetichus II, thus eliminating Egypt from the ranks of independent states. Six hundred and twenty-four years previously, in 1,149 BC, Rameses III had been able to defend this gateway successfully against the hordes of the Sea Peoples. It was the first serious setback to which the Pelethi were subjected. 'No land can withstand their weapons,' said a report on his opponents which the Pharaoh had drawn up: 'they laid their hands on all the lands to the four corners of the earth. Their hearts were full

of confidence and the assurance that "Our plans will succeed".'
But this time at least they did not succeed. Rameses's troops
were 'like bulls in the battlefield; his horses like falcons in the
midst of little birds'. Egyptian war-chariots, the magic weapon
copied from the Hyksos, tore through the ranks of the Pelethi;
infantry stormed their barricades of wagons; women and children,
who were crowded up among the fighting men, were slaughtered
like the Cimbri and Teutoni who at a later date attacked the
Roman legions with boulders. The tall warriors from the north
with their plumed helmets and round shields succumbed to the
small but better organized Egyptians. Their fleet, which had
sailed up one of the arms of the Nile, suffered the same fate.
Their ocean-going ships were becalmed and were outmanœuvred,
boarded or burnt by the paddle-driven Egyptian craft.

Rameses had what was left of the Pelethi driven into vast
prison camps, and later allowed them to settle in the Delta. He
allowed some to return to the Gaza strip, where they founded—
Act Five—the Philistine five-town league. A smaller number,
however, who must have eluded him, the seafaring tribes of
mixed barbarians and Kerethi, as Thekel, Weshesh and Shekelesh
rendered the Syro-Lebanese coast unsafe, finally coming to
terms with the inhabitants and integrating with them.

This is the process which so fascinated Dimitri Baramki. The
descendants of the poor Sinai Bedouins, of the relations of
Abraham and Moses, and the northern barbarians, who, some
historians consider, came from Denmark and should therefore
really be called 'North' Sea Peoples, together with the successors
of the Homeric heroes, became fused into the Phoenician people—
a fact of which the Greeks, their later rivals and arch-enemies,
were ignorant.

The intruders brought a number of valuable assets with them:
firstly their absolute supremacy at sea, which forced Egypt to
let the land of Canaan emerge from its former dependent state,
secondly their navigational skills, warships and trading vessels,
and finally the secret of how to extract iron and possibly also
the dye used by the people of Ugarit, for their purple cloth. All
in all, valuable initial capital for the firm of Baal, Sons and Co.,
which was thus founded.

CHAPTER V

They Lived on Man-made Islands

———————————

THE ARRIVAL OF the Kerethi, Pelethi and Sea Peoples did not bring equal benefits to all the towns on the Lebanese coast. It was detrimental to Byblos at first. She forfeited her position as the leading trading centre and had to look on while the younger towns of Tyre and Sidon overtook her and became the leading cities of the new Phoenicia. Neighbouring peoples now spoke of Sidonians or Tyrians, instead of Giblites, as hitherto, when they meant Phoenicians. Both the Bible and Homer refer to the trader race only under these two names. It is not possible to say for certain what brought about this reversal. But it seems likely that the Sea Peoples, whose invasion started the process, found greater possibilities for development in the two southerly lying towns than in the worthy timber port with its ossified social structures.

Quite apart from that the Tyrians seem to have been quite a different race of men from the Giblites. Some of the Amarna letters (see pp. 43-5) indicate as much. From the letters which Rib-Adi sent from Byblos, we get the impression of a fussy, obviously older man, who lost his nerve in the hour of crisis and fell prey to utter despair, whereas other letters, which his colleague Abi-Milki sent from Tyre to Ekhnaten, give a picture of a far more quick-witted and crafty politician, much more concerned with his own safety than with his duty as a vassal.

Admittedly the Tyrian goes in for the usual verbose forms of address, and expresses his abhorrence for the Habiru and all those—like the governor of Sidon for instance—who have made pacts with them, but he never relies on a verbal message alone: he sends presents to lend his words greater weight—and his method is successful. Ekhnaten, who so persistently ignored the unhappy Rib-Adi, grants Abi-Milki the favour of a reply. He even sends soldiers.

However, when it then becomes clear that the small Egyptian contingent is not equal to the Habiru and the Hittites, the Tyrian still does not lose his head, but coolly prepares for his flight and his new career in Egypt. In this too he reveals some clever refinements. He does not address himself to Ekhnaten, preoccupied with his heavenly thoughts, but, with the cunning of the well-informed courtier, to his eldest daughter Meritaten, who at that point had succeeded in ousting the lovely Nofretete from her position as first lady. He seems to think the grossest flattery will do. He assures the princess that she is his life, and calls Tyre 'her town'.

Then he announces: 'I am setting sail with all my ships. Let the King take care of his servants and protect them.' Abi-Milki spares himself beseeching entreaties, wailing and whimpers. When he sees that his position is no longer tenable, he shoves off and safeguards his position at the court of Akhetaten, the new capital which Ekhnaten had built near el Amarna, knowing full well that his presents and wooing will have prepared fruitful ground for him there.

What becomes of him in Egypt, is not revealed, but one obviously need not feel too pessimistic about his fate. The town governor, unlike his Giblite colleagues, was one of those people who always fall on their feet. The short historical episode in which he appears has, however, a distinctly provincial flavour. But in his day, of course, Tyre can indeed have been no more than a small provincial town.

What became of the town and its rival Sidon in the period after the Habiru revolt and the resulting Hittite wars, is barely mentioned in the available documents. For a time Tyre appears in the written exercises of Egyptian palace scholars only as 'a town in the sea, called the port of Tyre'; it is mentioned in the records of Egyptian border outposts as a place to which despatches were carried and in the romantic travel account of a man called Keret as a place of pilgrimage. The goddess Asherat, he says, was worshipped there, the Astarte of the Phoenicians, who later laid her spell on the Greeks too, and today probably lives on in the Maronite Mary cult of the Lebanon.

There is no record either of the goods with which the Tyrians and Sidonians traded, but they must have been largely the same

How they originally lived: nomads in the Sinai desert

Byblos today: an oval harbour in a 'Punic landscape'

The harbour at Byblos, as Renan found it

Renan was the first to dig here: the excavations at Byblos

as those on which Byblos thrived: wood from nearby Mount Hermon, papyrus from Egypt, their own and also imported earthenware; and, of course, food, cloth and metal. Tyre and Sidon were somewhat at a disadvantage compared to the more northerly trading town, because their people had to transport the cedar and cypress trunks from a greater distance than the Giblites, who had the forest growing right on their doorstep, and because they were only stopping places on the route from the Nile to the north of Mesopotamia, and not an end-point like Byblos.

But all that would change when the Sea Peoples introduced the Cretan style of ocean-going navigation on the Lebanese coast. The coastal route dwindled in importance beside a new westerly route which led to Greece, Italy and Spain. The main points of departure were not Byblos and its neighbouring ports but Sidon and Tyre.

Which of the two towns at the southern end of Mount Lebanon is the older, is a controversial point. Timaeus, a not very reliable Greek historian, has it that Sidon is the older, and that Sidonians built Tyre after their own town was destroyed by the Sea Peoples. But archaeologists—with Ernest Renan, who made searches here too during the Druze revolt, again giving the lead—believe they can refute this legend. Today they are fairly certain that Tyre already existed before 1,100 BC, the date of its supposed foundation by Sidon, and for some considerable time lay under the influence of Egypt, like Byblos.

But the real history of both towns seems only properly to have begun at about the time of the invasion of the Sea Peoples. Until then they existed at best on the perimeter of the political and mercantile worlds; now they made their presence firmly felt.

Hiram, a Tyrian king who lived in about 1,000 BC, transferred his town from the coast out into the sea. It was an immense but carefully considered undertaking, combining all the experience of the past centuries with the additional impetus of the Sea Peoples' policy of alliance with the sea.

Until the beginning of Hiram's reign the main port of Tyre, a settlement with the Canaanitish name of Usu, had lain on the mainland. On an island lying six hundred metres from the shore there were only a better fortified stronghold and some harbour docks. It was hardly even an island: merely two flat, partly submerged rocky ledges, a reef covered with seaweed, of which there are many on the Syro-Palestinian coast. It seemed quite unsuited for human habitation. Yet Hiram decided he must have his residence here, and only here. He set a massive building programme in motion. The narrow canal between the two rocks, on one of which the fortress stood (the other being somewhat lower), was filled in and the larger area thus obtained was used to build on. It was an exercise that must have kept thousands of men busy for years, since the rubble and boulders used as filling material had to be brought over from the mainland.

The whole enterprise was based on an extensive, carefully worked out plan. To the north of the man-made island the so-called inner or Sidonian harbour was made, by filling in and excavation, and to the south the outer or Egyptian harbour, by building quays and jetties. Over the smaller, newly won island— it lay to the east of the larger reef and therefore nearer to the coast—Hiram had a vast and handsome civic building erected, which was later called by the Greek name *Eurychoros*. The determined ruler seems to have pulled down most of the older buildings and re-used the material for this. The Jewish historian Joseph ben Mathit-jahu, who called himself Flavius Josephus, says at any rate: 'He [Hiram] also went and felled timber in the mountains which are called Lebanon for the roofs of the temple, and tore down the old temples and erected new ones to Heracles [Melqart] and Astarte.'

Tyre's reputation for being not only one of the strangest but also one of the most beautiful metropolises of the ancient world dated back to this time. It was hardly surprising, since Hiram employed descendants of the architects who had once built Mycenaean royal castles and the Cretan villa palaces. The then inhabitants of Tyre called their town Sor, which means 'rocks' in the Phoenician language. The present-day inhabitants also call it by the same name in Arabic: Sur. Both are right: Tyre was a town on the cliff, an artificially made stronghold in the sea.

If one is looking for a symbol of what Phoenicia would be from now on, one might well choose the town built by Hiram. It represents a tendency to take refuge on the sea and to trust the land as little as possible—with a thoroughness later emulated

only by the Venetians. The reason was obvious. On the one hand
the decline of Egyptian power after the invasion of the Sea
Peoples robbed the coastal towns of the Lebanon of their only
sure means of protection, and on the other their alliance with
the Cherethites enabled them to be so successful in trading that
they amassed riches in their towns which they could not hope
to defend with their own small forces against the great inland
powers. There was therefore no other practicable solution than
to put the sea between them and their potential enemies, as far
as was possible, and to trust themselves to that element, where
they were the undisputed masters.

Tyre was not the only Phoenician town which was so dependent
on the sea; it was just that it was more favourably sited than many
of the others, with those two miserable rocks off its coast, of
which it made such skilful use. Apart from Tyre, only Aradus,
about fifty kilometres north of Byblos, was able to expand onto
an outlying island. Sidon had to be content with a flat promontory
on the coast to move onto, Berytus clung to a cliff overhanging
the water, and Tripolis lay on the outermost tip of a small peninsula. But in every case they were places on the coast from which
a settler would normally recoil in horror: steep hillsides, slippery
crags and rocky bays.

In one of the smaller Phoenician ports, Ecdippa, north of
Haifa, this tendency was particularly noticeable. There, flat
terraces of rock project out into the sea. They are sometimes
covered by the tide, sometimes exposed, with whirlpools and
breakers in which even a good swimmer can easily drown. The
place seems quite inconceivable as a landing-place for ships. Yet
the Phoenicians built one of their intermediate bases precisely
here. They cut a semicircular basin out of the rock, built up the
remaining projections with a wall or boulders, and so achieved
a small harbour in which two or perhaps even four ships could
spend a peaceful night, well protected from wind and waves.
Behind this basin there is a small hill. Here there were probably
a tower and a few houses. The surrounding land was flat and
swampy. One could therefore see an approaching enemy a
long way off, and if necessary make a getaway—by sea, naturally,
because there one would be safe.

The price which had to be paid for such security was high,

admittedly. The construction and upkeep of these sea eyries demanded considerable technical skill.

The Tyrians for instance had no springs on their rocks, nor could they bore wells. They were therefore dependent on rainwater, of which there was plenty in the spring, but which quickly became brackish and undrinkable during the long hot summers. When the supply ran out, there was nothing for it but to bring the necessary liquid by boat from the mainland, a circumstance which made it difficult to defend the island fortresses, and which was probably their downfall at the time of the Habiru revolt.

In the letters which Abi-Milki sent to Egypt at that time, there is constant talk of the water and wood which it was hoped the Pharaoh would finally get sent from Sidon. From this it would appear that the scheming little small-town ruler was sitting in the sea fortress—the real island of Tyre had not yet been built—and that the mainland was occupied by the Habiru, that his cisterns were dry and that he and his people were freezing to death. If this was so, he would have to get water from the neighbouring town about thrity kilometres away. His successors in the town built by Hiram would have to contend with the same emergencies—unless a better solution occurred to them, of which we know nothing. We *do* know what was done at Aradus.

The people there, who also lived on a rock, overcame the drinking-water problem in a way which still arouses the respect and envy of modern engineers. As they had no springs on their rocks, they captured, as Strabo tells us, springs which gushed out of the sea-bed. From their boats they laid down-turned funnels over the freshwater sources in the salt water, so that the water was driven upwards by its own pressure and could be caught by means of a leather pipe. Fresh water from the sea is tapped in the same way today off the Peloponnesian coast and great pride is taken in the fact that, with the aid of all the resources of modern technology, it is possible to repeat this method successfully. The people of Aradus had mastered it three thousand years ago, and the Tyrians also possibly used it, because lack of drinking water was not a deciding factor in any of the monthslong sieges which they later had to undergo.

Quite apart from the fresh water, there were various other difficulties concerned with sea water which had to be overcome by well-trained and skilled engineers. One of these was the shifting sand on the sea-bed. The harbours in the shallow coastal waters were always threatening to become silted up if they were not regularly cleared. Today huge suction dredgers are used for the purpose. The Phoenicians had a simpler method. At Sidon, where the south-easterly facing harbour was especially endangered by the shifting sand-drifts, they constructed a system of tidal basins and canals, which in certain winds permitted clean surface water to be driven into the inner harbour. The silt-carrying water was thus pressed downwards and carried away by a deep outflow through another channel, and the harbour was automatically cleansed.

In 1935 when the docks at Saida—the present-day Arab name for Sidon—threatened to become silted up once more, a far more primitive method was used. A new mole was built, which simply blocked the silt-carrying water, and dredgers then had to be used. The Phoenicians' clever solution of the same problem was only discovered years later by underwater archaeologists.

Historians today are united in thinking that the Phoenicians were not only the best seafarers of early antiquity but were also among the most outstanding technicians of their day. They probably earned this reputation both because they were simply more gifted in a practical sense than many of their neighbours, and also because their special position and their permanently threatened existence forced them to exert all their mental resources much more intensely in this respect than those who could allow themselves, in view of their large population and secure tenure of land, to be somewhat more indolent. Apart from that they had for centuries had good teachers in the pyramid-building, mathematically expert Egyptians, and profited further from the learning they had accumulated from the emigrant Cretans, besides perfecting their knowledge and expertise all the time through their daily dealings with the sea.

One of the most valuable gifts which the immigrant Aryans brought them was the keeled boat. Its invention was equivalent to that of the wheel in land transport. The keel ship developed from the canoe, which was built up with planks until it became the backbone of a quite different kind of vessel. But its development was not an inevitable process resulting simply from the daily exigencies of coastal sailing. Until the eighteenth century

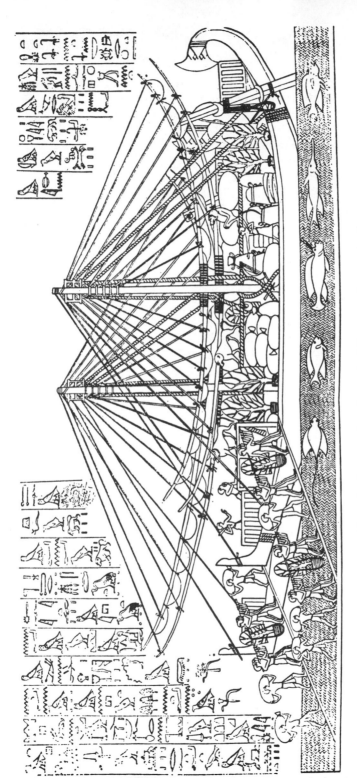

Egyptian ships—flat-bottomed and unsuited for sea-going navigation. Drawing after J. Dümichen.

the Polynesians from the coasts of Asia who settled in the Pacific islands used canoes which were only stabilized by outriggers or an additional hull. The discovery and use of the keeled vessel with all its advantages was therefore a completely exceptional phenomenon. It was possibly first demonstrated by the inhabitants 'of the islands and mainlands . . . at the edge of the ocean in the north'. At least one might assume so from a note of Rameses III, who apparently thought that the barbaric hordes of the Sea Peoples came from the North-sea area—and, as has been mentioned, some scholars agree with him in this because the keeled ship was already known there in the early Bronze Age. The Canaanites, who adopted it, quickly saw that one could hold a course better with this kind of boat than with a flat-bottomed craft, that it could also be steered against the swell without fear of pitching sideways, and that it did not so easily get out of control. They also learnt from the Sea Peoples that you can make better headway in a ship if you do not paddle facing the bows as they had done up till then, but put the oars in thole ports with the rowers sitting on benches facing aft. The Cretans had given them the rowing-boat as well as the keeler.

The towns of the Lebanese coast had three basic types of ship which developed from this technical expertise. First there was the war galley, a long narrow vessel with two banks of oars, a convex stern, a ram on the prow and a small sail. This type was enormously fast and easy to manœuvre in difficult situations. The crew hung their shields over the side of the ship, as the Vikings did later.

Then there was the merchantman, which was short and broad, needed fewer oarsmen, but had a large rectangular yard sail. It did not need to be particularly fast, but had to have a large hold, be easy to berth and, when necessary, get by with a minimum depth of water under the keel.

The third type was the so-called '*myoparones*' or mussel-boat, which had more oarsmen than the usual merchant vessel but not so many as a war galley. They usually had no sails and were used as auxiliaries to the war fleet, as buccaneering ships or as armed merchantmen in pirate-infested waters.

None of these ships, even the largest of them, can have been bigger than a nutshell by our standards. They were also smaller than the *Adoration of the Two Lands* ships of Pharaoh Senefru, because a keel—which the Egyptians did not yet have—could not very well be longer than the tallest tree which could be found in the forests, and cedars which could produce uniformly strong beams more than twenty metres long must have already been a very good size indeed.

None the less, all told, the Cretan-Phoenician boats made up a very good fleet with which to win supremacy at sea at that date. The neighbouring countries, even Egypt and Assyria, had neither such good ships, nor captains who could navigate by the sun and stars like the Cherethites and who moreover knew the eastern basin of the Mediterranean like the back of their hand.

However, even the new Phoenician squadrons rarely sailed a direct course across the open sea. Even they needed land bases at regular intervals, since they were not really up to weathering severe gales and therefore always had to be able to leave their set course, wherever they were, and seek a safe harbour. So they would go from, say, Tyre to Cyprus, and from there to the Anatolian coast and along that by stages to Rhodes. To the west of the Island of Roses there was then the Aegean, which could easily be crossed from island to island: from Tilos to Kos to Patmos and Ikaria, and finally over to the Peloponnesian coast or up to the Dardanelles.

It may seem a modest feat from our point of view, but for those days it was a considerable achievement. If you make the trip on a modern boat, you will hardly notice from up on the sun-deck how high the waves can be even in wind force two, as they roll towards a small rocking wooden craft. From down below it looks very different. I have tried it in a Turkish cutter, which must have been about the size of a Phoenician mussel boat (and I must admit I grew to love its put-putting, stinking diesel engine during the journey). I also now understand how a fight against the sea can be a back-breaking task, which makes a rest on dry land at least every two days seem more than justified.

CHAPTER VI

Establishment and Rise of the Firm of Baal, Sons and Co.

THE RISE OF Tyre and Sidon to become the leading towns in the Lebanon marks the beginning of the Phoenician trading empire. From wood suppliers to the Egyptians, always more or less duty-bound to pay taxes as vassals, they became wholesale merchants. Other customers from the islands and coastal areas of the Mediterranean now joined their main purchasers and contractors on the Nile.

It all began in a very primitive way, with methods which seem to us today more piratical than anything else. The Tyrians and Sidonians came sailing out of the azure realm they ruled with their ships, landed at strange beaches and harbours and spread out the wares they had brought with them in the market places. To the landsmen they must have seemed a cross between a fairground attraction and supernatural beings. They did not know where the seafarers came from, and so did not know how to treat them and were both terrified and fascinated by their appearance. The traders, on the other hand, who according to their reception behaved swaggeringly or servilely, regarded everything which the country they had descended on had to offer as potential booty and tried to get hold of as much of it as possible, either by barter or robbery. Herodotus tells us that they were always particularly interested in well-built girls and strong young men and had an evil reputation for being kidnappers in Greece. In a market in Argos, he recounts, 'on the fifth or sixth day after their arrival, when they had already sold everything', they fell upon the King's daughter Io, 'pushed her into a boat and made off in the direction of Egypt'. It is only one of the many stories which were told about the Phoenicians, and although it is very reminiscent of folk tales in which travelling gypsies steal children, there is little doubt that there is a hard core of truth in it. Trade was a harsh business in those days, and was carried out with no little brutality.

The wealth of the people from the Lebanon can hardly have been founded on such transactions, however. As they grew used to their new way of making a living the Tyrians and Sidonians must have realized that long-term profits were greater if one cultivated certain markets carefully and treated customers as partners, not (just) as objects to be exploited.

Another anecdote of Herodotus makes it clear that the principle of fair-dealing in business was so thoroughly adopted by them that they stuck to it even when it was not absolutely necessary. The Greek quotes a Carthaginian who had told him that the seafaring traders used to unload their wares in foreign parts and spread them out on the beach. 'Then,' he continues, 'they got back into their ships again and made a fire that smoked profusely. When the natives of the country saw the smoke, they came down to the sea. Then they laid down gold for the goods and went away again. The Carthaginians then disembarked from their ships to have a look. If the gold seemed to them to be adequate for the goods, they took it. If not, they went back to their boats and sat there. The others, for their part, would come down again and add more gold, until there was enough.'

In this way the first contacts were made. A counter-offer followed the first offering, and then the silent bargaining began, needing much tact, inventiveness and also honesty. The merchants did not want to spoil a possible new market before they had begun, a feeling apparently appreciated by their customers. Herodotus at any rate says, and his careful choice of words shows how amazed he was, 'Neither side ·cheated the other, because they [the sellers] did not touch the gold until it seemed to them to have reached the value of the goods, and the others [the buyers] did not touch the goods until they had taken up the money.'

It was thus a way of doing business which followed rules which we still rely on today. If one side profited more than the other, it was also for the same reasons which can be found today: an over-generous assessment of the cost, hidden faults, or wrong information as to the true value of the goods. But even that probably did not occur very often, because the delicate foundation of trust on which all trade is based was the life-blood of the Phoenician towns.

In the changeover from purely Egyptian to 'world' trade, there were many other essential requirements, which entirely altered the trading methods of the seagoing merchants as well as their life-style on the Lebanese coast.

First there was the recognition that bulk goods such as wood could be sent cheaply from Byblos to the Nile, but could never be transported for longer distances, or farther from the coast. Even the relatively near Cyprus can have been hardly accessible for the cumbersome coastal timber ships, not to mention more distant places such as Anatolia, Greece or Italy. The Phoenician boats, like the longships of the early middle ages, carried ten to twenty tons of freight at most, and usually less. It would obviously have been pointless to carry such a small quantity of timber on the arduous voyage from Tyre to, say, Argos. So it was therefore a matter of replacing the fragrant wood by expensive products, which it would pay to transport even in small quantities.

In fact the Tyrians and Sidonians, and naturally the Giblites and Arvadites too, consequently switched over to such products after 1,200 BC. The Bible states this in a report given by a prophet (Ezekiel 27:9–25), which, if one disregards the hymn-like style, might well have appeared in the trade pages of a modern newspaper as an economics article.

Ezekiel writes: 'All the ships of the sea with their mariners were in thee to occupy thy merchandise . . . by reason of the multitude of all kind of riches: with silver, iron, tin, and lead, they traded in thy fairs. Javan, Tubal, and Meshech [the Greek states in Anatolia], they were thy merchants: they traded the persons of men and vessels of brass in thy market. They of the house of Togarmah [Armenia] traded in thy fairs with horses and horsemen and mules. The men of Dedan [Arabia] were thy merchants; many isles [possibly in the Indian Ocean] were the merchandise of thine hand: they brought thee for a present horns of ivory and ebony. Syria was thy merchant by reason of the multitude of the wares of thy making: they occupied in thy fairs with emeralds, purple, and broidered work, and fine linen, and coral and agate. Judah, and the land of Israel, they were thy merchants: they traded in thy market wheat of Minnith, and Pannag, and honey, and oil, and balm. Damascus was thy merchant in the multitude of the wares of thy making, for the multitude of all riches; in the wine of Helbon, and white wool. Dan also and Javan [in Anatolia] going to and fro occupied in thy fairs: bright iron, cassia, and calamus, were in thy market. Dedan [Arabia] was thy merchant in precious clothes for chariots. Arabia, and all the princes of Kedar [also in Arabia], they occupied with thee in lambs, and rams, and goats: in these were they thy merchants. The merchants of Sheba and Raamah [Yemen], they were thy merchants: they occupied in thy fairs with chief of all spices, and with all precious stones, and gold. Haran, and Canneh, and Eden [in Mesopotamia], the merchants of Sheba, Asshur [Iraq] and Chilmad [Persia], were thy merchants. These were thy merchants in all sorts of things, in blue clothes, and broidered work, and in chests of rich apparel, bound with cords, and made of cedar, among thy merchandise. The ships of Tarshish did sing of thee in thy market: and thou wast replenished, and made very glorious in the midst of the seas.'

All in all, an impressive list. Ezekiel probably got the information for it in the markets and archives of Babylon, as he lived there in about 600 BC. His list of products can be divided into four main groups. There were the medicaments, cosmetics and spices like balm, and the calamus oil from the arum which is still used today in the preparation of medicines, together with honey and cinnamon. Then there was the group of dyes, and precious fabrics, to which the frequently mentioned blue and purple belong, as do the fine Egyptian linen and the brightly worked carpets from Iraq and Persia. Then group C: jewellery and other luxury articles. In this group are the precious stones from Syria, gold from the Yemen, silver from Anatolia, ebony and ivory from Africa or India, and naturally the beautiful Arabian 'clothes for chariots'. Finally, group D, the bulk goods, iron, tin, lead, horses, cattle, wheat, rope—and slaves.

If one looks at these groups in relation to their countries of origin, it is clear that foodstuffs and cattle came mostly from the areas close to the Lebanon, and were thus probably transported by land, whereas in long-distance and overseas trade it was mostly the precious goods which were exchanged, which would make a good profit even if sold in small quantities. Wood, the staple product of the Giblites, is only incidentally mentioned, as the building material for the ship to which Ezekiel compares Tyre. Many other products such as cowhides and papyrus, which are much in evidence in the Wen-Amon account, are not mentioned, although the Egyptian writing material at least was still an important item of trade in the fifth century BC.

Ezekiel's account is regarded as one of the most important documents concerning Phoenician economic history. What has made it of particular note, however, is not the list of wares, but the mention of the 'many isles', which one may suppose to have lain in the Indian Ocean, and 'the ships of Tarshish', which were held for a long time to be Spanish bound (which, as will be indicated below, is incorrect). Both points, however, do lead one to suppose that there was a trade network controlled by Tyre which spread over the Mediterranean and also included the countries round the Indian Ocean.

It remains to add that the words of the prophet are somewhat in advance of our account. They describe the situation when Phoenicia was at the height of her power. In the first few centuries after the invasion of the Sea Peoples her empire was only a half-realized concept. A people who simply traded and relied on a superior fleet would never have been able to come so far. Other political and economic factors must have played a part.

Bartering pure and simple, that is, trade that is carried on by buying certain goods somewhere and transporting them somewhere else to sell at a profit, is certainly profitable and lucrative. It becomes even more profitable if one does not just trade with these goods, but enhances them in one's own country—as by making copper vessels from copper for instance—adding on the cost of the workmanship. But most profitable of all is the sale of goods made in one's own land. There is a far greater concentration of wealth in industrial countries than in those which are merely trading centres, especially if both production and export-trade are combined. The merchants of Lübeck and Bremen recognized this in their day—not simply transporting French and Spanish wines from one place to another, but letting them mature to vintage wines in their cellars. It has been well understood by the Dutch, who include many of their own products in their world-wide trading network, from cheese to porcelain to electrical goods, and by the Swiss, who conveyed their own watches along the Nord-Süd-Strasse. And it was well understood, at the beginning of the first millennium BC, by the Phoenicians. They added to their range of goods more and more articles from their own workshops, and founded their own industries.

It sounds simple: to found an industry. But industry presupposes raw materials. What was there in the Lebanon? The small amount of copper and tin washed up by the mountain streams was hardly worth mentioning, and the possibility of finding its origin in the wild mountain country was slight. There was good clay soil here and there, but again not in any great quantity. There therefore remained—in addition to the forests, which of course did not grow again as quickly as they were cut down— stones, sand and the sea. Not a particularly favourable outlook; but the Phoenicians with their practical intelligence turned it to brilliant account.

First there was sand, which might seem not a very precious natural product. But only to those who do not know that in many cases—and the mountainous Lebanon is one such case— it contains a great quantity of quartz. Quartz is pure silicic acid in crystalline form, and silicic acid is the most important constituent of glass: an ordinary windowpane contains over seventy per cent and even a lead crystal glass sixty per cent. So if one mixes this waste product from the sea with sodium bicarbonate, which is found in the Egyptian soda lakes or can be obtained from the ash of salt-bearing sea and steppe plants, and then adds alkaline substances in the form of limestone, marble or chalk and heats the mixture to between seven and eight hundred degrees Centigrade, one gets, with intense vesication, that viscous, quickly solidifying substance which can be made into small beads or core-made flasks or, by blowing, into beautifully rounded, transparent vessels.

The process was already known to the Egyptians in the fourth century BC. They obtained an opaline, opaque glass from sand, plant ash, saltpetre and chalk, which they made into small liquid-containers and sold as a luxury article throughout the world.

The Phoenicians must at some point have succeeded in stealing the secret of their method of production (which one imagines

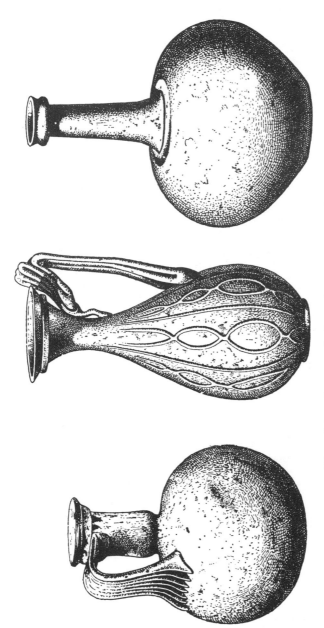

Phoenician glass vessels from the necropolis at Tyre.

was jealously guarded), and they developed their own glass industry on this basis. But they were not content with merely copying the process: they used all their ingenuity and tenacity in attempting to make the milky substance transparent. After much experimentation—and we can only guess at the time and difficulties involved—they did in fact succeed.

In Tyre and Sidon, particularly in the latter town, small glassworks were built, from whose furnaces came the first transparent glass in the history of mankind. Which means that if one can attribute the invention of glass to any one people, then it should be to the people living in the Lebanon rather than to the Egyptians. This is all the more justifiable since the Phoenicians later, in all probability, also discovered the technique of glass-blowing.

As spectacular as the discovery was the manner in which they commercialized it. They did not limit themselves to selling glass as a luxury article at a high price, but set up regular trade networks to sell it on the mass market. Cast, moulded or cut glass was sold so cheaply in Tyre and Sidon that it could be bought even by their less well-off contemporaries and so gradually replaced metal and clay goblets. The Phoenicians flooded the whole Mediterranean with their vessels, flasks, glass beads and glazed tiles and thus became the founders of mass production.

Besides the glass industry, another line of manufacture was developed which was to revolutionize contemporary taste almost as much: the manufacture of the Tyrian/Sidonian purple dye. The Phoenicians found the raw material for this right on their doorstep too, in the shallow water of their Mediterranean beaches.

Purple of a more beautiful shade than the Phoenicians ever achieved can be made today in a retort; it is a derivative of indigo. At that time they found the dye, without of course knowing its chemical composition, only in the glands of a small sea-snail of the Purpuridae family, which is found in nearly all warm seas. It is still found on the beaches of Saida and Sur, and there are dozens of small boys prepared to show admiring foreigners, for a couple of piastres, how they can dye a piece of white woollen cloth red with it.

The process is quite simple. You run the cloth over the underside of the small creature, where its secretory glands are, and

get a fleck of yellow, which, if it is sprinkled with lemon juice,
gradually turns blue, then red and then a deep dark red. But it
remains a tiny drop. The boy who showed me, used more than
twenty snails—and asked as many piastres—before the tip of
a fairly small woollen scarf was even spotted with red. Indeed
scientists have now established that, to make a few grammes of
purple dye, over ten thousand snails of the species *murex brandaris*
and *murex trunculus* must lose their lives.

As a result the Phoenician purple manufacture, unlike their
glass industry, could never be for a mass public but only for a
few of the rich. The purple cloth from Tyre and Sidon was
definitely a luxury article, which also explains why it was reserved
for a long time for kings, in Rome for senators and in later times
for those most loyal servants of the German government, the
chiefs of general staff. A purple stripe was always a sign of high
rank, and the colour itself a symbol of the highest authority—
and for this idea too the Phoenicians were responsible.

However, it was not they who discovered this method of
dyeing. The originators of the technique were possibly the people
of Ugarit, the Syrian town in which Hurrians lived together
with immigrant Canaanites and Amorites. A merchant from this
prosperous metropolis has left us a text in cuneiform script
which tells us that the big employers gave their woollen cloth
out to small homeworkers to be dyed. There was a good reason
for this: the workshops of the dyers gave off a powerful smell,
which, Strabo says, still infected the streets of Tyre in his day,
in the time of the Emperor Augustus. How the Tyrians themselves
came by the smell is not recorded, yet, as has been mentioned,
it is likely that the Sea Peoples learnt the secret of the dye in
Ugarit, when they plundered and destroyed the city, and later
taught it to their new Canaanite partners.

However, the purple dye did not smell to the Phoenicians, for
the same reasons that gold never smells. They grew rich on it,
and even more importantly, famous. It is thought that the Greek
word *Phoinike* is derived from *porphyra,* purple, and thus could
mean 'the land of purple'—but we have no proof of this, nor of
the theory that Canaan, also, may have meant 'the land of the
dark red people'.

Besides the purple-dye and glass industries, there were many other kinds of trade in the Phoenician cities, but none which could compare with them in size and importance—with the exception, of course, of shipbuilding.

In some of the dye factories clothes of a paler colour than the purple were made. The dye for this was obtained from insects which lived on oak trees. It was the 'scarlet' of the Bible. Besides this there were ivory carvers in small workshops who produced highly realistic trinkets from imported elephant or walrus tusks. Elsewhere artistic vessels of bronze, gold and silver were made, and pottery workshops produced dark red clay vases, with glazes which were almost as costly as glass. Phoenician craftsmen also made decorative weapons, bracelets and necklaces, but these were only additional articles in an economic set-up which specialized above all in luxury goods and only sold glassware to a wider market.

The Lebanon was a small country and the people there liked small things (especially if they brought in big profits)—which, incidentally, confirms a theory of the German political economist Werner Sombart, who holds that great fortunes, such as were amassed in Europe at the beginning of the modern era, always arise by catering to the needs of an élite and are only later invested in mass markets. His conclusion is: 'And so luxury led . . . to capitalism.'

CHAPTER VII

Dealings with King Solomon

THE PHOENICIANS ARE often reproached for having been so persistently silent about themselves and for having left no written history of their own. Everything we know about them comes from the annals of other races; they have only foreign advocates to plead their cause to posterity. The accusations usually culminate in the reproach that the people from the Lebanon simply had no feeling for the written word and therefore left no literature. They were nothing but clever philistines, and crass capitalists.

In the nineteenth century, which, with its need to draw colour from strange, and if possible exotic, climes, gave birth to a Phoenicia-cult, there was an attempt to reverse this judgement, but unfortunately by disreputable means.

In 1836 the German theologian Friedrich Wagenfeld published a book containing the writings of the Phoenician priest Sanchuniathon. He claimed to have rediscovered them in a translation by the Greek writer Philo of Byblos, and gave out that the document in question was a work of nine volumes in all, in which an account was given of everything concerning Phoenicia in the period around 1,250 BC. Naturally the publication of 'Sanchuniathon's Ancient History' caused immense excitement in the academic world. There was feverish hope of at last getting authentic information about the Phoenicians, especially as until now all that was known of Sanchuniathon was the little that the Byzantine Bishop Eusebius of Caesarea had told of him. Now he would be revealed in his own hand.

The popular scientific periodicals of the day launched into the theme of the Phoenicians with the same eagerness with which nowadays possible cancer cures are heralded. They discussed the subject in its widest context and even impressed Wilhelm Raabe, who made the hero of his novel *Abu Telfan* read

Sanchuniathon—behind locked doors, to heighten the mystery. But at the climax of the whole controversy—for there were naturally critics who doubted the authenticity of the documents— the affair burst like a pricked balloon. Karl Ludwig Grotefend was able to show, by means of the watermarks in the paper which Wagenfeld had used, that the letters in which a Portuguese colonel was purported to have offered the Sanchuniathon writings to their publisher were all faked. Wagenfeld was nothing but a highly gifted forger. He later became an editor of a small magazine and took to the bottle.

The deception, moreover, caused such disappointment to those of the public who were interested in the subject that any further discussion of the possibility of finding genuine documents on Phoenician history hardly got beyond the study-doors of the academics, and the Phoenicia-craze in general died a quiet death.

Today Sanchuniathon is still occasionally quoted, in the form handed on by Eusebius, but it is generally accepted that it is pointless to hope now that an original Phoenician commentator will be discovered, and felt that this vanished people will now remain silent for ever and that therefore reliable information about their travels on earth can only be obtained from the Greek and Jewish sources. The most exact information about a long section of the history of Tyre, Sidon and Byblos is given by the Bible.

Whether this circumstance justifies the accusation that the inhabitants of the sea cities were lazy writers, uncreative or lacking in literary talent is another matter. One cannot answer with a categorical 'yes', as even renowned scholars do at times, berating the Phoenicians for not even having given us Sanchuniathon. For the Jews, that race of great thinkers and visionaries, shared a part of their history in common with the Phoenicians, and were by no means only the leaders, but at times rather the led. The Phoenicians showed them the sea route to the kingdom of the legendary Queen of Sheba; they built up a vast copper industry on the Gulf of Aqaba for their King Solomon and gave them among other things the great sacred shrine of their people, the temple at Jerusalem. The Jews and Phoenicians were closely linked. Both came from Sinai, both had moved along the same paths towards the north, to the

Mediterranean coast and the fertile fields of Canaan, the promised land.

In about 1,500 BC the rocky plateau on the Red Sea was again the launching-ground for a massive migratory movement—the Aramaean. But the great tide also swept with it a group which was made up of Semites, Hurrians and people of Aryan origin. It was called the 'House of Joseph' and had by then already had a storm-tossed past.

At the time of the Hyksos' rule their forefathers had gone to Egypt and had been received there by the related occupying tribes with open arms. Their leader, a man called Jehusiph or Joseph, rose to high office and great honour, and his whole tribe lived richly on the 'fleshpots of Egypt' and quickly adopted Egyptian customs and the Egyptian way of life. However, this submission to the codes of a foreign civilization did not protect the immigrants from losing their houses and positions when King Amosis drove the Hyksos out of the Delta in about 1,570 BC. They fell together with their protectors, and over-night fine linen robes and slaves to fan their couches became things of the past. They were thrown into labour camps, groaned under the scourge of Egyptian overseers, and if one of them was killed, it was of little moment. The commandants of these slave prisons called their victims Aperu, which was probably the designation for a particularly low social class. In the Bible this became Ebrews or Hebrews.

But like every worm that is downtrodden the members of this luckless group finally turned. They struck back when they were beaten and then left the Nile country in a spectacular flight, to return across the Red Sea to the land from which they had originally come. A number of other groups of foreign workers joined them. The man who led the exodus is believed to have been called by the Egyptian name of Moses.

Sinai, of course, could be only a brief stopping place for the refugees. If they wanted to live even approximately as they had done in Egypt they had to join the Aramaean migration and press on towards the territory in the Jordan valley, where their fore-bears had probably lived. So we find them in about 1,100 BC in the hills to the west of the Sea of Chinnereth and the Dead Sea. Here they formed settler communities and gave themselves tribal names such as Ephraim, Naphtali, Benjamin, Zebulun and Asher. Thus Benjamin meant 'those who live in the south', and Zebulun, 'those who dwell by the shore'.

By 'settling' one does not necessarily mean that they took possession of the land by force, driving out the inhabitants and expanding over the territory they had won. They were often content to take over the spare land between the many small Canaanite principalities which had sprung up there. In doing so they came into contact with the people living there and also with the Phoenicians, who lived farther to the north. This was usually achieved in a peaceful way. The tribes of Zebulun and Asher, who lived in Galilee, not far from the present-day border between Israel and the Lebanon, sent their young men to Tyre or Sidon, so that they could be hired out as dockers. The Book of Kings also tells of a woman who went there. She married a Phoenician smith and bore him a son, who later became famous as one of the men who built the temple at Jerusalem.

Less happy than the relationship of the Jews to the peace-loving inhabitants of the Lebanon coast was their experience of the Sea Peoples. The Philistines pressed upwards from the south and tried to create a great empire that would include the whole of Palestine. They attacked the Hebrews, who had formed a holy covenant, an amphictyony of twelve tribes. This loose organization was naturally not ready for a major war. They had to form a state, which they did not succeed in doing straight away.

Saul, of the house of Joseph, which had in the meantime been named Israel, was the first king of the new, somewhat unstable, community. With the soldiers of the house of Judah he went to meet the Aryans in the valley of Jezreel, near the Sea of Chinnereth. It was a lost cause from the start. The Judaic warriors were as unable to withstand the Philistine contingents as any other group of farmers before or since an army of trained soldiers at the height of their military efficiency. They were utterly defeated at the foot of the hill of Megiddo, one of the classic battlegrounds of history. Saul slew himself with his own sword, and the people of Israel, or those who had not fled across the Jordan to the east, fell under Philistine rule. They were even forbidden to have their own forges, so that they could not make any weapons.

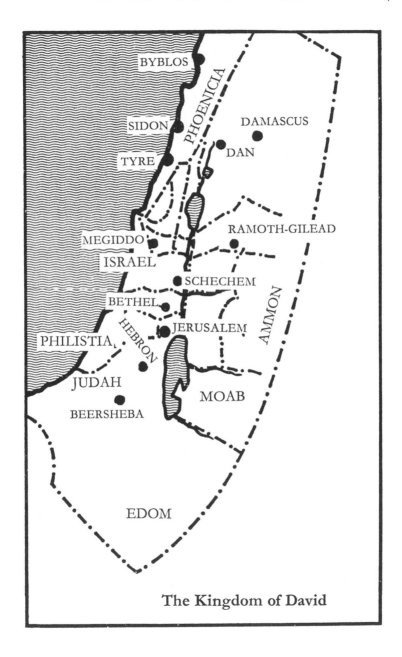

The Kingdom of David

It was only David, Saul's clever ex-adjutant, who was able to wipe out the shame of Megiddo. As a *condottiere* of a Philistine king, he built up a small private army under his very eyes, then let himself be chosen King of Judah, forcing the house of Israel to recognize him as their leader also. Finally he took possession of a small Jebusite mountain town then called Urusalim in the west Jordanian hills, renamed it Jerusalem (both names mean city of peace) and set up his throne there. Only then was the State of Israel really founded.

With the help of the confederation of the three half-sovereign states, Judah, Israel and Jerusalem, David was able to increase his small army and then inflict a decisive defeat on the quarrelling Philistine kings which erased them from the political map as independent powers. This had a decisive effect on Phoenician history. The Sea Peoples who had settled on the Lebanese coast had until now always had their brother tribes in Gaza and Ashkelon to fall back on and were therefore rather uncertain partners as far as the sea cities were concerned. Now, however, David's victory made them homeless and friendless refugees, who could no longer afford to alienate the goodwill of their hosts. They had to allow themselves to become integrated.

This probably gave the Phoenicians good cause to be pleased at the news of David's victory, and to consider the state he had created as a new ally—and in so doing they naturally thought first and foremost about new opportunities for trade.

Hiram in particular, the clever ruler of Tyre, soon realized that the new underdeveloped commonwealth in Palestine would turn to his people not only for their valuable products but even more for their fund of knowledge and experience. He therefore made haste to inform their king of the help and wares with which he could serve him. He sent him samples: cedar trees, carpenters and stonemasons (2 Samuel 5:11).

David gratefully accepted the offer. He wanted to make the small Jebusite town where he lived into a religious and political capital, but could never have found master-craftsmen among his own people who were capable of building a temple or palace. All he could do was to buy iron 'in abundance for the nails for the doors of the gates, and for the joinings; and brass in abundance without weight' (1 Chronicles 22:3). The rest he had to leave to the foreigners.

However the founder of the state of Israel did not live to see the building of the Jerusalem temple, or even its beginning. He died in 966 BC. His son Solomon, who was not nearly as wise as the Bible makes out, being in fact a rather ungifted ruler, was dutifully eager to carry out his father's plans. The first step was therefore a letter to Hiram of Tyre.

'Now therefore command thou that they hew me cedar trees out of Lebanon; and my servants shall be with thy servants: and unto thee will I give hire for thy servants according to all that thou shalt appoint: for thou knowest that there is not among us any that can skill to hew timber like unto the Sidonians' (1 Kings 5:6). All Phoenicians, to Solomon, or the authors of the chronicles of the Kings, were simply Sidonians.

Hiram was naturally highly delighted at the proposition. According to the Bible he was said to have cried out: 'Blessed be the Lord this day, which hath given unto David a wise son' (1 Kings 5:7). But this is fairly unlikely, since he was not a follower of the Lord and Solomon's commission was far from wise. A bulk buyer does not leave it to his supplier to name the price, especially when doing business on that scale. Let us therefore assume that in fact he only rubbed his hands. But he wrote back to Solomon by return of post to say he had received the order and would see to it promptly. In return he asked for and received twenty thousand measures, about seven thousand tons, of wheat and twenty thousand measures of olive oil, or about seven thousand hectolitres, for every year the building continued—a vast amount which must have been very welcome in the poor mountainous land of Phoenicia.

The undertaking of the building of the temple was itself a vast project. The Hebrew king was said to have mobilized thirty thousand wood-cutters, seventy thousand porters and eighty thousand stonemasons. The Tyrians, who only took on the architectural work, the supervision of the building and the finer stonecutting work, did not even have enough men for these tasks. They had to get help from the Giblites and probably the Sidonians also. Phoenicia hired out builders on a co-operative basis.

The joint building programme of Hiram and Solomon has been

invaluable to historians, particularly art historians. Thanks to the detailed descriptions of the temple of Jerusalem in the Bible we know today approximately how a large Phoenician building looked. None of the experts consider the great church to be an example of the Hebrew style of architecture—such a style never existed—it being generally accepted that it was made by the people from the Lebanon. It is all the more valuable as the Phoenicians themselves have left us only very few monuments in their own towns, which were continually destroyed and rebuilt. We would hardly have known how their own temples and palaces looked if there had not been a building contractor in Israel who invited them to work for him, and writers who described the result minutely.

Yet archaeological research does help in some respects. It indicates that the Phoenicians, who had already built large stone houses in the Bronze Age, then developed in the Iron Age (that is, after the arrival of the Sea Peoples), a model for public buildings. This is technically referred to as Bit-hilani by scholars today. Particularly characteristic of such buildings is a large outer courtyard surrounded on three sides by rooms, which were entered through a central audience hall—a gigantic *atrium* plus bungalows. But if it was part of a temple, the outer courtyard had a purely decorative function. It led to a single central door, that opened on to the tripartite holy place.

Solomon's temple was also built according to these two models. The biblical chronicle tells of a 'temple before it' and a 'house within'. This corresponds approximately with the Bit-hilani ground-plan: first an almost square vestibule, then a rectangular central room and behind that the small dark cell with the holy of holies.

In Jerusalem the outer courtyard surrounded the so-called 'molten sea', a vast basin filled with water, for the cleansing ceremonies. In the middle chamber was the altar of gold for the shewbread, the twelve loaves which are laid out every sabbath day 'in the sight of God'. The dark chamber beyond held the ark of the covenant, the throne of Jahweh, the invisible god of the wilderness, which was later used as a container for the tablets of the ten commandments and which is represented in synagogues by the Torah shrine.

There was another detail of the great building which, like

the division of the rooms, was typical of Phoenician architecture: the pillars of Boaz and Jachin, which towered skywards in the outer courtyard on the left and right of the entrance to the temple. Neither had any connection with any part of the Jewish liturgy, but similar designs were found in Canaanitish temples. Herodotus tells us, for instance, that the temple of Melqart at Tyre also had two pillars of the same kind, 'one of pure gold, the other of emerald, which shone brilliantly at night'. Besides which, bases of similar pillars have been found in a temple of Baal in Cyprus and in various Palestinian towns such as Samaria, Megiddo and Hazor. The decoration which covered the obelisk-like forms was probably derived from Egyptian prototypes, as Phoenician architecture in general was strongly influenced by the Nile.

The Phoenicians exported whatever seemed worth their while, including probably the largest building which they ever built. Those who received their goods were full of praise for their work. 'Hiram's builders', says the Bible, 'did hew them, and the stone-squarers: so they prepared timber and stones to build the house.' They must have carried out the work to perfection, for 'there was neither hammer nor axe nor any tool of iron heard in the house, while it was in building' (1 Kings 5:18; 6:7). All the pieces were cut to size in the quarry or in the timber-lands and only afterwards transported to the site—which apart from anything else meant that immensely precise measurements must be taken.

The quality of the finished work must have been equally exceptional. Josephus writes that the slabs for the temple walls were cut so smoothly 'that the onlooker could see no trace of hammer or other tools. The whole fabric seemed to have pieced itself together of its own accord without the help of such things.' The same applied to the carving of the great mass of cedar trunks. Solomon had the whole inner chamber panelled with this wood. 'All was cedar; there was no stone seen' (1 Kings 6:18). Finally the Tyrian textile industry also played its part in the decoration of the building. The curtain that separated the holy of holies from the central hall was 'of blue, and purple' (2 Chronicles 3:14).

Only one of the many craftsmen who worked on the temple

is mentioned in the Bible—once again a Phoenician. He was called Huram-abi and was the son of the woman from the tribe of Naphtali who had married a smith in Tyre. The pillars of Boaz and Jachin were shaped by Huram, also the molten sea and the vast number of cultic objects with which Solomon fitted out the church. The metalsmith must have worked for years to complete them all, but he received his due from the chronicler. 'He was filled with wisdom, and understanding, and cunning', he writes of the Tyrian (1 Kings 7:14). From this it is clear that the builders made a good impression in Jerusalem—at least at the court.

Whether they were quite so popular with the people is very doubtful. The remuneration which Hiram requested for his men was levied from the small country in heavy taxes. Israel's by no means inexhaustible supplies of wheat and oil were just sufficient to pay for the temple. The cost of the palace, which Solomon also ordered from Tyre—it was almost as big as all the rest of Jerusalem together—was beyond even his means. Hiram had to lay out 120 talents of gold (over 60 cwt.) in advance for the building and later had to write this off. The King's coffers were empty. He offered instead a strip of land in Galilee with twenty villages, which the Tyrian accepted under protest. But what else could Hiram do? He did not want to jeopardize future trade relations with the Hebrew ruler for the sake of such a trifle.

The friendship between the two rulers does not seem to have been seriously affected by the affair of the palace—according to a traditional eastern folk-tale. Josephus has handed it on to us. Hiram, he recounts, challenged Solomon to a riddle contest, since the latter was said to be so wise. He sent him a number of riddles and bade him solve them if he could. Naturally the lord of Jerusalem succeeded. 'None of the problems posed was too difficult for him. He solved them successfully by logical deduction and revealed their meaning, after he had discovered it.'

But it is only one version of the story, the one that was recorded in the Jewish archives. In Tyre it read very differently. Solomon, not Hiram, had begun the quizzing game and had laid a wager on the result. Whoever lost must pay. Hiram accepted, and lost. But then he found a wise fellow in his own town, called Abdemun, who thought up some difficult riddles for his king to send to

Jerusalem. And this time Solomon—naturally—failed. 'He paid Hiram back more than he had won from him.' It was now one-all in the match between kings.

The story is just a sidelight on the serious business of the Phoenician-Hebrew temple and palace building, a piece of the public relations waffle with which even then the less welcome realities were glossed over. It is only a pity that none of the riddles have come down to us with the anecdote. One would love to know what the two mighty men of the day were racking their brains over—and whether one could have competed with them.

CHAPTER VIII

Baal and Sons, and Israel

SOLOMON AND HIS state must have proved a godsend for Hiram. Nothing could have been more opportune than this customer who spent his money so freely, and his kingdom which served as a fruitful hinterland to Hiram's small community without burdening it with any administrative costs.

For Israel, on the other hand, Tyre was a doorway to the open sea and to world trade, for we have no record of the Hebrews having sailed forth from their own shores on long trading voyages. They were primarily farmers and shepherds, not a mercantile and industrial nation like the Phoenicians.

The fact that despite this they launched their own fleet in the Red Sea, also in the time of Solomon, can probably be attributed to the influence of Tyre, and would have been of equal benefit to both countries. The ships of the squadron were only nominally Israel's; their crews would have been exclusively recruited in Phoenicia. They were the mysterious 'ships of Tarshish' mentioned by Ezekiel, which sailed from Aqaba to the even more mysterious Ophir, among other places, and brought back 'gold, and silver, ivory, and apes and peacocks' for Solomon (1 Kings 10:22).

The two names, Ophir and Tarshish, together make up one of the most insoluble riddles the expounders of Phoenician history have to wrestle with. Ophir presents the lesser difficulty. Scholars are now on the whole satisfied that this region lay somewhere at the end of the Red Sea and was therefore either the Yemen, the *Arabia felix*, from whence the Queen of Sheba also came, or the African coast somewhere in the region between Ethiopia and present-day Tanzania. In any case it was a country which could be reached from the Gulf of Aqaba. Tarshish is more of a problem. Where was this place—if it was a place?

The most popular interpretation is that Tarshish was Tartessos in Spain, near present-day Cadiz, a town (or region) which is also often associated with the Atlantis legend. But this solution is more than dubious. If Tarshish was in fact one of the Iberian ports later founded by the Phoenicians, the question arises of how ships which also went to Ophir, got there from Aqaba. The Suez canal was not in existence. Or did Solomon have a second fleet in the Mediterranean?

This last idea is rather unlikely. The Phoenicians, on whom the King was dependent for all his maritime activities, had built the Jews a fleet because the latter had had a port in the Gulf of Aqaba since the time of King David, and because this gateway to the east opened up interesting trade routes for them too. It would be to underrate their intelligence, however, to think that out of pure friendship they also built and organized a Jewish fleet in the Mediterranean. It would have been in direct competition with their own. It thus follows that Tarshish can hardly have been in Spain.

The most likely, and also most original, answer is that suggested by the Dutch Jesuit Father Simons. According to his theory, the word Tarshish does not stand for a place but is derived from the Akkadian word *rashashu,* to melt or be melted. Simons rests his evidence mainly on the discoveries of the American archaeologist Nelson Glueck.

In 1939 this scholar set about elucidating the verse of the Bible in which there is talk of Solomon, who 'made a navy of ships in Ezion-geber, which is beside Eloth, on the shore of the Red Sea, in the land of Edom'. So Glueck went from Jerusalem to the Negev, as Edom is a strip of land to the south of the Dead Sea which David took from a neighbouring people, the Edomites, and the Red Sea refers to the Gulf of Aqaba. Ezion-geber, the port of the Hebrew king, must therefore have lain somewhere near the spot where today a Jordanian and Israeli town smoulder in hostile propinquity under the same sun, the sleepy El 'Aqaba and the far more cheerful Eilat.

Glueck's assistants began digging in a mound of rubble at Tell el-Kheleifeh, near the former of these two towns. They hoped to find remains of shipyards or shipping equipment or something of that kind. But instead, to their amazement, they found copper utensils, moulds and finally the remains of a surprisingly large smelting works. Naturally they were astonished, as anyone would be who thinks he is on the trace of something and then suddenly finds himself face to face with something quite different. There is only an occasional mention of copper in the Bible, and then in quite a different context from Ezion-geber.

What was the explanation of their finds? Further excavations brought new discoveries. Near the copper workshops the archaeologists also found a massive gateway. The fortifications removed any remaining doubts as to whether they had discovered the town near Eloth in the land of Edom. Only this Ezion-geber was not only the great port of Solomon as described in the Book of Kings, but also an important industrial city, a copper-mining and smelting centre, in short 'the Pittsburgh of Palestine', as Glueck announced with understandable euphoria. His euphoria lacked a solid archaeological basis, since it has not yet been proved that it was Solomon who invested there. But this objection is only of importance if one considers the biblical chroniclers to have been extravagant fabulists.

If one takes them seriously it becomes clear why Simons thinks Tarshish could be derived from the Akkadian word for smelting. The ships of this name would then be simply vessels based in the mining town of Ezion-geber with its smelting furnaces, which travelled from there down the Red Sea and possibly also across the Indian Ocean. The Lebanese historian Nina Jidejian has followed up this theory with the suggestion that there were probably many places in the territory occupied by the Tyrians and Sidonians which were called Tarshish. From which it follows that Ezion-geber too may possibly have been named thus in the Phoenician language.

A relatively simple explanation for one of the favourite myths in Phoenician history! And the facts which remain are sensational enough. Phoenicians and Jews together founded a maritime empire which reached from Aqaba as far as the countries of the Indian Ocean, and they also had a thriving industrial centre in this dusty corner of the desert which was among the largest of its kind in the ancient orient—for none of the experts has suggested that the Hebrews were in a position to build, on their own, blast furnaces as elaborate as those which Glueck found there.

The copper mines on the Red Sea must have been one of the Phoenicians' greatest assets in their trade with Israel. The inhabi-

Foundations of the hippodrome at Tyre

The cedar woods were their capital—one of the remaining trees

They hung their shields over the ships' sides like the
Vikings: Phoenician warships and merchantmen

Sidon, Byblos's rival: today a humble fishing port

tants of ancient Byblos had also traded in copper; the search for copper later led Tyrians and Sidonians as far as Cyprus and Spain. Copper was then, as it still is, one of the most precious raw materials. And they had found it in Ezion-geber.

The Bible—as has already been seen—is unfortunately rather inarticulate when it comes to describing the predecessors of present-day Aqaba and Eilat. This is probably because by the standards of the day, the Negev was a long way from Jerusalem, where the chroniclers were, and still farther from Babylon, where both the Books of Kings were later edited. The information which filtered through from there to the writing rooms of the day was probably considered to be half mythical, and was moreover only used as material with which to fill out the glorious (but false) picture of Solomon which is given in the Bible. In fact the industrial town of Ezion-geber was far from a fairy-tale place. Its factories were sweat-shops.

Among other things Glueck found a smelter, which cleverly adapted an old forging technique, being built so that the prevailing winds of the region would force the necessary oxygen into the furnace through suitable flues. He also discovered huge smelting crucibles with a capacity of almost five cubic metres and a large number of copper- and also iron-mines.

He came to the conclusion that Ezion-geber was not a place which had grown up more or less organically and therefore untidily round the copper mines, but was 'built with considerable architectural and engineering skill at one time as an integrated whole'. This sentence alone conjures up a picture of Phoenician engineers with surveyors' staffs and rolls of plans in their hands, supervising and chasing up the hordes of workers recruited by Solomon during the building process. It can hardly have been a pleasant task for either party. The sun there shines down through hot shimmering air masses, and is reflected back from the rubble. Admittedly the air is cooled from time to time by the recurrent winds, but only at the cost of unpleasant dust-storms, with particles which get in one's eyes and grate between one's teeth. It must have been still worse when the furnaces were finally finished and fed by the sweat-drenched workers, in the combined heat of the fire and that from the murderous heavenly star.

We do not know exactly what living conditions were like in

Ezion-geber, but life there must have been much the same as it is in present-day Eilat. Adventurous types, seldom wearing more than shorts and shirt, crowd the shoddily furnished bars, wander down the sandswept streets and see themselves as heroes, but also as rejected by their country, both of which are true. Israel does not send her most law-abiding citizens to the Gulf of Aqaba, but on the other hand she repays their stint on the edge of the Negev with considerable tax reliefs. Besides being an outpost on the Jordanian border, Eilat is also one of the most important copper-mining centres in the Jewish state. The Israelis have exploited Glueck's discoveries in their own way. They dig their mines where Solomon's workers once wielded their picks.

Thus the biggest souvenir shop in Eilat is called 'King Solomon's Mines', the second-best hotel the 'Queen of Sheba'. The tradition is kept alive. But that does not apply to the quality of the service offered. The Queen of Sheba would certainly not have patronized the hotel named after her for more than one night.

The copper mined in Eilat now goes north to the Israeli industrial region, to be wrought there. Again, we can only guess at what they did in ancient times. They probably loaded just small quantities onto camels to be transported up to Jerusalem. Most of the copper must have been worked by smiths on the spot. The ships of Tarshish were then loaded with the vessels, implements or whatever else was made from the non-ferrous metal, and sailed to the market-places of the distant Ophir. There the goods were mostly traded for gold, silver, ivory, sweet-smelling woods, panther skins or for the spices for which Southern Arabia was famous: incense and myrrh, a sweet-scented gum-resin which the Egyptians particularly loved.

It was only because of this profitable export trade that it was possible to use King Solomon's mines economically. The copper was made into easily transportable articles, which were then sold at a vast profit. One can judge how large this was from a record which has come down to us, which states that the Mesopotamian Chaldeans burnt incense to the value of ten thousand talents of silver every year, or two hundred and sixty tons, the equivalent of an incredibly large sum of money, even by today's standards.

The copper mines were so profitable that in spite of his extravagance, Solomon was saved from national bankruptcy, and the

Phoenicians, 'Hiram's servants' as they are called in the Bible, must have had a great deal to do with this.

However, the business which they carried on down there was not without its problems. The transport of the wood alone, for keels, masts and ships' sides, from the Lebanon to the dockyard on the Red Sea—it takes a good day and a half by car from Haifa to Eilat—must have been a very wearisome business. Before Roman times there was not a single road in the area. So all the trunks and planks must have been loaded onto camels, none of which would have been able to carry very much more than two hundredweight. Which would have made it necessary to use several thousand animals. Friedrich Wagenfeld, alias Sanchuniathon, who obviously racked his brains over this problem, states unhesitatingly that there were eight thousand. From the wood which they carried, he continues in biblical tone, 'a fleet of ten ships was built.'

But whether his perhaps fairly realistic assessment was approximately accurate or not, it still leaves one question unanswered: how were the over-twenty-metre-long trunks transported, from which the Phoenician shipbuilders cut the keels for their boats? In ox-carts? By several animals roped together? Again we are left without any information. The authors of the relevant books of the Bible had little interest in such technical details. It is left to our imagination, and we can only conjure up those endless caravans which the not unthoughtful, if over-inventive, Wagenfeld would have us see plodding across the Negev. We must conclude that the technically gifted Phoenicians solved the problem, as they had done others in Tyre or Aradus.

At any rate the fact which emerges most clearly from all the above points is that without the technical and mercantile skill of Hiram's people the Jewish king would not have been in a position to exploit the Ezion-geber copper deposits in an economically viable way or to develop his overseas trade. On the other hand without his help the Phoenicians would not have been able to reach the East African and Indian trade routes, which were very profitable for them too. The teamwork between Tyre and Israel can therefore be defined in almost biological terms. It was not an alliance or syndicate, but a symbiosis—two different organisms living together for the mutual benefit of each—like that between hermit-crabs and sea anemones.

Needless to say, things have altered a lot since. The present-day descendants of Solomon and Hiram, the Israelis and Lebanese, face each other across barbed-wire barricades and minefields. And anyone who imagines that in a country where the past has so much bearing on the present as it does in the Near East, one or other side might occasionally remember the good old days and wish them back, will be sadly disappointed.

In spite of the praise given to the Phoenicians in the Bible, modern Israeli historical scholars do not speak at all kindly of their one-time neighbours, even if this is for religious rather than economic reasons.

The same applies in reverse to the Lebanese. Dimitri Baramki almost began to hiss when I mentioned the old friendship. And the Munich-born Israeli religious historian Schalom Ben-Chorin, with whom I spoke about the same subject in Jerusalem, reacted in the same way. Certainly, he said, one was grateful to Hiram and his people for the help which they had given the young Jewish state, and one would be very happy to have equally good trading relations with the present-day Lebanon, if the barbed-wire barricades at the borders came down, but—here he could not suppress a sigh—one could not altogether regret that there was no close working relationship between Beirut and Jerusalem, because even in the past no good had come of it. 'Remember Queen Jezebel!'

I could not quite follow Ben-Chorin's train of thought at the time and must have looked rather puzzled, because the small, round little man began, in an earnest tone, which I cannot adequately reproduce here, to give a lecture in the five-o'clock crush of the King David Hotel on the only aspect of the Jewish-Phoenician relationship which had any importance for him. The upshot of his argument was that economically it was excellent, but that politically and from the theological point of view, and therefore ideologically, it was almost catastrophic for Israel. The Tyrians had not only represented a state which was far in advance of the Jewish operationally, but also a religion which, with its seductive, sensuous, spiritual splendour, far outshone the then still very primitive Jahweh-cult and was therefore highly likely to lead Moses' people away from their own God. That would however have been fatal for Israel, because it was only their worship of the invisible Lord which held the tribes together.

Ben-Chorin was almost exhausted when he had finished this lecture on religious history. Although as a non-Jew (and for obvious reasons pro-Phoenician) I had not entirely agreed with his theory, it did confirm my belief that besides being able to deal with reality in an impressive way the people of the Lebanon had also come to grips with the supernatural, or at least had been able to represent it in a manner which must have given them an almost Lucifer-like allure in the eyes of their neighbours.

Once again we see that they were not the boors or crass materialists that they are so often held to have been. They were also the creators of a religion, and myth-makers of a high order, and helped to shape the imaginative world of the Jews and Greeks and even of western Europe far more powerfully than the schoolbooks would have us believe.

However, Ben-Chorin is quite right: Queen Jezebel of Tyre is one of the many witnesses in this case whom posterity must judge.

CHAPTER IX

The Tyrian Whore

THE AUTHORS OF the Books of Kings make no bones about the fact that Jezebel was a merciless dictator, a wily intriguer and a shameless trollop. Besides which (but this is only hinted at), she was a whore.

When one of Jezebel's citizens refused to sell his vineyard to her husband, she ordered him to be accused by false witnesses and stoned to death. When the prophet Elijah contrived an uprising of the people against the Phoenician priests of Baal whom she had imported, in which the latter were killed, she threatened to have him killed and drove him out of the country. When she later met the man who had just killed her own son, she had the gall to ask him how it felt to be a murderer, where-upon he promptly had her killed.

One of the worst curses in the story of the people of Israel, which is certainly not lacking in terrible execrations, was flung at her and swiftly came to pass. 'In the portion of Jezreel shall dogs eat the flesh of Jezebel,' thundered Elijah the Tishbite. 'And the carcase of Jezebel shall be as dung upon the face of the field in the portion of Jezreel; so that they shall not say, This is Jezebel.' Which is exactly what happened. She was thrown out of the window by her own eunuchs, 'and some of her blood was sprinkled on the wall, and on the horses: and he trode her under foot.' And when, having killed her, the man felt some compunction and decided to have her buried in spite of the prophet's words, 'they found no more of her than the skull, and the feet, and the palms of her hands' (2 Kings 9). The dogs had taken the prophet at his words. As I said, this is the Bible story.

Anyone reading the chapter which tells of the rise to power, fall and terrible end of the Phoenician woman, must be struck by the violent hatred shown, a hatred which has not lost its impact in more than 2,800 years. It is for precisely this reason that the namesake of all Isabels deserves at least a second hearing of her case. The accusations of the biblical chronicler are not very convincing, and are hardly supported by any factual evidence. The worst that can be said of the Phoenician woman is that she betrayed Naboth, who was so unwilling to sell his vineyard; all the rest is pure hearsay. That she was wanton and a witch, sounds like servants' gossip, that she loved to adorn and paint herself, may have been thrown up at her by puritans; and that she threatened to kill Elijah was certainly not very nice, but on the other hand not totally unjust, since the angry man of God had previously put 450 priests of Baal to the sword. The whole weight of the accusation thus rests on the Naboth affair, which cost him his life and would have justified a sentence of death. But it does not justify a curse which went beyond death itself.

Why was she thus damned? Why was there so much venom on the lips of her accusers? The answer is quite simple: Jezebel was not sentenced according to the rules of an ordinary court but by a revolutionary tribunal, and since the revolution was in the name of God, it was also a spiritual body before which she stood. And inquisitors, whether they be called Torquemada or Robespierre or Vishinsky, seldom give sentences according to the book. The Jews did not do so in their day either; they did not even think it necessary to hear the accused. The result was a foregone conclusion.

Jezebel came from the palace of Hiram of Tyre, who had done so much business with Solomon; her father Ithobaal, whom the Bible calls Ethbaal, King of the Sidonians, had been a priest of Astarte before he usurped the throne of Tyre. His neighbours the Jews were still among his best customers.

However, by this time, the beginning of the ninth century BC, they had lost part of the inheritance won by David. After Solomon's death the artificially united empire had fallen into two halves: Judah, with the metropolis of Jerusalem in the south, and Israel, with a rapidly changing sequence of capitals in the north. In about 875 BC, when the story of Jezebel begins, a strong warrior king, former commander Omri, who was probably of Arab origin, had stabilized the latter state to some extent by means of bloody internal and external wars, and had built the strongly fortified capital Samaria.

But besides being a gifted commander, whose fame had spread as far as Assyrian Mesopotamia, Omri was also a far-sighted diplomat. Among his political goals were reconciliation with the brother state of Judah and the establishing of good relations with neighbouring Phoenicia. To achieve the latter he suggested to Ithobaal a union between Ithobaal's family and his own. Jezebel, the daughter of the Tyrian usurper, should marry Ahab, his eldest son.

Ithobaal, who knew he was on to a good thing with the Jews, agreed and so did the Israelite crown prince. Jezebel must have been a beautiful woman; she had grown up at one of the most liberal courts of the day, was mistress of all the tricks of feminine seduction and intrigue and must have caused a considerable stir in the rather provincial Samaria. Ahab obviously fell for her completely, because from the day of the wedding she did what she wanted with him. Yet he was no weakling, but a brave soldier and good leader like his father.

The people—or more precisely two large groups of Israelite society, the farmers and the military nobility—were less pleased with Jezebel. The farmers felt they were being exploited by a rich merchant class, and they had to sell their heavily mortgaged lands and themselves retreat in poverty to the towns. To them the Phoenician woman was just another member of the entrepreneurial class, the representative and agent of foreign capital. The soldiers, however, who already saw their privileges threatened by the absolute ruler Omri, thought that Jezebel, the daughter of an autocrat, could only cause the nobility to be further crippled.

It was thus almost inevitable that sooner or later an alliance should be formed between the peasantry and the military class, with the overthrow of the ruling house as its aim. The common ideological basis for both—obviously, in such a conservative grouping—was the good old tradition, and that in Israel meant of course the religious tradition. Jezebel herself set the tinder to the fire. When she married Ahab, she changed her nationality but not her faith. And furthermore, she not only proceeded to ignore Jahweh and cling to the gods of her own people, which could perhaps have been forgiven in a priest's daughter; she

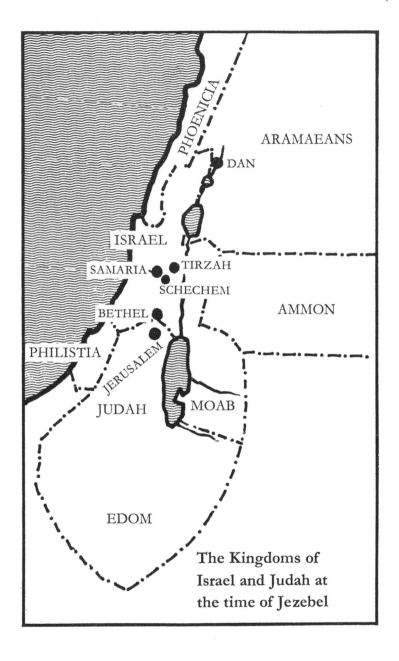

The Kingdoms of
Israel and Judah at
the time of Jezebel

also strove with all her might to introduce the Phoenician religion into Israel.

Even this, it was true, was neither illegal, nor did it contradict the usual political rules in the ancient Orient. A union between the princely houses of two kingdoms was always also regarded as a union between different religions. The union in the royal bed symbolized a mutual cultural and spiritual interchange between two communities, as Solomon had well understood. Each of his many wives and concubines from foreign countries had been allowed to worship the gods of her homeland, and if she also had missionary zeal, the king at least had not complained. At the time of David's son there was a famous altar of the Phoenician Baal in the Ben-Hinnom valley, directly beneath the walls of Jerusalem, and the Emperor Vespasian later found a place of worship on Mount Carmel, which resembled those of Byblos in every detail. In the Jewish kingdom many religions flourished side by side.

It was quite another matter that the prophets, the representatives of the Jewish national conscience, never condoned such practices. As long as they had things firmly under control, the kings did not need to pay any attention to the voices of these admonishers. But the prophets mostly held them on a loose rein. They occasionally had to grit their teeth while foreign priests moved freely around in their age-old territory, but when their time came they swept their enemies aside on the tide of the people's anger. And their time always came; their mills ground slowly but finely. So eventually they managed to demote the Ben-Hinnom valley from a place of sacrifice to a dumping ground, and were also partly responsible for the fact that the name Ben-Hinnom was changed to Gehenna, the New Testament name for Hell.

Even Jezebel could not count on the Jewish conscience tolerating her for long. Apart from the common unrest amongst farmers and nobles, sooner or later a new prophet was bound to arise, who would uphold the cause. And so it was. The prophet was called Elijah; he embodied the anger of the true believers; he was the idol of the suppressed and the secret hope of the dissatisfied. And he was more than this.

Behind the peasant preacher from Tishbe were the nobility and landowners, but also the critical intelligence of the Israelite state. He was not merely a puppet of powerful interested parties, but a power in his own right, a product of Jewish history.

The people to whom he belonged drew their strength from the fact that they were different from other people. Unlike their neighbours, the Jews honoured, in place of many specialized individual gods, a single heavenly lord responsible for everything, who, moreover, did not even possess a visible form. Even the names which he bore told very little about him. He was originally called Jahweh, which, according to Moses, meant only 'I am', and later Eloah or Elohim, or simply God; later still Jahu or Jehovah and finally just Adonai, 'Lord'. All these names seemed to obscure rather than reveal him. The closer one approached to him, the farther he receded. He demanded followers who completely negated their sensual powers of imagination and contented themselves with the purely abstract.

Jahweh-Jehovah really took concrete form only in the stern laws which he had given to his followers. Devout Jews were, and are, asked to respect absolutely for every hour of every day, no less than 613 different laws and injunctions. They are not asked to believe but to act, and through their actions to be something special: members of the chosen people. The community to which they belong is in fact an order of a sternly intellectual kind, whose rules make those of the Trappists look like the rules of an elegant club.

How the Jews came to worship their stern and strange God is one of the great mysteries of history. It is now popularly held that they learnt about Jahweh during their wanderings in the Sinai desert, where they met the Kenites. It is thought from fragmentary bits of information which we have that this nomad tribe worshipped a faceless, formless fire spirit, and infused the ex-slaves from Egypt with their belief in him.

Sigmund Freud puts forward a more subtle argument, however, in stating that Jahweh was originally an Egyptian conception. Moses, he thinks, was not a Hebrew but one of the few remaining followers of the monotheist Ekhnaten. Disappointed in his own people, he approached the forced labourers of the house of Joseph and promised them freedom if they accepted his doctrine, and this they naturally did. Freud supports his theory by a number of obscure traits in the portrait of the great lawgiver. His name for one thing, he says, indicates his Egyptian origin. Mose means the child, as for instance Ramses or Ra-mose, means the child of Ra. Then again the man who led them across the Red Sea probably did not speak Hebrew at all, or spoke.it very little, and therefore used his brother Aaron not as a mouthpiece to formulate his orders, as the Bible suggests, but as an interpreter. And finally, contrary to the accepted custom, he had been circumcised very late, which would also go to show that he did not come from a Jewish family.

All these very penetrating observations do little to lighten the darkness that surrounds the God Jahweh, but they do make it quite clear that he was indeed an amazing and mysterious phenomenon. No normal race, so to speak, in the ancient Orient, would have had the idea of recognizing a supernatural power who could only be perceived in fire and as an inner voice, who must be worshipped in great empty temples and who watched jealously to see that his complicated laws and commandments were kept.

However it was just this 'abnormal' situation which confronted the Phoenician woman, and she probably could not quite understand it. She came from a country where the gods, as everywhere else, were neither so anthropomorphized that they were conceived as super-egos, nor so inhuman that one had to fear and respect them on purely human grounds. Gods had to rule like kings, with carrots and whips, with good harvests and hailstorms, with favourable winds and tornadoes, sunshine and thunder. They had to be an order into which one fitted, not a law which laid claim to the whole man.

The Phoenician pantheon was so ordered that any modern person of a rather humanistic bent could easily feel at home in it, and so probably could any good Catholic who manages to regard the holy trinity as a pure phenomenon, not seen merely in liturgical terms. For there was a trinity of gods who ruled over the inhabitants of Tyre, Sidon, Aradus, Byblos and the one-time Ugarit. At the head of this triple formation was a father god, El, whom the Greeks later sometimes identified with their Kronos. Beside him was his wife Asherat or Astarte, who in Byblos was called Baalat (which can be roughly translated as 'our dear lady'). Then there was their son, the god Baal, whom the Giblites also called

Adon, Adoni or (Graecized) Adonis, the Lord; while the Tyrians worshipped him as Melqart and the Sidonians as Eshmun.

Each of these three heavenly rulers represented and embodied a number of definite natural forces and phenomena. They were also closely related to beings in all the other eastern heavens. El, who was called Baal in Sidon, was the mightiest of the three and the most uninteresting. He seems to have had such great and far-reaching powers that people rarely dared to consider him more closely or give him human attributes. He is merely characterized in a few texts from Ugarit as being, like Zeus, an unfaithful husband. Apart from that people were content to consider him simply as lord of the earth and to keep their distance, which prevented him making any direct contact with them.

It was different with his wife Asherat, who was also called Asherat-Yam, the lady of the sea, and who thus ruled the sphere which was most important to the Phoenicians. It was known that she assisted as an adviser at the council of the gods but, like a good wife, only offered an opinion when she was asked to do so. Although Asherat-Baalat, like her husband, could not be approached directly but only through other, lesser gods, she stood appreciably nearer to men than the intangible El. This may have been because she was a woman and as such also symbolized the fruitful earth, or fertility in general. People prayed to Baalat for good harvests, children and a long life. 'May our dear lady of Byblos,' a Giblite ruler implored her, 'bless Yehaumilk, King of Byblos, may she let him live long and prolong the days and years he rules over Byblos, because he himself is only a prince.'

Asherat-Baalat was not an original Phoenician creation, but a being derived from other ancient eastern deities. She was known to the Sumerians as Innin, to the Babylonians and Assyrians as Ishtar and to the Egyptians as Isis. Men saw her also as a mother in the heavens or an earth-mother, who could satisfy their instinctive need for security and warmth.

Even nearer to the faithful than the mother stood the son, however. Baal-Adon-Eshmun-Melqart is without doubt the most interesting figure in ancient oriental mythology. He could not be sure of his immortality—which was unusual—but had to die once every year and be resurrected. That this special godly fate is none other than the mythical representation of the yearly fertility cycle is obvious, but does not alter the strangeness of his destiny. In the summer, when the ripe harvest had been brought in, the young god died, in order to return to the earth by the spring at the latest, with the new seeds. But although this started with something so primitive and earthy, Baal's story as a whole led to a rich development and later to abstraction, which finally left nothing but the idea of a god who suffered death as a sacrifice for mankind. It was probably the most influential of all non-Jewish mythological concepts in the east and doubtless also prepared the ground for the later flowering of the story of Christ's death and resurrection.

Baal was clearly the special favourite of the Phoenicians, just as previously he had played a leading role with the Canaanites. His image was decked out with the most fantastic features, and he himself represented in so many other guises that he finally almost entirely superseded his father El or was sometimes fused into one being with him. He was worshipped as Baal-Shamim, the lord of the heavens, Baal-Lebanon, the lord of the mountain, Baal-Rosh, the lord of the promontory, and as has been noted above, as Melqart in Tyre, where he also gradually took on the status of a sun god.

In a Canaanite legend he fights at the edge of the wilderness with a kind of Minotaur, a bull-headed monster, and is killed (originally he usually seems to have died without rising again). In a hymn from Ugarit he is praised as the conqueror of the turbulent sea: 'The mace in the hand of Baal,' it says, 'swoops down like a vulture in his fingers. He beats Prince Sea across the shoulders and Ruler River on the breast. The skilful one takes a mace and reads out what is written on it: "Thy name, yes, thy name is He-Who-Expels, oh, He-Who-Expels!" Let him expel Sea! Let him drive Sea from his throne and River from the seat of his sovereignty. You shall swoop down in the hand of Baal, like a vulture in his fingers! He shall strike Prince Sea on the head, Ruler River between the eyes! Then will Sea sink down and fall to the ground. Now the mace swoops down in the hand of Baal, like a vulture in his fingers. He strikes Prince Sea on the head, Ruler River between the eyes. Sea sinks down, falls on the ground, his hips tremble, his body buckles. Now Baal destroys Sea and drives Ruler River to his end.'

However, Baal is not only a great fighter against the sea which threatens man, but also a great lover. He boasts that he has embraced his beloved Anat seventy-seven times. 'Yes,' he says, 'I loved eighty-eight times'—in one night, one imagines. No wonder that Anat buried him with ceremony, on the mountain of Saphon, after he had suffered one of his many deaths, and then wreaked a bloody vengeance upon one of his many murderers. 'Anat siezed Mot, the god's son. With a sickle she cut him, with a shovel she winnowed him, with fire she scorched him, in a mill she ground him up. She scattered his flesh over the field as food for the birds, so that his fate was fulfilled.'

But she could not alter Baal's fate. When summer came, he had to go 'down into the belly of the earth, and the fruits on the trees were abandoned to the terrible heat of the sun'.

Below the godly trinity in the Phoenician heaven, which one may assume was recognized to a greater or lesser extent in all the towns of the Lebanese coast, there was a whole row of lesser heroes and demigods, to whom carefully limited areas of the real world were apportioned as their territory. Thus Chusor ruled over the sea with Asherat and watched over the punctual succession of the seasons. Resheph had power over thunder and lightning, Aliyan, a son of Baal, controlled springs and under-ground water, Dagon was the god of corn, Shadrapa the patron of doctors and Hijon of craftsmen and industrial workers, while Sydyk and Misor personified justice and righteousness.

Besides these the books of the legendary Sanchuniathon tell us of a number of other mythical figures, but only by their Graecized names. The priest wrote, as Eusebius, who learnt this from Philo of Byblos, recounts: 'Genos, the son of Aion and Protegenos, fathered mortal children, who were called Phos, Pur and Phlox. These discovered fire by rubbing two bits of wood together, and taught men how to make it. They begat sons of great size and strength, whose names were given to the mountains round about. So the mountains are called after them Cassius, Libanus, Antilibanus and Bratu. By coupling with their mother these men begat Memrumus and Hypsuranius. The women of that time had intercourse with any man without shame, whoever he might be. Hypsuranius lived in Tyre and devised huts made of reeds, papyrus therefore. He fell out with his brother Usus, who first thought of clothes for the human body;

he made them from the skins of wild animals.' Other offspring of this Promethean family then invented the ship, iron-mining, the fish-hook, the sail, the craft of building and various other useful things.

The world over which these heavenly beings and heroes ruled, was created, if Sanchuniathon has informed us correctly, from a primeval egg, which opened one day, separating the waters from the sky. Then the gods appeared and after them the founders of human civilization. According to another version El created Ulomos, a Greek name which contains the Hebrew word 'ōlām, the world. He somehow fashioned the primordial egg and set plant and animal life in motion.

We cannot reconstruct the Phoenician cosmogony more exactly. The available sources are too few and far between. Besides which the priests in the individual sea cities frequently remodelled the existing gods to suit their own ends and arranged their relationship one to another to fall in with the political needs of the day. This was then the customary practice throughout the Near East.

Thanks to archaeologists we are rather better informed as to the religious customs of the Lebanese communities. The gods were preferably worshipped on mountains, the 'heights' of the Bible, and by springs, rivers and in woods. But there were also temples—small, unobtrusive buildings as a rule, made of limestone and richly furnished with vertical stone columns, which according to oriental tradition represented the heavenly beings without portraying them. Like the Jews, the Phoenicians in their early days obviously only rarely dared to give the gods human or animal forms. The Obelisk-Temple which has been excavated in Byblos is a large collection of upright, carved pieces of rock. On the other hand, another shrine of later date which the American James B. Pritchard found in 1972 near Sarepta between Tyre and Sidon had an altar and fragments of Egyptian holy images. Its size was three metres by eight—not a very monumental building therefore.

Baal seems definitely to have been a mountain god. The people of Byblos worshipped him on the nearby hills of Aphka, the Sidonians on the hillsides round their town, whereas Asherat-Baalat favoured stone houses in the settlements. But there was at least one place where both the son and the mother were worshipped together. It was on the Adonis River, the present-day Nahr Ibrahim, which rises twenty kilometres east of Byblos and flows into the sea quite near the town.

The valley of the Nahr Ibrahim must be one of the most beautiful canyons in the world. The narrow tarmac road which leads to it curves dramatically through vineyards and orchards, through small Arab villages with white-washed houses, and then winds up to a plateau, from which there is a dizzy view to the valley below. The step-like walls of the river valley are a gleaming brown and almost violet at the top, sprinkled with flashes of green. Towards evening these colours blend together with the red of the sunset and the trembling waves of light which the giant mirror of the Mediterranean throws up towards the sky. At the end of the plateau the road shoots steeply downwards, passes a half-ruined Roman temple, skirts a rock-face in the middle of which there is a great cave mouth. A broad stream of water gushes from the cave. It falls into a stony river-bed and laps past a second ruined temple into the redly glowing ravine: the Nahr Ibrahim, Adonis's River.

In the cave where it rises or near by, Baal-Adon is said to have died. According to the legend, he fought with a wild boar, which wounded the god on the inside of his thigh and thus killed him. His death, the great Greek writer Lucian tells us, is echoed by nature at regular intervals: 'Every year it [the river] is coloured blood-red and loses its normal colour, shortly before it flows into the sea: it colours a great stretch of the sea red and thus lets the people of Byblos know that it is time to mourn. They say that during this time Adonis is wounded and that the nature of the river is changed by the blood which runs into the water.'

On the day of the strange transformation, the women of Byblos, Lucian further recounts, began the 'secret rites' of the Adonis cult in the temple of Baalat, whom he calls Aphrodite. They beat their breasts, cried and wailed, and then 'when they have finished wailing and weeping, sacrifice to Adonis, as to one who has departed this life. Then they announce that he lives again, and set up his image in the open air. Then they begin to shave their heads, like the Egyptians when they mourned the death of Apis. Those women, however, who refuse to have their heads shaved, have to undergo the following punishment: for a whole day they have to be prepared to sell their bodies. Only strangers are allowed access to the place where this takes place. An offering to Aphrodite is bought with the money derived from the traffic with these women.'

Two gods were thus honoured in Byblos with a religious festival, Baalat-Astarte, offerings to whom were also thrown into the water of the Adonis spring (if they sank they were regarded as accepted), and Baal, the dying, resurrected hero. The celebration had its climax in an orgiastic ceremony which is echoed in Shrovetide carnivals in some countries today. Women became prostitutes for one day, and gave themselves to foreign guests, thus probably representing the fruitful earth, which receives new seeds.

Lucian, though a sceptic with a slight tendency towards cynicism, was nevertheless so impressed by the whole proceedings that he sought to get to the root of the matter. He came across the Egyptian Osiris, who like Baal, but also the Sumerian Dumuzi and the Babylonian Tammuz, was killed and afterwards passionately mourned by his sister and wife Isis. The place of his death was said to be Byblos. 'I will tell you,' the Greek writes, 'why this story seems credible. Every year a human head floats from Egypt to Byblos. It takes seven days to get there; the winds, moved by some godly influence, blow it on its way, it never loses its course, but comes by a direct route to Byblos. The whole affair is very astonishing. It is repeated every year, and it also happened when I was in Byblos, and I myself saw the head in this city.'

It will never be known what Lucian really saw. He himself claims that the strange head was made of 'Egyptian papyrus', whereas a later witness, St Kyrillos, thought that what was borne towards him by the wind looked like a small boat. But certainly the Greek scoffer is right in thinking that in the old Egyptian-influenced timber ports several legends merged into one and that Baal, alias Adonis, was at least closely related to the Nile god.

The blood which flows in the waters of the Nahr Ibrahim, however, can still be seen every spring—though even Lucian was not quite able to believe in its godly origin. 'This river, my friend and guest,' he has a Giblite recount, 'flows through the Lebanon, a mountain in which there is a great quantity of red earth. The strong winds which occur regularly at this time, blow great quantities of the vermilion dust into the mountain streams. And it is this earth which colours the river, not blood as they maintain.' Lucian adds that that may well be so, but that the whole natural phenomenon smacks of the supernatural all the same. The Greek did not know that other rivers in the Lebanon also sometimes take on this red colouring, the Nahr al-Awwali for instance, which flowed past a temple of Baal-Eshmun in Sidon and gave rise to similar legends there.

Lebanese farmers' wives still agree with Lucian, however. They attribute healing powers to the water of the Nahr Ibrahim and offer holy candles to Adonis from time to time. It is true they do not call him by his old heathen name any longer but, if they are Christians, Saint George, and if they are Mohammedans, Al Khadr. Asherat's son lives on in both saints.

What made the Phoenician religion appear in rather a dubious light to western eyes was not so much the whole cycle of legends surrounding Baal-Adonis, which the Greeks and Romans also adopted, but accounts, such as Lucian's, of temple prostitution, and rumours of human sacrifices carried out during the holy ceremonies.

The former is now generally accepted as having taken place. It was an ancient oriental custom for 'respectable' women to prostitute themselves in the temples. Herodotus also speaks of this happening at the Ishtar temple in Babylon and, in what is most probably the most often quoted passage of his *Babylonian Logos,* is comically shocked by it: 'The following,' he writes, 'is the most shameful practice in Babylon. Every woman born in the country must sit in the temple of Aphrodite (Ishtar-Astarte) and associate once in her life with a strange man. . . . They sit with a wreath of braids round their head in the holy precinct. There are many women, some coming, some going away. Straight paths are made between them in every direction, along which the strangers can walk to make their choice. When a woman sits there, she may not go home until one of the strangers has thrown money in her lap and associated with her outside the holy place. . . . But when she has given herself, she has fulfilled her holy duty to the goddess and returns home, and however much she is offered thereafter, she is not to be won. All those who are beautiful and well-made quickly return home, but the ugly ones have to wait a long time, until they can satisfy the custom, many having to wait for three to four years.'

The Greek world traveller, who was more interested in the retelling of piquant exotic details than in the underlying explanation, makes no attempt to unravel the meaning of this custom, and modern historians also tend to dismiss temple prostitution in a few embarrassed sentences. It was all part of a fertility rite, they say. Through submission to or intercourse with the Hierodules—the holy servants who worked in the temple as male or female prostitutes—men communicated with the godly power.

Oswald Spengler is one of the few who venture to give a more detailed interpretation. The symbol of the phallus which was also representative of the Ishtar-Asherat cults, was, he believes: 'The expression of a sexuality which was completely given up to the moment and forgot both past and future in it.' Man, in the ancient Orient, felt himself to be a part of nature, a plant, and 'gave himself up to the spirit of growth without will or care', whereas concern about a dark future is a characteristic trait of later western civilization.

Admittedly even this interpretation must of necessity remain rather vague. We have no way to conceive of liturgies which pertained to sex; which saw the working of godly powers in generation and conception. We know too much about the pure mechanics of sexual intercourse to be able to see the process of copulation as a mystery. Yet the ancients seem to have been in complete control of this act. 'If it has such importance in the life of individuals, why should it not be declared a sacred public institution?' they may have argued. And in so doing they must have avoided and forestalled much difficulty and misplaced prudery and spared themselves at any rate the elaborate uncertainty which can give rise, as in our case, to a whole literature.

It remains to say that temple prostitution and the public offering of virginity occurred in all eastern temples between the Mediterranean and the Indus valley. Hierodules even worked in the older Jewish churches, where they were called Kedeshim, consecrated ones. Strabo recounts that in a single town in Cappadocia (present-day Turkey), there were no less than six thousand of these temple prostitutes. And they were customary in Phoenicia too. In Byblos and Tyre no one would have stepped aside if he met one of them next day.

It was only the arrival of Christianity which caused a break in the tradition. Amminanus Marcellinus, a friend of the Byzantine Emperor Julian the Apostate, who had become a heathen once more, described the Adonis celebrations at Byblos prosaically as 'a feast, which symbolized the ripening of the crops'. Whereas his older contemporary Eusebius of Caesarea uses quite different terms to describe the Astarte temple of Aphka, which seems still to have been in use in the fourth century: 'It was,' he writes, 'a school of godlessness for those dissipated men, who had ruined their bodies in the pursuit of luxuriousness. The men were soft and effeminate, were no longer men; they had betrayed the honour of their sex; they believed they must worship their god with impure lust. Dishonest traffic with women, secret obscene proceedings, dishonourable and indescribable things took place in the temple, where there was no law and order, and no guardians to insist on the observation of the rules of good conduct.' It is possible that in Eusebius's day the Astarte cult had already become degenerate and that the temples had in fact become brothels. Yet the militant bishop was regarding them in the wrong light, even if this was the case. Our morality would have been incomprehensible to the Phoenicians. And even our idea of the sanctity of human life was unknown to them. As has been noted, not only temple prostitution, but also human sacrifice was among the religious practices for which they have been criticized.

'And they [the people of the State of Judah],' it says in the Bible (Jeremiah 7:31), 'have built the high places of Tophet, which is in the valley of the son of Hinnom, to burn their sons and their daughters in the fire; which I [Jahweh] commanded them not, neither came it into my heart.' And in another place (2 Kings 23:10) we read: 'And he [King Josiah of Judah] defiled Topheth, which is in the valley of the children of Hinnom, that no man might make his son or his daughter to pass through the fire to Molech.'

Both passages have greatly puzzled Phoenician scholars because from these texts it appeared that the children of Israel had taken over these terrible sacrificial rites from other people, especially from those with whom their kings worked so closely. Human sacrifice was forbidden to the Israelites themselves.

Moses had already stated: 'And thou shalt not let any of thy seed pass through the fire to Molech' (Leviticus 18:21), and the story of Abraham's sacrifice illustrates this commandment very vividly. When the patriarch was about to kill his son as a burnt offering, a ram was sent by Jahweh. This meant that in future every firstborn who was dedicated to God, could be 'redeemed' by an animal.

Thus a stringent ruling was made against the age-old custom, accepted throughout the east, of offering men to the gods— although it does not seem to have been very easy for the Jews to give up what was, so to speak, their most effective way of bribing the super-terrestrial beings. For it represented one of the most elementary weapons in the eternal battle with the demoniac powers. The Phoenicians—as Philo of Byblos also tells us— never gave up the practice. At Carthage, excavators have found thousands of urns full of the charred bones of children and dozens of *stelae* which marked the place where such containers had been buried.

Gustave Flaubert used all these details and other unconfirmed reports which have filtered down through the centuries in his terrible picture of the sacrificial automaton Moloch. In his novel *Salammbô* he describes this god as a brazen idol, whose glowing, mechanically operated hands shovelled living children into his insatiable jaws, to be burnt to ashes. 'To satisfy him,' so his story goes, 'they heaped the sacrificial victims in his hands and laid a chain round them to hold them together. To begin with the pious had wanted to count them to see whether the number corresponded to the days of the solar year, but more and more were added, and it was impossible to recognize individuals in the vertiginous movement of the ghastly arms. It lasted for a long, an endlessly long time, until evening. Then the inner walls grew darker. It was possible to see burning flesh. Some even thought they recognized hair, limbs, entire bodies.' It is a grisly description and a reflection of the flawed image which the world has had up till now of the Phoenicians and Carthaginians. Johann Gottfried Herder was so struck by this that he compared the Tyrian colony in North Africa to a jackal, which the Roman she-wolf had to destroy. The question is whether it is a correct image or not.

Archaeologists, who now know a little more about the Phoenicians than they did in Flaubert's day, give us a down-to-earth answer. The 'topheths', they state, which are mentioned in the biblical accounts, did in fact exist. They were altars which were erected in the open air, mostly on mountains. Among other places, they have been found in Carthage and on Mount Sirai in Sardinia, though not in old Phoenicia itself. However, we know for certain that they also existed there, possibly even in Canaanite times. Moreover, it can be taken as proven that children were sacrificed on the topheths, because charred human and animal bones have been found in their neighbourhood. The answer must therefore be, yes, they practised this custom.

A more difficult question to answer is who or what was the Molech mentioned in the Bible, that proverbial horror which we also mean when we say Moloch. Hebrew scholars have tried to solve the riddle. They know that Molech can be roughly translated as kingship (one can see traces of the word in Melqart, a name which can be translated as 'king of the town') and they took it that a god with this name must be a ruler of heaven and earth. It was an explanation which seemed so appropriate that they stuck to it, even when they had been unable to discover a single Molech or Moloch in the entire Phoenician pantheon. They simply found a way out by using the composite name Baal-Molech or Moloch-Melqart, and continued to regard their explanation as the only possible one.

Meanwhile, another theory has begun to gain ground. 'The Phoenician and Punic word for sacrifice in the topheth is *molk*,' writes Sabatino Moscati, and his British colleague, Warmington, adds: 'The Hebrew word, the same as the Phoenician word on many of the commemorative stelae from the sanctuary at Carthage, was MLK and meant something like "sacrificed offering", and so "to Moloch" should really be rendered "as a sacrifice". . . . In Roman times in North Africa, the Phoenician word survived in a compounded MLKMR which was transcribed in Latin *molchomor*, and meant "sacrificial offering of a lamb". . . . More important', he concludes, 'is the misunderstanding in the translation "to Molech" (or Moloch); there was no such god.' The brazen monster conjured up by Flaubert's vivid imagination may well have existed, however, even if it was not quite so technically perfect as he supposed.

Another suggestion is that the Phoenicians and Carthaginians considered that to offer living men was the highest form of sacrifice, but that as a rule they held back from the full sacrifice, burning a lamb instead of a child, like Abraham, and only carrying out the rite literally in dire emergencies. This new theory does not lessen the bloodthirsty luridness of the whole practice, but recognizes that they were not acting in a thoughtlessly inhumane way, even if they did sometimes observe the letter of the law and tear their young ones from their breasts. Their belief that they must do this was perhaps their secret tragedy; it marks the point at which they became vulnerable, helpless and uncertain, a prey to the unknown powers which no human mind can comprehend. Like Jacob they were beset by dark angels and harrowed in their innermost beings, but this ever-open wound was also the sign of their humanity.

The journalist and historian Albert Wucher sees it quite differently. 'I can't help it,' he writes of the Sardinian topheth; 'the Carthaginian ritual sacrifice seems to me to be a sign of an oppressive, imposing piety.'

Yet Wucher, an expert on church history, might have come to a more immediate understanding of the phenomenon of human sacrifice if he had paused to glance at his own religion. Biblical scholars have for a long time seen the attempted sacrifice of Isaac as a prophetic allusion to Christ's sacrificial death, and so, with justice, have compared the one with the other. But the church was in fact never really in a position to come to terms with the offering of the body on the cross in this original sense, and has therefore always tended to speak and sing of Jesus as the 'Lamb of God'. In so doing it was reacting in much the same way as the Phoenicians, who said *molk* when perhaps they meant men.

Jewish philosophers sometimes go even one step further when considering the significance of the original Christian sacrifice. Schalom Ben-Chorin once confided to me that when he hears the words at the beginning of the Sacrament, he can never avoid a slight shudder: 'Take, eat; this is my Body.' For taken literally, he said, it is a human body which is being offered as a sacrifice.

Ben-Chorin's thought echoes one of the strongest Jewish taboos and can only be understood in that context. The children of Israel were the first to break with the idea that man is only a part of nature, who could be sacrificed by his fellow men like an animal or plant. It was enough, their teachers asserted, to honour Jahweh by what they were and did. In so doing they laid one of the cornerstones of modern civilization. The Phoenicians, on the other hand, still belonged to an older era and never progressed beyond it. It was for this that Jezebel had to pay.

What made the Tyrian princess appear so dangerous to the intellectuals and prophets in Samaria was the fact that she set a bad example. It must have been hard to follow Jahweh, so that many, and particularly the rich, liberal Jews, would have gladly siezed the opportunity to seek absolution in an easier way by following Baal. Baal was present in flowers and plants, his story offered food for the imagination, and was enhanced by a sensuous radiance. He paid nature her due: in blood, seeds, orgiastic intoxication. By performing a few easily comprehensible rites men could partake of his glory.

The temptation to be converted was all the greater since the Israelites were surrounded by the remnants of the older Canaanite culture and were closely bound up with it. They must all, down to the poorest shepherd, have been spiritual giants if they were able to be constantly mindful of what was unique and of particular significance for them in the cult of Jahweh. They were about as much in a position to do so as the Western European heathens who only found monotheistically structured Christianity to their liking when the Holy Trinity had been decked out with a teeming Olympus of saints and angels.

But since the Hebrew prophets stood on firmer ground than the first popes, long passages of the Old Testament are made up of an account of the battle of the godfearing teachers and zealots against 'Baal'—a battle, however, which they did not always win, since it often had to be resolved by a compromise.

In order to imbue the idea of their one and only God with life and a visible presence the Hebrews borrowed from nearly all their neighbours. They took their cosmogony from the Babylonians, and also their flood and their Gilgamesh, which became Nimrud; from the Assyrians the winged bulls which they changed into cherubim; from the Persians their hierarchy of angels and archangels. But from the Phoenicians they borrowed among other things the newly interpreted pastoral feast of Mazzoth, at the beginning of the barley harvest, the Sukkoth, the Feast of the Tabernacles, and also the kingdom of heaven, a number of hymns which were changed to psalms, and their temple architecture.

It was no wonder that the rulers in particular (but also the priests) were happy to rely on the Canaanite-Phoenician traditions; their own people had nothing similar. One can see this clearly with Saul, who was able to call his son Esh-baal (Jonathan's son was Meri-baal), thus honouring Jahweh's Phoenician rival. But the pious David also decorated the walls of his house with Phoenician fetishes. When at the beginning of his career he was pursued by Saul, his wife Michal took one of these 'teraphim' and laid it beside her in bed, saying it was her sick husband.

One can conclude from all this that on her marriage Jezebel came to a palace where the people were familiar with Canaanite customs. Her husband Ahab's willingness to do what was 'evil in the sight of the Lord', that is, to allow temples to be built for Baal and Asherat and to permit human sacrifices to be made when Jericho was being rebuilt, was not caused by her alone—there were historical reasons for it and there had been famous precedents.

The prophets who rose up against the house of Omri were probably aware of this and therefore only struck when Ahab had fallen in battle and the foreign woman could be put away as being the only representative of non-Jewish ideas. Elisha, a highly educated, clever intellectual took over Elijah's role after his death and opened battle with Jezebel by promoting an adherent of the true faith called Jehu as a rival candidate to Ahab's son Ahaziah, and then let the young king be murdered by him. And so the ageing queen, who had had a firm hand in the government in the name of her son, came into Jehu's direct line of fire. When she reproached him for the dastardly deed— Ahaziah was killed from behind—he had her thrown out of a window and then killed the rest of her children. His reward for this bloody act was the kingship, for which Elisha had chosen him. He was the last prophet to anoint a Jewish king.

But Jezebel's family had not yet been completely stamped out. Her beautiful daughter Athaliah reigned in Judah, and was a veritable monster. After the death of her husband and his son who succeeded him, also called Ahaziah, she had all the rest of the house of David killed and set herself up as Queen in Jerusalem.

But it could not last long. A conservative *fronde* was formed in the country and began to say the same things about her which the Israelites in Samaria had said about Jezebel. It is significant that they not only accused Athaliah of worshipping Baal but even found it reprehensible that she had made her son build Tarshish ships in Ezion-geber—that is, work with the Phoenicians. The established nobility and the farmers wanted an end to this business alliance because it had only profited the merchants, not themselves. And so, with the downfall and murder of Athaliah, they also put an end to a well-considered power-sharing and trade policy, which David had begun, Solomon had continued and Omri had tried to revive.

The victory of the revolutionaries was a victory for Jahweh over the foreign gods; it was sealed with a thorough purge and religious reform. The people stormed the temple of Baal and 'brake it down, and brake his altars and his images in pieces, and slew Mattan the priest of Baal before the altars' (2 Chronicles 23:17). Later they also broke the betyls, the high places in the topheths: 'cut down the groves, and threw down the high places and the altars out of all Judah and Benjamin, in Ephraim also and Manasseh, until they had utterly destroyed them all' (2 Chronicles 31:1). Then they appointed new priests.

That was only one result of the religious conflict in Israel and Judah; there was also a complete and irrevocable break with the Phoenicians. For the sake of their Jahweh and religious independence, the Jews had sacrificed all the opportunities which would arise from their world-wide trade with Tyre and Sidon, the treasures of Ophir and the profit from the Tarshish ships.

During the first forty years after Athaliah's murder (in 831 BC), Israel and Judah lived fairly peaceably together, but then it began to be evident that the revolutionaries had also unwittingly disturbed the alliance between three countries so cleverly contrived by Omri, and that they now stood alone and had to face singly attacks from armies which were far larger and more powerful than themselves, the Assyrian and Babylonian. The leaders of these were to conquer Phoenicia as well as Israel and Judah, and to destroy Jerusalem. The independent Jewish state was thereafter (with the exception of a brief interlude) a thing of the past—another sacrifice to Jahweh, from which he in fact profited.

CHAPTER X

From the Lebanon to the Edge of the World

THE GORY TALE of Jezebel took place in an era which Dimitri
Baramki calls the golden age of Phoenician history. The cities
on the Levant coast had never been richer than in this ninth
century BC, their supremacy at sea hardly ever more secure.
Great fortunes were piled in the treasuries of Tyre, Sidon and
Byblos; the storehouses were full; hardly a day passed at the
docks without heavily laden cargo ships arriving or departing
from the quays. At night the streets resounded with the shouts
of drunken sailors and with the sound of shawms from the
merchants' palaces, where they were feasting richly.

This prosperity was naturally regarded askance by the neighbouring countries. 'Thine heart is lifted up,' Ezekiel lets his
Jahweh say to the King of Tyre, 'and thou hast said, I am a God,
I sit in the seat of God, in the midst of the seas . . . With thy
wisdom and with thine understanding thou hast gotten thee
riches, and hast gotten gold and silver into thy treasures . . . by
thy traffick hast thou increased thy riches, and thine heart is
lifted up because of thy riches' (Ezekiel 28:2–5). Elsewhere the
prophet compares the town to a ship 'of perfect beauty', and then
continues: 'They have made all thy ship boards of fir trees of
Senir [a peak on Mount Hermon]; they have taken cedars from
Lebanon to make masts for thee . . . the inhabitants of Zidon
and Arvad were thy mariners: thy wise men, O Tyrus, that were
in thee, were thy pilots. The ancients of Gebal and the wise men
thereof were in thee thy calkers' (Ezekiel 27:3–9).

If one takes this lyrical account literally, one gets a picture of
a dazzling metropolis before which all others paled. Tyre appears
to have surpassed even her Phoenician neighbours, possibly to
have been their ruler. Ezekiel at any rate sees Sidonians and
Arvadites as servants of their mighty sister and only allows the

worthy people of Byblos an advisory role at the Tyrian court. They are alleged to have been there to repair ships, which perhaps means that they worked as building contractors, wharfmasters or engineers.

The god of the city of Tyre, Melqart, also appears to have put all other Phoenician gods in the shade at that time, and this is confirmed by the leading status of his birthplace. He was even recognized in Aramaean Damascus, which Tyre considered his place of origin. Ben-Adad I, ruler of this city, had a stele of Melqart erected in 850 BC near Aleppo, with an inscription stating that he honoured the god thus portrayed. In so doing he gave posterity its first likeness of Melqart. It shows a half-naked man, wearing a conical hat and carrying an axe on his shoulder. Nothing comparable has been found in Tyre, and indeed the original appearance of the city is very difficult to reconstruct.

In spite of all their efforts, archaeologists have not been able to discover where and how Melqart was worshipped in Tyre itself. They only know that he must have had a magnificent temple, because the Roman author Horace, describing it almost a millennium after the death of Hiram (who probably built it), wrote: 'I saw this shrine, richly adorned with a great number of offerings; amongst other things it contained two stelae, one of pure gold, the other of emerald, which shone very brilliantly at night.' These two pillars, which Herodotus and Aristotle's pupil Tyrtamos (called Theophrastus) had already described and which were reproduced as Boaz and Jachin in the temple at Jerusalem, are the most frequently mentioned details in accounts of the temple. What they really were is the subject of endless conjecture for historians. Amazing theories have been put forward. For instance it has been suggested that the emerald stele—Tyrtamos calls it the biggest piece of corundum in the world—was really a tube of green glass in which a flame was kept burning, as only that would explain why it shone so brightly. Hardly anyone has suggested that it was made from genuine precious stone, and it is generally doubted that the other pillar was of pure gold. The only thing on which the experts are agreed is that the pillars had evolved from two holy stones which once lay under a tree dedicated to Baal Melqart. In the vast mythology of history both have survived as symbols of the most fabulous wealth and immense sanctity.

Melqart, without doubt, made his own city a Phoenician Jerusalem, the 'centre of a religion, whose adherents kept their eyes tirelessly turned towards their temple', as a modern historian has written. They sent offerings from far and wide, loaded their god with precious metals and jewels and in this way amassed capital against which they could borrow when the need arose. There was as yet no difference between a bank and a temple, and the distant worshippers would have mostly been exiled Tyrian businessmen, who had a cool head for figures.

But if all that we know of Tyre's most famous shrine is only what we can glean from the writings of a few classical travellers, we know far less about the location of the other famous temples which are also mentioned. Where was the temple of Asherat with its stone fallen from heaven? That of Baal-Shamim, which also had a golden pillar? Where were the royal palace and the royal necropolis? How large was mainland Usu and where was the causeway to the island? Since the days when Ernest Renan excavated in Tyre, archaeologists have unearthed from the sand near Sur whole cities of the dead, stadia, temples, and columnated streets, but hardly one stone which could be said to have been hewn by stonemasons in Phoenician times. Romans, Byzantines, crusaders and Mohammedan kings built and rebuilt the town time and time again; and as Beirut grew, it was used as a quarry. So today we know only—thanks to Strabo—that at the beginning of the Christian era Tyre must have had an amazingly modern appearance. The houses, the Greek geographer writes, were taller than those in Rome, where they were limited by law to twenty-one metres. This means that the island city was in fact a miniature Manhattan, with conglomerations of small-scale skyscrapers looking far out over the sea.

Thanks to aerial photographs and underwater geography we also know the rough outline of the city and its great harbours and can see that the Greek poet Nonnus (fifth century) was not indulging in a flight of fancy when he compared the town to a young girl bathing in the sea who stretches out both her arms (the jetty walls) in the water with her feet resting on the shore. Moreover we can be sure that his ecstatic description of Roman Tyre also reflects some of the magic of the older Phoenician town. 'O city,' he rhapsodizes, 'well esteemed by the world, a picture on earth, the image of heaven. Never have I seen such

beauty. What god built this town? What godly hand designed it?'
His metaphors were not entirely of his own making, as Ezekiel,
who probably knew the old Tyre, waxes equally eloquent when
he celebrates the trading metropolis even while cursing it. 'Thou
hast been in Eden the garden of God; every precious stone was
thy covering, the sardius, the topaz, and the diamond, the beryl, the
onyx, and the jasper, the sapphire, the emerald, and the carbuncle,
and gold: the workmanship of thy tabrets and of thy pipes was
prepared in thee in the day that thou wast created. . . . Thou wast
perfect in thy ways . . .' (Ezekiel 28:13–15).

If Tyre was beautiful, Sidon was no less so, although in a
different way. Less magnificently ornamental than her rich
neighbour and less strongly fortified, she had the benefit of large
residential areas which were shaded by green, luxuriant gardens.
The Greeks called Sidon 'the kingdom of flowers' and told the
story of the gardener Abdelonymos, who had just dug one of his
flowerbeds when a deputation came to offer him the crown of the
city state.

Phoenician scholars have been more richly rewarded for a
different kind of digging in the park area of the old port than they
have been for their efforts at Tyre. In 1855 they found in
Mogharat-Ablun, south of Sidon, a perfectly preserved sarcophagus in the Egyptian style and saw from the Phoenician text
engraved on it that it was the resting place of Eshmunazar, a
ruler who reigned during the sixth century BC. Today this
impressively gleaming exhibit is one of the major attractions
at the Lebanese National Archaeological Museum in Beirut,
together with the so-called 'anthropoid' or human-shaped
coffins in white marble which were found near Ain al-Hilweh
on the edge of the garden city of Sidon, and the famous ship
sarcophagus of Roman times, which has a relief of a one-masted,
high-boarded sailing-boat on the front.

Even less is known about Aradus, the third important Phoenician settlement, and old Berytus, than about Tyre and Sidon;
it is only of Byblos that we have a more precise picture. She must
have been as rich as her neighbours in the south, but was less
brilliant, and already had a sober, elderly air, derived from the
parochial, unhurried merchant families who still kept records
from the old Egyptian days in their archives.

Whether and how these Phoenician cities worked together is

equally matter for conjecture rather than certainty. There are theories which suggest Tyre acted as the capital of a kind of Phoenician federation of states, whose members all felt they belonged to the same nation, even if personally they only identified with their own home towns. But, as I have said, there is no proof of this. The only supporting evidence is the fact that it would have made sense for the Phoenicians to form such a confederation. The area jointly ruled by the sea cities was not particularly large. It stretched from Acre in present-day Israel to a point north of Aradus in southern Syria, corresponding more or less with the territory of the modern Lebanese Republic. Lengthways one could travel through the entire country by car in one day. To go across it a cyclist would take half that time, if it were not for the mountains.

The Phoenicians had virtually no hinterland. Their realm was a coastline, a small strip between mountainside and Mediterranean, where the sea was the main highway. If it had not been so, they would have had no means of communicating with each other. Nearly all these city states lay sandwiched between two torrential mountain rivers: Aradus between the Nahr Markieh and the Nahr al-Abrash, Byblos between the Nahr al-Jawz and the Nahr Ibrahim, Berytus between the Nahr al-Kalb and the Nahr al-Damur, Sidon between the Nahr al-Awwali and the Nahr al-Litani, Tyre between the Nahr al-Litani and the foothills of the Ras en Naqura, which were also called the Ladder of Tyre, and Akko between these foothills and the Yam Kinneret. There was no road in existence to link all these places and cross the rivers; it was not until Roman times that one was built.

If therefore a Phoenician alliance *did* exist, it must have been formed in the face of many different obstacles. In such small, clearly delimited cantons isolationist and separationist ideals are more likely to flourish than dreams of an overall national unity. Town dignitaries become self-important and eager to defend their rights. They bandy about the concept of freedom; but they can hardly then have meant that individual 'liberty' which we mean when we say freedom.

The Phoenician towns were ruled by kings, who—somewhat like Ahiram of Byblos, whose coffin Montet discovered—regarded themselves as the earthly representatives of the gods. Ahiram's sons Ithobaal, Abibaal, Yehimilk, Elibaal and Shipitbaal—the last-named ruled in about 880 BC—addressed themselves to posterity in exactly the same way as their father, in equally pharaoh-like tones. When a new public building was erected during their reign, *they* were regarded as having built it, not the town or the religious community. 'This is the temple which Yehimilk, King of Byblos, erected,' it says in an inscription which was found in Gebeil. 'May Baal-Shamim and Baalat-Gebal and the whole assembly of the holy gods of Byblos prolong his days.' Or: 'This is the statue which Abibaal, King of Byblos, son of Yehimilk, King of Byblos, had brought from Egypt for Baalat, his lady. May . . .' Or: 'This is the temple wall which Shipitbaal, King of Byblos, son of Abibaal, King of Byblos, son of Yehimilk, King of Byblos, had built for Baalat-Gebal, his lady. May . . .'

Always the same phraseology, revealing priest kings or monarchs by the grace of God. The dynastic principle is stressed and seems to have been respected for a relatively long time in Byblos, at least until 880 BC, the year in which the last Ahiramid known to us by name sat on the throne.

That things could also go very differently, we can see from the history of Tyre. There, as Josephus tells us, after the death of Hiram's nephew Abdastratus (a Latinized name), bloody palace intrigues broke out which in 875 BC brought the priest of Astarte, Ithobaal, Jezebel's father, to power. These disputes, the chronicler makes quite clear, are entirely in keeping with the idea which writers of romantic Gothic novels have of history. The four sons of his nurse conspired against Abdastratus, for instance, while one Astharymus was killed by his brother Phelles, until finally the priest intervened and founded a dynasty which lasted nearly a century.

Once more, we can only conjecture about the class structure below the throne thus won. To start with, one has to remember that there was no aristocracy in the classic sense, since there was not enough land for extensive estates. Phoenicia had no feudal era in that sense, only a strong middle class. A patriciate of rich merchants, who certainly lived like lords, decided the fortunes of the cities, while all rough work was done by servants and all lowly tasks by slaves. If the patricians allowed their kings to ill-treat them it was only because they were the

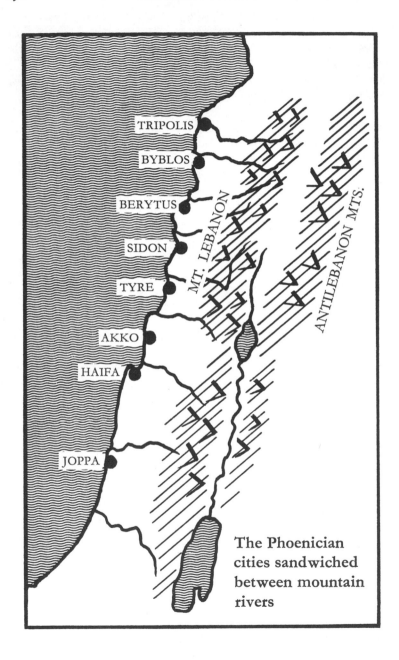

TRIPOLIS

BYBLOS

BERYTUS

SIDON

TYRE

AKKO

HAIFA

JOPPA

MT. LEBANON

ANTILEBANON MTS.

The Phoenician
cities sandwiched
between mountain
rivers

representatives of the gods, who must not be crossed. But there must also have been powerful oligarchies in all the Phoenician ports, with councils of elders who acted as a supervisory board in trade transactions. The basis of life was business, which automatically limited tyrannical methods. When it is a question of money, profit is the only deciding factor, and cannot be manipulated.

This was still more evident in the Phoenician colonies. Carthage, the largest, probably never had a king and was ruled as democratically as any other mercantile republic of later times. Financial returns decided the ballot.

There is another factor which differentiates states working on an entrepreneurial basis from others: providing they have not developed the imperialistic urge, they are reluctant to wage wars. Wars are too expensive. So the people of the Lebanon almost entirely eschewed this political expedient.

In all the accounts about them there is only one mention, by Josephus, of the Phoenicians having sent a strike force. The Jewish historian writes that Hiram of Tyre sent a punitive expedition to a distant colony, which for a long time was thought to be Utica in North Africa. The experts are now inclined to think that it was Kittim or Kition, now Larnaca, in Cyprus. This is more likely because the island was near enough for troops to be sent there from the Lebanon and by the turn of the century it had probably already been occupied by Phoenician outposts for a long time and was considered as almost part of the motherland—another legacy from the Sea Peoples, who had ruled parts of Cyprus from Crete.

There are further grounds for thinking that Cyprus was the first and most important colony of the Tyrians or Sidonians, or both. Phoenicia was an industrial state. Its factories desperately needed raw materials, particularly copper, and—as has been mentioned—there was very little in the Lebanese mountains. However, the nearby island offered inexhaustible supplies of this non-ferrous metal. It probably owed its name to copper—a derivative of the Greek *Kypros*—or alternatively gave its name to the metal.

If you go along the Troödos mountains, the central Cypriot massif, today, you continually see great dross-heaps, in which archaeologists have carried out excavations. They have found two levels, a red and a black. They attribute the former to the Phoenicians, who were the first to smelt copper there, the latter to the Romans. However, they know that copper was mined in Cyprus a long time before 1,000 BC, the time of the first Phoenician colony. This can be seen from the Amarna letters, in which a King of Cyprus tells the Pharaoh: 'See, my brother, I have sent you five hundred talents of copper . . . and I will send you [in the future also] as much copper as you like.'

The Tyrians and Sidonians, therefore, had not taught the original inhabitants how to work mines, as was previously thought, but had bought themselves into existing concerns and then ran them under their own management—for example at Pendaya on the north coast of the island. There an engineer of the American Cyprus Mining Company proudly showed me that the vast hole in which his men were then preparing to blast had earlier been an equally large mountain, on whose summit the Phoenicians had uncovered their mines. Then the enterprise was directed from Tyre, today its directors are in Los Angeles. The modern tycoons derive their income from the same substance from which their colleagues nearly three thousand years ago made their living. And Hiram, in sending a punitive expedition to protect these mines, was not behaving very differently from the Americans who aim to control the eastern Mediterranean with their Sixth Fleet.

Copper was vital to the Phoenicians. To get it, they came to an agreement with Solomon, and also founded at least five mining towns and ports on Cyprus. The most important was probably Kittim; the others were called by the Greeks Amathos (near Limassol), Tamassos (present-day Politiko), Idalion (by the village of Dali) and Lapithos near Kyrenia. Besides which the people from the Lebanon laid the foundations for the huge Graeco-Roman temple at Salamis, as their Baal was much esteemed throughout the island. One of the few likenesses of him was found in Engomi near Salamis. It shows the god as a man with bull's horns on his head.

From all this it is apparent that Cyprus was not just a staging-post for the Phoenicians, but territory which they occupied as a civilizing power and organized in the same way as their home-land. In Kittim there was a whole dynasty of resident kings,

Stele with a prayer from Yehimilk to Baal

Obverse and reverse of a Tyrian coin of the Hellenistic era

Relief of a Phoenician ship of Roman times, found near Sidon

with names like Baalmilk, Osbaal and Baalram. The most famous citizen of the later Larnaca, the philosopher Zeno, founder of the Stoa, certainly had Phoenician blood in his veins. A bust of him, in Naples, shows a distinctly Semitic head. Yet Cyprus was an exception among the colonies of the settlers from the Lebanon. They generally saw no point in burdening themselves with large tracts of land in foreign countries. It was contrary to their ideas of what was economical.

If a group of merchants in Tyre decided that for one reason or another a new base must be established, they made their plans in a systematic way, so systematically in fact that archaeologists only have to repeat their prudent thought-processes to find new sites to excavate. The Frenchman P. Cintas was the first to recognize this. In a report on Carthaginian Morocco he writes: 'When I began my research, I never asked myself where I should dig: I simply pre-supposed certain facts of scientific archaeology. Thus I ignored the places which the classical authors may have had in mind, and instead ranged over the country and the coastal region looking for a "landscape", a certain type of landscape—a "Punic landscape". A Punic *facies* exists both on the Moroccan coast and in the interior; we can imagine it if we consider what were the essentials necessary to the primitive life of the Carthaginians. This gives us a basic idea of the manner and method in which they went about it.'

What these essentials were, is in fact not too difficult to imagine. Sabatino Moscati lists them. First, he deduces, a Phoenician harbour had to be not farther than a good day's journey from the next, because Tyrian and Sidonian captains were reluctant to spend nights at sea. Furthermore it is known that they preferred promontories, islands close inshore and shallow bays, which allowed them to pull their ships on land. Third, they needed a minimum of fertile land, on which the garrisons could live, with at least one spring. And finally they also liked a few rocks, as their dead were not thrown into the sea, but buried in vertical shafts cut in the rock, of the kind which Pierre Montet discovered in Byblos.

So if one finds a rocky bay with a little vegetation round it anywhere on the Mediterranean coast, with a spring and some small tomb entrances nearby, together with the carefully cut slabs with which they were closed, one may feel hopeful of finding other traces of the Phoenicians there too. A bay, a spring, rocks and arable soil—this is the Punic landscape which P. Cintas was thinking of, similar to that in which the Phoenicians had built their cities at home. On the basis of these deductions it is possible to work out a network to pin over the whole Mediterranean. Starting from a few known harbours, one can discover where the others may well have lain. Cintas has had great success with such methods.

There are conflicting opinions at present as to when the Phoenicians began to open up their trade routes in the Mediterranean. There are two opposing schools of thought. One insists that the Phoenician colonizing era did not begin before the eighth century BC, thus occurring at the same time as the Greek expansion. The other proclaims the merchants of the Lebanon to be the earliest colonizers in the Mediterranean, who set forth in their ships to distant shores long before the Hellenes. The first group mostly quotes the archaeological proof, pointing out that there are no finds which go back before the eighth century, while the second relies more on the classical authors, who put the founding of the North African colony of Utica (north-west of Tunis) in 1,101 BC and mention even earlier colonies.

Today the chronicle-followers are doing rather better than the archaeologists. The relatively recent recognition of the importance of the invasion of Phoenicia by the Sea Peoples turns the scales in their favour. It seems only logical that the fusion with the Aegean Aryans was not only the trigger moment which gave the impetus to the nautical expansion of the people of the Lebanon, but at the same time also marked the beginning of their expansion overseas: the Cretan Thalassocracy no longer existed, the sea was free, and they also possessed good ships and daring captains. What was there to prevent them expanding their trade operations directly and tapping new markets in the Mediterranean?

So Moscati thinks that Cyprus was possibly occupied as early as the second millennium BC, certainly by the beginning of the first. A little later, in about 1,100, the Phoenician merchants settled in Camiros and Ialysos on Rhodes, and at the same time founded staging-posts on Thasos, Cythera, Thera, Crete and

Melos. They are even said to have played a part in giving the last-named island its name. 'The Phoenicians were its first inhabitants,' wrote Stephanos of Byzantium; 'it was then called Byblis, because they came from Byblos.' In fact the island was originally called Mimblis, which may have been derived from Byblis. This became Mimallis and eventually Melos.

Travelling in the other direction, along the African coast, the Tyrians and Sidonians had to use more cautious tactics than in underdeveloped Greece. They came first to Egypt, a country where they could not just occupy bays and set up their trading posts. Instead they had to find lodgings in ordinary houses and respect the laws of the state. This they did. Herodotus recounts that there was a district in Memphis called the 'Tyrian quarter'. There was also a temple there 'which is called that of the foreign Aphrodite', and was therefore an Asherat-temple. In addition Phoenician pottery has been found in various Delta ports, which leads one to believe that they had quays and warehouses there.

In spite of this the Phoenicians probably did not play a very major role in the kingdom of the Pharaohs. Their colonies only really blossomed in politically weak areas, which certainly could not be said of Egypt.

More famous than their quarter in Memphis, then, was their Libyan base at Leptis Magna, which the Roman Sallust said was founded by refugees from Sidon, and also Hippo and Hadrumetum in Tunisia, which the same author assigns to the Tyrians; then a place called Auza, which Ithobaal was said to have founded in the ninth century (we do not know where it was), and Utica; and finally Gades, now Cadiz, on the Atlantic coast of Spain near Gibraltar. The date of its foundation is thought to be 1,110 BC. Opposite it on the Atlantic coast of Africa lay Lixus, which according to Pliny was older than Gades and therefore, if he is right, the earliest Phoenician colony of which we know.

The list of Phoenician towns in the Mediterranean does not end here. Yet this gives us an idea of an undertaking which is among the most outstanding in the history of mankind.

If one thinks about it, they were members of an almost laughably small race, who, while only possessing a minute piece of Mediterranean coastline and living in gull-like nests on cliffs and rocks, set forth on expeditions of which none of their more powerful neighbours had even dreamt. They got into their cockle-shell boats and sailed off across a stretch of water of two and a half million square kilometres, about which they knew less than we know of the moon's surface. They knew neither where this sea would end, nor how deep it was, nor what dangers it hid. If the picture of the earth which they had has been correctly handed down to us, i.e. that it was like an opened egg, they must have also been afraid that they would reach the edge of the world at some point; what might lie in wait for them there was beyond the powers of human imagination. Yet they still set forth.

They were not, admittedly, taking an absolutely uncalculated risk. Their captains had the benefit of generations of accumulated experience, and were as much at home on the sea as we are in the jungle of city traffic. Besides which they felt their way along the coast in short stages and must certainly have taken years to get to know the whole stretch from Tyre to Gades. As they had no maps they had to get their bearings from characteristic headlands, peninsulas or estuaries and must therefore have had excellent visual memories. But there is little doubt that such an enterprise took a high toll in human lives, and that countless ships' crews were overtaken by sudden storms and ended in a watery grave before the voyage became a routine journey.

What was all this sacrifice for? Pure profit? It seems unthinkable that a whole gifted nation would have involved itself for such a reason. There must have been more to it than that: an inherited Bedouin *Wanderlust*, the joy of discovery, the will to find something different, to adventure, to dare. However much the merchants at home may have profited from these journeys, those who undertook them were certainly more than mere businessmen. They must have been men who strove for self-realization and self-fulfilment. If for this reason only, one must regard the opening-up of the Mediterranean as an important cultural achievement, even if the feat was not glorified by the figure of a Semitic Odysseus.

Of course the reasons which we can discern for undertaking such voyages were primarily of an economic nature, but that does not alter the foregoing conclusion. It cost money to equip the ships, and this capital had to pay dividends. As in Cyprus, the Tyrians and Sidonians looked mainly for copper, tin, gold and silver in the countries where they landed. But even if one only regards the whole enterprise in this light, it is still impressive enough. Until such materials were discovered somewhere, enormous sums had to be paid out, and therefore they were speculating on an unprecedented scale. Anyone who has ever taken the risk of investing a large sum in an uncertain venture will know what this means—even if it was only on the racecourse.

For the people of the Lebanon the risk paid off well. At the end of the long trans-Mediterranean route they found, in Spain, the rich silver mines of the Sierra Morena, which were worked by the indigenous Iberians. Diodorus Siculus, a rather superficial Greek historiographer, relates that these men were so ignorant that they did not know what to do with the precious metal, 'until the Phoenicians on their trading voyages offered them small amounts of their goods for the silver'. But that is rather improbable if only because they would hardly have dug for the ore if they had not known how to use it. Moreover it is known that they also eagerly prospected for tin, that they traded with England and Ireland and possibly even went there. The Phoenicians thus met a relatively civilized people at the southern tip of the Iberian peninsula, with whom they could do solid business. Consequently they immediately set up their outpost at Gades. It was—as its name seems to indicate—a fort on one of the small offshore islands they so loved.

Before doing so, they would have passed through the Straits of Gibraltar, and seen that beyond it stretched another endless ocean, far more stormy than the one they knew, and moved by tides. This was a phenomenon which also amazed Alexander the Great in India centuries later. There were no tides in the Mediterranean. How the Phoenicians reacted is not recorded. They appear to have simply grown accustomed to the fact and were soon feeling their way down the Atlantic coast of Africa. According to as yet unconfirmed theories they then even veered westwards and sailed as far as America. Professor Cyrus H. Gordon of Brandeis University in Boston at any rate put forward the supposition that the Melungeons, a light-skinned Indian tribe in East Tennessee came, as they themselves believe, from Phoenicia. Two and a half millennia before Columbus these ancestors of theirs landed on the shores of the New World and became settlers there. Anyone who has studied the Tyrians and their voyages for any length of time will be inclined to think that this theory is likely. They were an amazing people. The things they have not recounted would fill at least as many volumes as all that the Greeks have told so volubly.

With the founding of the two colonies at Gades and Lixus, which are both the farthest from Tyre and the oldest, the most important part of the mineral prospecting enterprise seems to have been concluded. Now it was time to consolidate and safeguard the route there; that is, to set up bases, supply-stations and refuge-harbours in many of the places at which the explorers had stayed overnight and rested on the voyage out. This project naturally went hand in hand with further expansion.

Thus in about 600 BC the Phoenicians built a trading station on Ibiza; a little earlier they were already installed in Malta and the neighbouring island of Gozo. We know that there were at least three Phoenician settlements in Sicily, at Motya, Panormus and Soloeis, all on the northern tip of the island. In 1972 Phoenician graves of the seventh century BC were also discovered near Mozia, on the west coast of Sicily, in accordance with Thucydides's account stating that the Tyrians had more or less had the whole island in their power. Until then no one had believed him because his account was not corroborated by any other contemporary author. Now archaeology appears to back him up.

By the ninth century BC the Phoenicians had already settled in Sardinia, which opened the way to the northern Mediterranean and a second route to Spain, and there in Sardinia they embarked upon an active building programme. Their oldest settlement was Nora, and they also laid the foundations for the Sardinian capital Cagliari, for Bythia, Carloforte, Tharros and Sant'Antioco, all in the south of the island. They seem to have particularly liked Sardinia, as anyone will understand who knows the island. The round bay of Sant'Antioco is a more or less classic 'Punic Landscape'. The Phoenicians built one of their forts on Monte Sirai, which overlooks the bay—a small stronghold, whose ruins are not particularly impressive. Small streets between narrow stone houses, a little temple and an uneven wall, that is all. Yet anyone who was up there could overlook the whole stretch of sea below him, could see every sail which appeared on the horizon, and was thus in a position to warn in particular the priests of the topheth opposite and keep them informed. Today the small site is manfully defended against all-comers by a grim-faced Sardinian war veteran, but a five-hundred-lira note works wonders.

With the occupation of Sardinia the Phoenicians had perfected their trade system. Their ships could now return from Spain either along the North African coast or, if they wanted to avoid that because of the dangerous currents in the two Syrtes, via Sardinia and Sicily and along the Greek coast, where they had strong bases and also gold mines in Bithynia and Thrace (on the shores of the Bosphorus), and then via Rhodes, Asia Minor and Cyprus to the home ports.

Altogether this whole network was an amazingly modern achievement, an empire which depended, not on vast territories, but on a fleet, a system of well-fortified staging-posts and on the goodwill of their customers. The last was essential. The Phoenicians never felt strong enough to enforce their claims and transactions.

The trade network directed from the Lebanon could not really be called complete until they had succeeded in creating a sea route between the Mediterranean and the territories on the Red Sea. The two were separated by the bridge of land between the Sinai Peninsula and the Lower Nile Valley. The Tarshish ships had to unload their cargo in Ezion-geber and transport it to the north by camel caravans. The operational sphere of their owners was severely limited by the anti-Phoenician and anti-trade Jewish policy of Ahab's successors. Possibly trade with Ophir came to a complete halt during their rule, because the Phoenicians no longer commanded the Gulf of Aqaba. Only a Suez canal could really have saved the situation, allowing both systems to be directly linked. But it did not exist.

The Phoenicians asked why.

They went on asking this until the year 609 BC. At that time their country was once more under Egyptian sovereignty—but this did not worry them: King Necho II (also called Nikau), their new ruler, was a man who was passionately interested in all

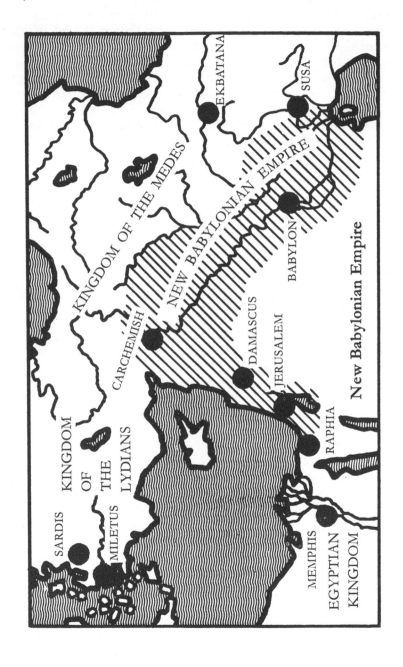

nautical and overseas trade matters and therefore well disposed towards the people of the Lebanon.

Herodotus recounts that he had ordered 'Phoenician men . . . to sail home through the Pillars of Hercules into the northern sea and so back to Egypt.' He therefore did not want them to return to Tyre from Lixus or Gades along the Mediterranean route, but to sail round Africa. Risky as it appeared, the Phoenicians carried out his orders, at least in the reverse direction. They launched forth, writes the father of all sensationalist journalism, 'from the Red Sea and sailed across the southern sea. When autumn came round, they landed and sowed their crops, finding themselves in Libya [Africa] each time, and there they waited for the harvest. When they had brought in the grain, they sailed on, so that after two years they came in the third year through the Pillars of Hercules and back to Egypt again. They said—which I do not believe, but many others do—that on the voyage round Libya they had the sun on their right.'

The last detail, the reverse position of the sun which Herodotus doubted, is in fact clear proof of the fact that this journey must indeed have taken place. None of the Mediterranean people could have learnt from their own observation that the great orb, which in the northern sphere always turns south of the zenith, i.e. on the left, in the southern sphere would have to pass to the north of the celestial pole, i.e. on the right. So this means that long before Vasco da Gama, the Phoenicians succeeded in an enterprise—the voyage round Africa—which even in the fifteenth century so impressed the civilized world that they honoured the Portuguese count as one of the most renowned sailors of all time. The people from the Lebanon achieved this with primitive means and in their own way, sailing by short stages and seeking out 'Punic landscapes' where they could rest. They saw the Table Mountain at the Cape of Good Hope, the jungle-swamped mouths of the Congo and the Cameroon rivers, came across strange black tribes and suffered from yellow fever, malaria and sleeping sickness. An eye-witness account of the journey would have been one of the most exciting adventure stories of all time—but it too was never written.

King Necho, however, must have been so impressed by the tales of those who had sailed round the continent that he decided to put in hand another great undertaking, the building of a canal from the Mediterranean to the Red Sea. He must certainly have used Phoenician specialists for this, and it seems reasonable to suppose that the original idea came from them too. Inevitably Tyrians would have gained the most from it.

The work was started some time after the year 600 BC. A line was planned which would run from the most easterly arm of the Nile near present-day Es-Zagazig, to the sea near Ismailia. From there, going round the Bitter Lakes, it followed roughly the course of the modern Suez Canal. However, shortly before the work was completed, Necho lost heart and called a halt. An oracle had warned him that he was working for 'the foreigner', but had omitted to add that the latter would only appear about seventy-five years later, in the form of the Persian King Cambyses, who conquered Egypt.

In the years after Necho's death the canal was alternately open and closed. Ptolemy II (third century BC) later put it in working order again, and gave it a lock. The last ruler to have it dug clear was the Muslim general Amr ibn al-As, who conquered Egypt in AD 640. It finally fell into disuse in the eighth century AD. We do not know if the Phoenicians were able to resuscitate trade with the Red Sea by using it, and sailing directly from Aqaba to Tyre, but it is possible. And if they did succeed in doing so, they put to shame the men of the nineteenth century, who greeted the opening of de Lesseps's canal on 17 November 1869, with music by Verdi, as an epoch-making feat.

The high point of Phoenician expansion was not, however, the building of the first Suez canal, but an event which took place about two hundred years earlier: the founding of another colony, which at first was only one among many. The first settlers called it, unimaginatively enough, Carthage, the new town. They came from Tyre, but according to the many legends, appear not to have sailed from there with any fixed intention, but rather to have been rebels or otherwise dissatisfied in some way.

This indicates that the Phoenician trade empire was not always so organically and methodically conceived as it might appear. The seafarers who had grown rich may well have kicked against the injustices of their kings. A way of life, and of looking at the world, which they had learnt abroad, may have made it difficult for them to identify with what those who had stayed at home thought and considered to be right. Quarrels, attempted coups, internal struggles for power would ensue; possibly blood flowed, prisons were filled, heads rolled. Yet it could also work in reverse. The sea heroes could form themselves into a conservative élite, and as often happens in colonies, hold more stubbornly to the old customs than the rich business magnates at home who had adopted liberal views, and thus may have revolted against them.

Carthage at any rate, the new colony which was founded by Tyrians against Tyre, was later to guard her old-Phoenician character far more jealously than those at home. If at home there was a noticeable current of frivolity and urbanity, and people flirted with Egyptian, Assyrian and Persian customs and gods, over in Tunis it was very different. There the entrenched 'pieds noirs' flourished, who on the one hand wanted nothing to do with the home kingdom, but on the other were far more willing to give Baal what he demanded, i.e. human sacrifices.

The founding of the new town therefore marks a break in the development of Phoenicia, and the beginning of a new era. It is the equivalent of the founding of the United States of America in European history. From former colonies, a newly independent state emerged; from trading posts, an independent power. Yet that would hardly have been possible, if, towards the end of the sixth century, Tyre, Sidon, Byblos and Berytus had not lost their independence for ever.

CHAPTER XI

The End of a Golden Age

GOLDEN AGES, HOWEVER golden, must all come to an end. That of the Phoenicians had in fact lasted for a small eternity of about three hundred years. Born in about 1,150 BC, from the fusion with Cherethites and Pelethites, it was nearing its end by about 850 BC. Indeed it is a wonder that it lasted so long. For three hundred years the cities of the Lebanon had been independent and had become rich solely on the basis of a few small ports and a coastline of about two hundred and fifty kilometres, a bare minimum of land and possessions. Seen in this light, 'wonder' is inadequate to describe their achievement.

The Tyrians, Sidonians, Giblites and Arvadites owed their long run of luck principally to the fact that there was no major power anywhere which would have been strong enough to extend its boundaries to include them.

In the south, Egypt, since the death of Rameses III, was only a shadow of the kingdom it had once been, with, it is true, a brilliant late flowering of culture, but politically unambitious and militarily weak.

In the sphere of the Mesopotamian north, on the other hand, there were kings who for thousands of years had been entirely occupied in defending their mighty states against even mightier neighbours. The ancient Assyrian kingdom was superseded by the Chaldean Babylonian empire, and the latter was torn asunder by the invading Hurrians from Armenia. Then Assyria rose to power again, to shine for three hundred and twenty years, expanding, and then finally shrinking again to its central territory on the upper Tigris. Phoenicia remained almost completely unaffected by all these events. She did business with Assur and Babylon, but kept out of their inner and external conflicts.

To her immediate neighbours, the two Jewish states centring

on Samaria and Jerusalem, and the Aramaeans in Syria, the tiny state may have occasionally seemed a tempting prey. But all had enemies enough to keep them fully occupied, and were moreover happy to know there was a land nearby which was useful to them in trade and banking matters, and which would give them technical help when necessary.

As has been indicated, this era came to an end in the ninth century BC. Up in the north a new power had arisen which outshone all its predecessors—the new Assyrian kingdom of Assurnasirpal II. Admittedly, this realm also had opponents enough, particularly the Medes, who had advanced to the centre of Asia Minor, but as the Persians were soon hanging on their heels, Assyria had its frontiers free for the time being and could turn to the south. Naturally her eyes lit on Phoenicia, small, powerless, and unashamedly rich.

It was thus the kings of Assur who gradually put an end to the happy state of affairs in the Lebanon—for good, because when they had passed the zenith of their power the Assyrians were followed by the Babylonians, who had meanwhile grown even stronger, with the Persians hard on their heels, and the proud merchants in Tyre, Sidon and Byblos had to fit in with each new power without an interim break. They found it hard enough. They did not bear the Assyrian or Persian yokes as calmly as they had done the Egyptian, and they rebelled continually against their new masters. In this perpetual struggle their strength was diminished and their supremacy at sea was lost. By the time the Persians disappeared again, the Phoenicians of the eastern Mediterranean were only a third-class trading power. At least two others had surpassed them, the Greeks and the Carthaginians.

This period of slow decline lasted half a millennium, from 850 until about 350 BC. It did not begin with a catastrophe, but with tremors which they were easily able to cope with. And it was not a rapid deterioration, but on the contrary was concealed by many resurgences and upward swings. But they were only distortions of a curve whose basic downward direction was unalterable.

In spite of this their eclipse did give rise to at least one positive result, which might never have occurred in happier times; namely the new-found recognition, which they had avoided for so long, that all Phoenicians belonged to a single nation and must therefore form a common state.

The first of the northern kings with whom the Phoenicians came into direct contact was Assurnasirpal II. It was still in an entirely friendly way. In 877 BC the Assyrian undertook a campaign which led him via Carchemish to the north of the Lebanon. The kings of the sea cities, who of course knew that they could be hopelessly crushed by his war machine, made no attempt to prevent him advancing farther but hurried to greet him in the only sensible way: they sent a well-supplied deputation to his camp and made the most neighbourly advances, which the neatbearded ruler received with great satisfaction. He made his court scribe note that: 'I received the tribute of the sea coast— of the inhabitants of Tyre, Sidon, Byblos, Makhalata, Maisa, Kaisa [other smaller ports], the Amurru [Amorites] and Aradus— an island in the sea—consisting of gold, silver, tin, copper, copper vessels, linen robes with many coloured borders, big and little apes, ebony, boxwood, ivory and walrus tusks—thus even a product of the sea—and they kissed my feet.'

This promised well for future trade. Assurnasirpal was just about to build a vast palace at Kalakh near Nineveh on the upper Tigris. He needed great quantities of cedarwood for it, which only the Phoenicians could supply. They declared themselves ready to do so. That led directly on to the next official contact. Years later, when the building was finished, representatives of the sea cities were invited to the Assyrian residence and entertained in princely style.

'After I had had the Palace of Kalakh built,' his official chronicle announces, '47,074 male and female workers from all the provinces of my land were invited; together with five thousand important representatives and delegates from Suhi, Hindani, Hattina, from the Hittites, from Tyre and Sidon. . . . For ten days I entertained the happy men from all these countries together with the citizens of Kalakh; I gave them wine, I let them bathe, I anointed them with oil and did them honour. Then I sent them back to their countries in peace and goodwill.'

The Phoenician tactics seem to have succeeded. As they were not in a position to live on terms of enmity with the Assyrians, they gave them an assurance of their friendly intentions and then let them see their business potential, and so were taken up as trading partners.

The same methods also bore fruit with the followers of Assurnasirpal. Neither Shalmaneser III, nor Shammuramat, whom the Greeks called Semiramis, made any attempts to encroach on the independence of the sea cities. Even Tiglath-Pileser III, the all-conquering founder of the Assyrian world empire, did not attack them, although it would certainly have been possible for him to do so. When he had progressed as far as north of Aradus in the course of one of his campaigns, he was content to accept the usual tributes, including '. . . elephant skins, blue-coloured wool, red-coloured wool (and thus purple cloth) . . . stretched red-coloured lambskins, stuffed blue-dyed birds, horses, mules, calves and deer, male and female camels with their young'.

It was not until the reign of Sennacherib, who came to the throne in 704 BC, that this era of peaceful coexistence came to an end. And the Phoenicians were themselves partly to blame. They had joined an anti-Assyrian coalition of Aramaean towns and were grimly punished for this. Sennacherib descended on the south with an army which included the new weapon, cavalry. The report he had written reads: 'On my third campaign I marched against the Hittite land [Syria]. Luli, the King of Sidon, whom the terrifying splendour of my majesty had overcome, fled over the sea and perished. The fearful effulgence of the army of Assur, oh God, conquered his strong cities, Great Sidon, Little Sidon, Bit-Zitti, Sariptu [Sarepta], Mahalliba, Ushu [the part of Tyre on the mainland], Akzib [Aczib] and Akka, all his fortified places, which were surrounded by walls and well stocked with food and water for their garrisons. They [the besieged] threw themselves at my feet in submission. I put Tuba'lu on the royal throne over them and exacted tribute from them, presents for my majesty, which they should continue to pay to the end of all time.'

This campaign, which clearly cost Sidon its independence and gave it an Assyrian viceroy, must have taken place in about 700 BC. We know from other sources that Luli, the Sidonian town ruler, fled to Cyprus, but he was registered there as 'King of Tyre', so it is not quite clear whether Sennacherib actually conquered the more northerly or southerly of the two ports or both. The most likely theory is that he took Sidon and the neighbouring towns, but only that part of Tyre which lay on the mainland.

Josephus also seems to think this was the case. He recounts that after this lightning victory of the Assyrians, the other Phoenician towns turned against Tyre and placed a fleet of sixty ships at Sennacherib's disposal so that he could also besiege the island city. But he could not take it even with their help. The sea fortress built by Hiram held out for five years and then finally defeated the enemy armada in a bloody sea battle. The town therefore remained independent and could boast that it had withstood the greatest military power of the day, although it had to accept the fact that its entire hinterland had fallen under the sway of the viceroy Tuba'lu, who ruled henceforth as Ithobaal II in Sidon.

Why the other Phoenician towns had joined forces against the unofficial capital of their country, we cannot now know. Possibly they acted under pressure from the Assyrians. Perhaps, however, they had always wanted to shake off the overlordship of the arrogant Tyrians and simply seized what seemed like a good opportunity of doing so.

That in doing so they were cutting off their own right hand, they must have seen only when it was too late. For Sennacherib was determined to contest the Phoenicians' right to their own particular territory, the sea. From the tributary towns he ordered ships, which were broken up into their various parts and transported piecemeal overland to Assyria where they were put together again on the Euphrates. From there they sailed down to Chaldea to seek out the remaining followers of the Babylonian kings in the swamps of the Shat el-Arab and put them to flight. The boats were naturally manned with 'Tyrian, Sidonian and Cypriot seamen, my prisoners', as Sennacherib said.

There were other boats, however, which were soon sailing across the Mediterranean under the Assyrian flag, where they rapidly formed a large fleet with which Sennacherib was able to conquer and occupy Cyprus.

The island of Tyre, then, stood as a lonely monument to Phoenician power, looking out over the sea which it no longer ruled. But then the pendulum swung sharply in the other direction.

Under Sennacherib's successor Esarhaddon it was the turn of the

Assyrian viceroys of Sidon to revolt against the kingdom in the north, and this time Tyre was on the side of the Mesopotamians. Esarhaddon attacked as ruthlessly as his ancestors. 'I razed Sidon to its foundations,' it says in one of his war reports. 'I pulled down its walls and houses and cast them into the sea. With the help of Assur, my lord, I caught Abdi-Milkutti [the successor of Ithobaal II], who had fled before my weapons, like a fish from the sea, and had him beheaded. . . . Then I reorganized the whole province and set up one of my commissioners as governor over them. He imposed a greater tribute on them than before. Some of his [Abdi-Milkutti's] towns, such as Marubbu and Sarepta, I gave to Baal, the King of Tyre.'

Now it was Sidon's neighbours who had won in the complicated game of power and survival, but the victory had its bitter side. In spite of it the Tyrian ruler Baal had to sign a treaty with Esarhaddon which virtually made his town a subject of the Assyrian kingdom. A governor of the King of Nineveh and a council of elders were to see that the treaty was kept. The Syrian ports at which ships from Tyre might call were carefully listed, and trade with them had to follow precise regulations.

In the long term this arrangement does not seem to have particularly harmed Tyrian trade. There is a record of further rebellion against Assyria, which resulted in Usu being devastated once more, but it is reported so ambiguously that it can also be interpreted as having been instigated by Assyria in order to increase the tribute payments.

Since Esarhaddon's time, moreover, Phoenicia had been divided into two provinces, the north and the south. Within this framework, at least Tyre, Aradus and Byblos could act fairly freely. The Mesopotamian control of the whole of the Lebanon must have also guaranteed a certain unity, which is always advantageous to businessmen, especially when they are engaged in anything as uncertain as overseas trade.

The Phoenicians' towns therefore continued to prosper, their colonies flourished and their craftsmen worked, as previously in Jerusalem, in the palaces of Babylon and Nineveh. Assyrian notables also occasionally came to Tyre, as Assurnasirpal II had done, to engage in a sport, which today would have the animal protection societies and television viewers of the entire world up in arms—the hunting of '*nahirus*', or dolphins. If in spite of these good relations the Tyrians still kicked over the traces now and then, they usually got off with an increase in tribute or had one of the almost routine punitive expeditions inflicted on them which the Assyrians primarily instigated in order to impress seamen for their ships.

Esarhaddon's successor Assurbanipal, however, soon had no time to worry about the distant sea province; he had other burning problems—family feuds, internal unrest, attacks by the Scythians. The new Assyrian empire was falling to pieces in his hands. In 612 BC Nineveh was overthrown by the rebellious Babylonians, and its heyday was over for good.

The palace scribes had by now made no mention of Tyre, Byblos and Aradus for a long time. Fortune had granted them their independence again—one of the upward curves in the graph.

The sea cities now strove more energetically than ever before, opening up new trade routes, doing business with all the Mediterranean peoples and also approaching their old protectress Egypt, who offered them an ideal colleague and overlord in King Necho II. Now they were sailing round Africa, building the first Suez Canal with him, at the brilliant summit of their career, as described by Ezekiel.

But this short moment of independence and peace was only a brief interlude. Up in the north Assyria had been superseded by the new Babylonian empire; in its capital, the most important centre of civilization in the ancient world, rose the legendary tower, and its builder, Nebuchadnezzar II, was by no means inclined to give up a prize which his predecessors on the throne of Nineveh had held so securely in their hands. In the year 605 BC he advanced on Egypt, met Necho's army near Carchemish and routed the Pharaoh, whose troops stampeded. Phoenicia was once more at the mercy of the Mesopotamians, but was reprieved for another seven years. Nebuchadnezzar had to return to Babylon because his father had died and the succession was being disputed. But during this stay of execution his shadow hung threateningly over the whole land. It reached as far as Jerusalem, where Jeremiah and many of his compatriots trembled before it.

The Tyrians reacted differently from the Hebrews. They

decided to stop the encroachments of the northern powers once and for all, and to build up an opposing force. It was a foolhardy plan, which can only be explained by the fact that they may have had inadequate information. If the Phoenicians had known who this Nebuchadnezzar was, they would never have had such an idea, but would have speedily remembered the old recipe from their grandfathers' day and sent heavily-laden envoys with unsolicited tribute to the Euphrates.

The Babylonian lives on in history as one of the most powerful potentates of all time. He dreamt of an empire which would stretch from Anatolia to the Nile Valley and where there would be no national differences, but only citizens with the same rules, the same status, the same rights, who would look submissively towards his glorious capital. And he was certainly not in the mood to be hindered in carrying out this plan by a tiny merchant state on the edge of the Lebanon.

The Tyrians, as has been explained, knew nothing of all this, but Jeremiah knew of it—that level-headed, realistic politician who lived in Jerusalem and entreated his King Zedekiah not to become involved in any anti-Babylonian activities. 'Bring your necks under the yoke of the king of Babylon,' he wailed, 'and serve him and his people, and live . . . wherefore should this city be laid waste?' (Jeremiah 27:12 and 17.)

Jeremiah spoke from experience, knowing what his people had suffered under the Assyrians. The State of Israel had been conquered and completely depopulated by Sargon II in 721 BC; Judah too had felt the weight of Sennacherib's fist. Zedekiah, however, did not want to be reminded of that. He did not listen to Jeremiah, but to his rival Hananiah, a raging nationalist, who announced his Jahweh with wild delusions of grandeur: 'I have broken the yoke of the king of Babylon' (Jeremiah 28:2). Then he joined an alliance, to which Egypt belonged, and also Edom, Moab, and the Phoenician city states. The league was led by Tyre, whose King Ithobaal had personally enlisted the support of his Jewish colleagues.

The sealing of the treaty between the ailing empire on the Nile and the few Syro-Palestinian midgets was, whichever way you looked at it, the prelude to suicide. Ezekiel, who was then already languishing as a prisoner in Babylon, thought he could see how it must end. 'Therefore thus saith the Lord God;' he wrote, 'Behold, I am against thee, O Tyrus, and will cause many nations to come up against thee, as the sea causeth his waves to come up. And they shall destroy the walls of Tyrus, and break down her towers: I will also scrape her dust from her, and make her like the top of a rock. It shall be a place for the spreading of nets in the midst of the sea: for I have spoken it, saith the Lord God: and it shall become a spoil to the nations. And her daughters which are in the field shall be slain by the sword; and they shall know that I am the Lord. For thus saith the Lord God; Behold, I will bring upon Tyrus Nebuchadrezzar king of Babylon, a king of kings, from the north, with horses, and with chariots, and with horsemen, and companies, and much people. He shall slay with the sword thy daughters in the field: and he shall make a fort against thee, and cast a mount against thee, and lift up the buckler against thee. And he shall set engines of war against thy walls, and with his axes he shall break down thy towers. . . . With the hoofs of his horses shall he tread down all thy streets: he shall slay thy people by the sword, and thy strong garrisons shall go down to the ground. And they shall make a spoil of thy riches, and make a prey of thy merchandise . . . and destroy thy pleasant houses: and they shall lay thy stones and thy timber and thy dust in the midst of the water. And I will cause the noise of thy songs to cease; and the sound of thy harps shall be no more heard' (Ezekiel 26:3–13).

It was a precise description by a precise author of that which must come to pass; and yet it did not happen. Nebuchadnezzar did advance in 598 BC with an army whose terrible size justified all Ezekiel's adjectives, but it only smashed Judah, took Jerusalem and carried off its inhabitants into captivity in Babylon and also defeated the armies of the Egyptian-Edomite-Moabite-Phoenician coalition. He failed in his attempt to take Tyre by joining it to the mainland with a dam and using his battering rams to crush it. Which was almost miraculous.

For thirteen years, from 585 to 572 BC, the largest army of the day lay before a tiny island fortress and was unable to take it. 'Every head was made bald' (from wearing helmets), Ezekiel says, 'and every shoulder was peeled (from carrying weapons and armaments); yet had he [Nebuchadnezzar] no wages, nor his army . . .' (Ezekiel 29:18).

The Tyrians, getting their supplies by sea, countered each assault, defeated every attempt to build a dam and bore with incredible staunchness the inevitable hardships of a siege. Which shows that they could also fight when necessary, and that they were not always prepared to sell their independence—that they knew the value of freedom, that it cannot be valued too highly.

However, they did not manage by this tremendous feat of endurance to achieve a return to wholly normal conditions, or the unconditional withdrawal of the Babylonian army. They had to compromise in order to survive. Fragments of Phoenician annals, which Josephus has handed on to us, lead one to conclude that Nebuchadnezzar gained at least a formal surrender and the handing over of hostages from the siege. Only when he had done so did he give up the attempt to take Tyre, which was equally hopeless from his point of view, and hand the prisoners over to some of his officers, to be 'escorted back to Babylon together with the heavy troops, and the rest of the siege equipment, while he himself returned to the Euphrates through the desert with a small troop of men. . . . And now that he was lord of the whole realm which his father [Nabopolassar] had possessed, he gave orders that after their arrival the prisoners should be allowed to settle in suitable Babylonian provinces.' There they did not fare too badly. They were registered by the powerful bureaucracy and given generously apportioned benefits.

The royal bookkeepers mention in their list as having received quotas of oil, 'the King of Tyre, the King of Gaza, the King of Sidon, the King of Aradus', and '126 men from Tyre'. So there were Phoenicians who sat down 'at the waters of Babylon' with the Jews and wept for their lost homes, or who made a new life for themselves in the new land—although Ithobaal, Nebuchadnezzar's antagonist, who had formed the anti-Babylonian alliance, was, in spite of the above mention of him in the list, not among those deported to Babylon. He died in Tyre, and bequeathed the throne of the badly shaken city state to his son Baal, who was later overthrown by revolutionaries and supplanted by a judicial body from Carthage. This provisional government only operated for a few years and was then replaced by a prince called Baalator, who also seems to have succeeded in founding a new royal dynasty. The last member of it was once more called Hiram.

He had to be fetched back from Babylon, where he had been living with the other prisoners, by a delegation.

But by the time this happened Babylon's star was already on the wane. Cyrus II had conquered Nebuchadnezzar's empire— in 539 BC—and made it a Persian province, part of an empire which would soon surpass all the earlier realms of the Near East in size and strength. Phoenicia too surrendered almost at once.

The Persian fetters do not seem to have been particularly oppressive. Under Cyrus the Phoenicians again enjoyed a relative independence, and his followers did not subject them to too many regulations. The towns could breathe more freely.

Their first large commission under their new masters was a building contract. The conquerors of Babylon had set the captive Jews free. They had returned to Jerusalem and were now anxious that the town should be rebuilt in all its old glory. But this was still not possible without the help of Phoenician architects and craftsmen. So they gave, the prophet Ezra writes: 'money also unto the masons, and to the carpenters; and meat, and drink, and oil, unto them of Zidon, and to them of Tyre, to bring cedar trees from Lebanon to the sea of Joppa [Jaffa, near present-day Tel-Aviv], according to the grant that they had of Cyrus, king of Persia' (Ezra 3:7).

Indeed, the Tyrians badly needed this contract because things were not going too well for them in the first years of Persian rule. They had not yet recovered from their heroic stand against Nebuchadnezzar, had fallen far behind their rival Sidon and were only slowly getting on their feet again. To make matters worse they had then lost their important colonies in Cyprus. King Amosis II of Egypt had occupied the island, probably fearing the Persians would otherwise use it as a base for a naval attack on his own country. Which was exactly what they were planning to do. Cambyses II, Cyrus's successor, was determined to get the whole eastern Mediterranean basin under his control. To do so he would first have to conquer Egypt.

And he also needed a fleet. But as Persia was no more a sea-going nation than the defeated Babylon had been, he could only get the necessary ships and men from the Phoenicians. It was the second lucky break for the sea cities, and naturally they made the most of it. Their kings made an agreement with Cambyses which guaranteed them almost complete independence, in return for which they promised to place their whole naval force at the Persian's disposal, although under their own command. This gave them the status of allies, but on the other hand also committed them to supporting Persian foreign policy. The two roles were not compatible, however, for any length of time, and this soon became apparent.

When Cambyses advanced on Egypt in 525 BC, Phoenician contingents were among his troops and fought reluctantly, one imagines, against their oldest friends, who had helped them shape their own civilization. But when shortly afterwards the Persian also wanted to attack their daughter city of Carthage, the Tyrians went on strike and forced him to give up the idea. Without the ships of Tyre and Sidon the great commander was powerless. 'Cambyses's whole navy,' Herodotus writes, 'was dependent on the Phoenicians', and the great king knew this. He laid less heavy taxes on them than on all his other subject peoples. Moreover the *Pax Persica* gave the merchants of the Lebanon exactly what they so urgently needed if they were to prosper— peace and order. In addition there was also an excellent post and road network and—since Cambyses's successor Darius—a single monetary unit on the Lydian pattern, the so-called 'daric' (a Greek word).

The Phoenicians were again trading with Judah—which displeased the prophet Nehemiah, because they disregarded the Sabbath day—and had a flourishing goldmine on Thasos. Herodotus claims to have seen it. Their prosperity in the shadow of the Persian throne was only disturbed by a new development in the Aegean, which must have caused many headaches among the city elders of Tyre, Sidon, Byblos and Aradus. For there a rival power was developing, with men who soon knew as much about seamanship as themselves and were as good, if not better, traders—the Hellenes. The sea cities had every reason to distrust these people. And the opportunity to fight them came soon enough.

When in 500 BC the Ionian Greek towns of western Asia Minor, which was part of the Persian empire that then reached from the Bosphorus to the Indus, raised a rebellion—doomed before it started—against Darius, they were met not only by the king's army but also by a fleet under Phoenician command.

The first sea battle between the Greek squadron and those from the Lebanon took place off Salamis in Cyprus, which had also revolted. It was fought on both sides with considerable bitterness and great tactical skill, but the Hellenes proved themselves the better fighters. Tyre and Sidon, until then the unchallenged queens of the sea, suffered a humiliating defeat. They were only saved from total destruction by the fact that the Ionians withdrew from the battle prematurely.

They only retrieved their honour months later off the coast of Asia Minor. There Darius had gathered six hundred ships, which he launched against the contingents of Samos, Chios, and a few other islands. It was a sea battle in the classic style. Both sides advanced towards each other in long lines and then tried to smash their opponents' oars or ram them. 'From now on,' Herodotus reports, 'I cannot say exactly which of the Ionians were brave or cowardly in this battle. The Samians (at any rate) are believed to have . . . unfurled their sails and—except for eleven ships—sailed back out of the battle order to Samos.' They fled at the height of the battle and so helped the Phoenicians gain an easy victory, one of the few in their encounters with the Greeks. In his next action against Greece Darius lost a large part of his Phoenician ships in a storm off Mount Athos and was only victorious on land. This was followed by an encounter culminating in the battle of Marathon and an equally humiliating withdrawal of his fleet.

Then in 480 BC Xerxes I made his famous attempt to conquer European Greece. Again Phoenicians were appointed to prominent posts and Xerxes planned his campaign with utmost care. As he did not want to risk losing his fleet in a storm, he decided that this time he would cut a channel through the narrow strip of land joining Mount Athos to the mainland, in order to spare his ships the dangerous journey round the cape. The only people who were able to solve adequately the technical problems involved in this gigantic project were the men from the Lebanon.

Herodotus illustrates this in the following extract: 'The barbarians [Persians] divided the place by peoples, after they had drawn a straight line near Sane [a town on the isthmus]. When they had dug to a certain depth, the ones standing at the

Ivory carving from a Phoenician workshop (*c.* 715 BC)

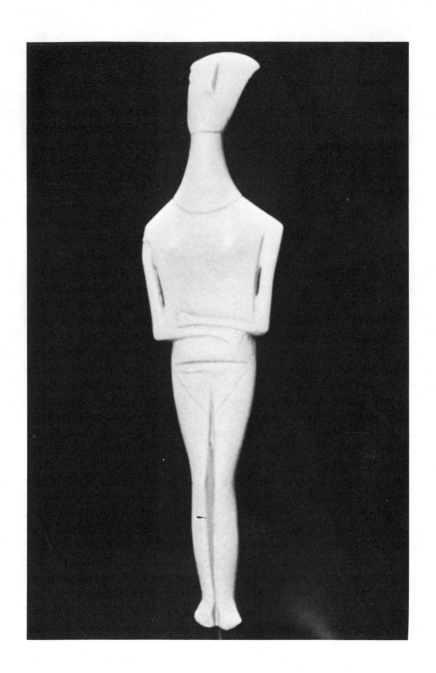

Two Aphrodites: sex symbols of the pre-Classical era

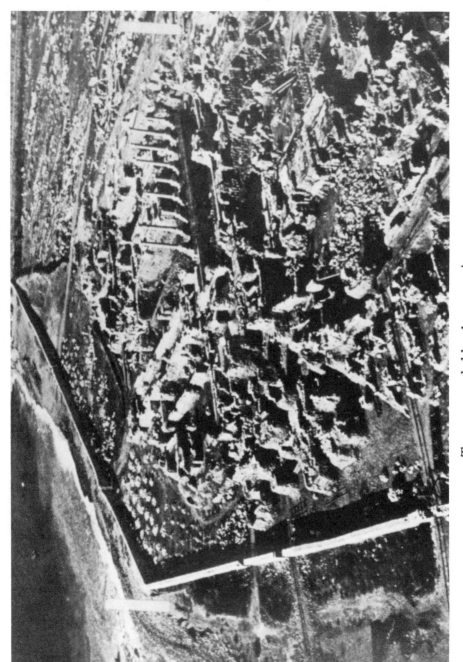

Tyre, as revealed by the excavations

bottom went on digging and others handed the earth dug out to those who stood above them . . . these lifted it out and threw it aside. With the exception of the Phoenicians, they experienced great difficulty with the sides of the canal; as the upper and lower sides were the same width apart, they kept falling in. But the Phoenicians showed their skill here as elsewhere. They dug leaving the upper opening of the cutting twice as wide as the canal would be, so that the sides of the cutting slanted obliquely inwards, and thus were finally the same distance apart at the bottom as those of the other peoples.' They were the only ones who knew the correct angles at which to build a dam, and dig a canal. However, even their store of knowledge was of no avail. The burdensome undertaking ended with the battle of Salamis near Athens.

The evening before the battle, the Persian king held yet another splendid council of war. 'When he had come in,' Herodotus writes of the meeting, 'and had sat on the throne, the despots of each of the [vassal] states appeared before him, together with the commanders of the naval units, and they sat according to the rank which their sovereign had bestowed on them: first the King of Sidon, then the King of Tyre, and then the rest.'

The Phoenicians accordingly acted as First Lords of the fleet, a rather doubtful honour as would transpire at the battle. The 1,207 ships which they commanded were opposed by only 310 Greek vessels, but these were carrying out the orders of one of the greatest strategical geniuses of all time. Themistocles, supreme commander of the Greek forces, represented at sea by the Spartan Eurybiades, had seen that his people would only have a chance if they succeeded in preventing their opponents, in the narrow bay of Salamis, from deploying their fleet. And this they did. The Persian ships, crowded together in a dense group, could make no sweeping attack, and hindering each other as they manœuvred, were shamefully put to flight.

Xerxes, who had watched the whole spectacle from the mountain of Aegaleos—he sat there on a throne with silver feet— naturally vented most of his anger on those he considered responsible for the defeat, his Phoenician commanders. When some of them came to him to justify themselves he ordered their heads to be cut off, 'so that they who had themselves been cowardly should not slander the brave' (Herodotus). At which other captains from the Lebanon were so horrified that they left the fleet forthwith and sailed off.

It was the best thing they could have done. In doing so they were at least spared from taking part in a second naval battle off the Mycale Mountain near Miletus, which also ended in disgrace for the Persians and their Phoenician admirals.

Altogether the unfortunate Greek campaign of Xerxes seems to have rather damaged the renown of the Tyrians and Sidonians. After Salamis and Mycale no ships of either town took part in a battle against the Hellenes for fifteen years. It was not until 465 BC, when the victorious Athens wanted to take Cyprus, that they appeared once more at the side of their sovereign, who had taken the island from the Egyptians, to drive their rivals back to the Aegean. The fear that they might lose their valuable copper mines seems to have inspired them with greater courage than Xerxes's extravagant dreams of glory.

More important than the news of the belated sea victories off Cyprus was another report which we have from that date. It comes from Diodorus Siculus. He wrote: 'There is an important town in Phoenicia, which is called Tripolis [Three Towns], and this name describes its nature, for there are three districts in it, each a stade [192 metres] distant from each other and which are called: the towns "of the Arvadites", "of the Sidonians" and "of the Tyrians". This is the most famous of all the towns of Phoenicia, because the city elders held their general councils there and decided matters of the greatest importance.' Then he adds that Tripolis could therefore be called Phoenicia's first 'parliament'.

If what he says is correct—he is rather unreliable—then the sea cities must have at last decided, after their participation in the Persian-Greek conflict, not to contend against each other any longer but to work together on a national basis. Besides being ratified by a treaty, the decision was also strengthened by the creation of a central institution, the permanent council of Tripolis.

As Diodorus also informs us, the town which is present-day Tripoli in the Lebanon (in Arabic, Tarabulus), was said to have been founded in the fourth century by Tyre, Sidon and Aradus in conjunction. To look at, it was one of the usual little Phoenician sea towns, lying on a small promontory, but it had the status of a federal capital, whose existence did not, however, threaten the position of any of the great metropolises. It was thus the result of a clever official compromise.

It is easy to guess what drove the people of the Lebanon to take this uncharacteristic step. They realized that the sea no longer belonged to them alone, that they had to reckon with at least two new rivals between Gibraltar and their native shores: their own colony of Carthage, and Greece. Moreover, it must also have become clear to them that with their tiny city states they could no longer muster the necessary political strength against the great Persian empire; and they also finally seemed to realize that there were ultimately a whole series of common problems, fears and interests, which could more easily be controlled, mastered and pursued by uniting than by maintaining an aggressive independence. In short, they had discovered their national identity. This was a great step forward since the days when Sidon had allied herself with the enemies of the Tyrians, or Tyre with those of the Sidonians, to achieve their own limited ends.

In 352 BC the union was even ratified by a kind of declaration of independence. The city elders gathered in Tunis solemnly pronounced the secession of Phoenicia from the Persian empire; but they had once more over-reached themselves. Sidon, which following this heroic ceremony drove out the imperial garrison and burnt their cavalry fodder, was at once attacked by King Artaxerxes, treacherously delivered into his hands, and burnt by the angry citizens. At which Tyre, having already attempted a rebellion thirty-five years before, did not dare to take up the revolutionary flame, or attempt to follow up the declaration of independence by a war of independence.

After this outbreak both towns were content to bend to the will of their masters once more, and to enjoy the peace this brought. They even minted their own coins—with Tyre choosing Melqart riding on a seahorse as its heraldic device—and in general went their own way.

Unfortunately, there is no extant record of what became of the Phoenician federation of towns in the final years of the Persian era. So we do not know whether they ever achieved their political aim and whether one can therefore call them the precursors of the present-day Lebanese Republic. But it is not entirely improbable. Tripolis, the capital of the federation, rapidly blossomed. She provided herself with a series of important temples, and was still enjoying considerable renown in Roman times. From this one may perhaps conclude that she was more than just another sea port in the shadow of the mountains—but one must stress the word 'perhaps'.

However, one thing certainly remained from the Phoenicians' attempt to achieve national unity (it was also probably the cause of their trying to do so): their rivalry with the Greeks. Henceforward the latter were not only their rivals, but since the Phoenician participation in the Hellenic Persian campaigns, their sworn enemies, and dangerous ones at that. The Greeks, as voluble as the Phoenicians were silent, saw to it that the people of the Lebanon went down in history as a crowd of avaricious, thieving, deceitful traders. To all intents and purposes they have only been rediscovered through modern research.

CHAPTER XII

Admired and Hated by the Greeks

IT IS NIGHT. In a wretched hut on the island of Ithaca two men sit and tell each other stories from their eventful pasts. One of them is a swineherd, the other a nameless vagabond with a marvellous gift for telling a story.

For seven years, the man in rags recalls, he lived in Egypt, but suddenly in the eighth year, a 'Phoenician man came, who had evil in his heart, a wretch who had already harmed many men. He cunningly persuaded me to join him, and took me to Phoenicia, where his houses and possessions were. There I remained with him for a whole year.' Then, the story-teller continued, his master persuaded him to go on another journey, on the pretext of giving him the job of cargo-master on his ship. In reality he wanted to sell him as a slave. But the plan miscarried. The ship was struck by lightning: 'it was filled with sulphur. And all the men were thrown overboard.' Only one was able to save himself, the story-teller.

It is a fine, well-rounded story, at once sad and consoling. The swineherd nods understandingly. He too can tell a tale or two about these Phoenicians, and naturally he does so. He is really, he says, a prince. His father ruled on the 'island of Syria', and he would probably have been the ruler there himself now if the following had not happened to him one day: 'Some Phoenicians came, notorious sailors, rogues, and brought all kinds of gewgaws in their black ship. Now in my father's house there was a Phoenician woman, large and comely, who knew how to do fine work too. The crafty Phoenicians led her astray. First one of them made love to her when she went to wash the clothes, and seduced her by the empty ship—which makes women lose their heads, however honest they are. Then he asked her who she was and where she came from, and she at once named the high-roofed house of her father: "I am proud to come from Sidon, the town rich in ore, and I am the daughter of Arybas, who is very rich. But robbers carried me off as I returned from the fields and sold me into the household of this man [the King of Syria]."'

Her lover, the story continues, rogue that he was, at once scented business and asked the woman if she would not like to return to the Lebanon with him. Naturally she, also being a rogue, agreed, and moreover promised to bring the young prince who was entrusted to her care with her, for 'he may fetch you a fortune anywhere where you like to sell him'.

Thus the plot was hatched on the bed of love. It was carried out. After the Phoenicians had remained a whole year in Syria and had traded there—they sold amber necklaces among other things—they came to fetch the woman and the boy and take them both to the harbour. 'There was the swift ship of the Phoenicians. They climbed aboard at once and, after they had taken us in, sailed off across the water.'

But the seduced abductress did not reach the Lebanon. Her end came on the sixth day of the voyage. 'She fell and plummeted down into the water in the hold like a gannet. And they threw her out to be carrion for the seals and fish. But I,' thus the swineherd ended his story, 'remained behind with a heavy heart. They, however [the Phoenicians], travelled on through wind and water and came to Ithaca, where Laertes bought me in return for goods.' So the prince ended up with the pigs. It was another dramatic and pleasantly sad story. It was now the vagabond's turn to nod sadly and sigh. The public, reading the account of both stories, may well have done the same. The author, Homer, knew very well what trite clichés were popular and must therefore be trotted out. He even included them in the *Odyssey*. Anyone who did not already know, learnt from the mouth of its title-hero—the vagabond—and from the faithful Eumaeus—the swineherd—that the men from the Lebanon were rogues and deceivers.

Admittedly they were not only that. They had their better points, as even the Greeks allowed. When someone gave costly presents, he would casually add, to enhance their value, that they came from one of the sea cities. This can be seen in Homer too. In the same epic poem in which the two stories of abduction are told, Menelaus of Sparta gives to Telemachus, Odysseus's son, a precious vessel and remarks as he does so: 'I had it from my royal friend, the King of the Sidonians.' It was a good indication of the quality and worth of the article. 'Made in Phoenicia' was a recognized seal of merit.

The picture which Homer gives of the Phoenicians was rounded out, and justified ideologically, by Herodotus in his own way about 300 years later. He also used a rather unfair narrative trick.

Seeking to find the causes of the Persian-Greek conflict, he arrived at the conclusion that the whole thing was a war between Asia and Europe; two opposing worlds had fought each other. To demonstrate this, he rehashed the old kidnap theme again, although without professing to believe it himself.

In days long ago, he recounts, the Phoenicians had carried off Io, the daughter of the King of Argos, and taken her to their country. Then the Greeks, to avenge themselves, had abducted Europa from Tyre; and in retaliation another Asiatic, the Trojan Paris, had in turn stolen the beautiful Helen from Sparta and so started the Trojan war.

'In this way,' he then continues, 'the Persians explain how it happened. They attribute the beginning of their enmity with Greece to the sacking of Troy.' He himself, however, is much too clever to take this extravagant nonsense seriously, or believe that because of the abduction of Helen the Phoenicians had really started the European-Asiatic conflict. But in using the short and probably popular story as a peg on which to hang a more searching account, he nevertheless brought it to the attention of his readers, while cunningly implying that it perhaps could have happened like that. He had also (and this was probably the main point of the exercise) made it clear that the Phoenicians in any case belonged to the hostile oriental world and so had nothing in common with Europe, which was 'rather more self-reliant and quite different' from Asia.

Yet he may not have felt very happy about this subtly promoted propaganda story. If this Europe which he described was so different from the Asia of the Persians, why did it happen to have the Semitic name of a Phoenician princess?

If Herodotus is in a rather unenviable position with regard to the limited possibilities for argument at his disposal—he admits himself that he does not know exactly how our continent got its name—modern scholars who try to elucidate the matter are equally at a loss. Whether they like it or not, if they want to get to the root of the problem, they must plunge into the tangled web of mythology, and in so doing always end up with the story which began in Tyre and which their classical colleague had already puzzled over.

Who was this Europa?

Two things seem to be certain: she was a Phoenician, and she was beautiful. Her father Agenor (in Phoenicia he was called Canaan), according to the Greeks a son of Poseidon and the nymph Lybia, ruled over Tyre, and fortune smiled on him.

Then his luck came to an end. One day terrified women ran from the washing place to his palace and cried that his favourite child, Europa, had been carried off. A magnificent bull with a snow-white forehead and snow-white coat, large belly and small jewel-like horns had been responsible. Europa, they told breathlessly, had approached the splendid animal timidly, and stroked it, and as it did not seem to wish her any harm had played with it. She wound garlands round its horns and finally even climbed on its back. The bull, still friendly, carried her around a bit but then suddenly trotted off down to the beach, into the sea and—incredible as it seemed—had swum away with the girl on its back. The last thing the washerwomen had seen was an utterly bewildered Europa, with a wreath in her hand, growing smaller and smaller and finally vanishing on the horizon.

Of course the educated reader knows at once what all this means. The bull was Zeus. He had fallen in love with the Phoenician beauty, taken the form of a bull in order to approach her unnoticed by his wife, and had carried her off to Crete, where they still show you the spot at which he climbed ashore. It is near Gortyna on the south coast of the island. Italian archaeologists have unearthed an ancient town there. Tourists, however, are still led to the grove where the lusty god ravished the beautiful maiden.

You could say, and the Cretan guides of course do say, that this is where the Europa myth was born. But why our continent should owe its name to a bawdy affair of this sort—Herodotus suggests that the saga was based on an actual event—no one knows. As I have said, scholars are hard put to it to find out what the word Europa really means. Some say it means 'broad-faced' and that it is another name for the moon goddess, the bestower of life and death, which was also given to the Phoenician Asherat-Astarte. Others believe that if the word is pronounced eu-rope, not eur-ope, it can be translated as 'good for pasture' or 'well watered', while a third group puts forward the theory that Europa is derived from the Semitic 'ereb', dark.

In fact all the explanations are rather disappointing. Whether we now live in an area which was simply called dark because, seen from Phoenicia, it lay in the west where the sun went down, or whether the people of the Lebanon saw the west as merely well-irrigated pastureland—neither explanation is very satisfying. But this much is clear: we owe the name Europa to the Phoenicians.

And indeed the story of the ravished maiden and the hour of love in the olive grove is by no means finished.

Agenor, the bereaved father, sent four of his sons to look for Europa. The first, Phoenix, went across Libya to Carthage and then returned to the Lebanon, whose inhabitants—according to the Greek story—called themselves Phoenicians from then on in his honour.

Cilix, the second, came to Asia Minor and gave the Cilicians their name. He had no success in finding his sister either.

Thasos, the third, went to Olympia, erected a statue to Melqart, whom the Greeks called the 'Tyrian Heracles', and then colonized the island called after him, with its rich gold mines, which Herodotus mentions as still belonging to the Phoenicians in his day.

Finally Cadmus, the fourth son, sailed to Rhodes, built a temple, and then went on to Delphi, to ask the oracle where his sister was. But the Pythia, knowing that Zeus was mixed up in the affair, advised him to give up the search and to go instead to Boeotia, to found a city. The Tyrian followed her advice. He reached the place where Thebes later stood, called it Onga and began to build. But then unfortunately his companions were killed by a dragon. However, when he had killed the monster and sown its teeth in the ground, new warriors grew from the teeth, and immediately began to fight among themselves. He chose the five who were left as his new companions and finished the task with their help.

The story of the beautiful Europa thus took an unexpected turn. A Phoenician, who had set out to look for his sister, founded instead one of the most famous Hellenic towns, the place where Heracles, Dionysus, Oedipus and Antigone were later said to have been born—a demi-god, a god, and two of Greece's most important mythical figures.

This, with the information given by Homer and Herodotus, makes up a very confusing picture. The Greeks regarded the Phoenicians on the one hand as sharks, seafaring gypsies and the instigators of a war which had almost destroyed them, and on the other hand as the co-founders of their own tradition. One wonders how the two could be reconciled. The answer lies in Greek history.

When in 1,950 BC the Dorian people, the founders of 'classical' Greece, then still a group of half-wild mountain tribes, came from northern Greece to settle in the Mycenaean territory which had been disrupted by the onrush of the Sea Peoples, they had to adapt not only to a new world around them but also to the hidden world of ideas. Conquered territory is more than a static thing which is simply taken over from predecessors and then shaped to fit one's own needs. There are men there who have their own values, customs, habits and traditions, which cannot simply be abolished, as the warriors from Illyria discovered.

In Hellas they found a civilization which was far in advance of their own. The Achaeans who had remained behind and who had not left with the Sea Peoples could read and write, construct domed stone buildings and build and sail ships. The Dorians could do none of these things, and could not appreciate them. After their arrival, therefore, knowledge of the complicated Cretan script—the archaeologists' 'Linear B'—died out, only wooden buildings were put up at first, and sea-going navigation was reduced to coastal navigation.

More difficult to suppress than these techniques were the age-old Aegean myths, legends and pantheon of gods, and the tales of the Mycenaean captains about their voyages, which lived on in a distorted and garbled form. In them was reflected the image of a world which the barbarians from the north could not hope to match with their own descriptions, because they had no knowledge of the lands beyond the jagged Greek coastline.

They knew nothing of the Egyptian necropolises, their vast pyramids and sphinxes, nor of the cities of Canaan, where intoxicated priests celebrated orgiastic religious rites and women offered themselves to strangers without being regarded as whores. From the rumours they heard of all these places and things they were forced to accept that there were men who lived in other Mediterranean lands who were more skilled, wiser and cleverer, and also less moral, than they were—people in any case from whom they could learn.

At the beginning of the Dorian age these reports and ideas seem to have resulted in a kind of Phoenicio-mania, similar to that experienced for a short while in the nineteenth century. After the Egyptians, the people of the Lebanon were hailed as the fathers of civilization. It was difficult to imagine that they had not had a hand in the creation of Dorian culture.

These early Daniken-style theories, which were not entirely unjustified—Phoenicians built the town of Corinth and introduced the Greeks to gold—found shape in sagas such as that of Agenor's sons, who colonized Thasos and founded Thebes. But they are also reflected in the *Iliad*, which appears to be older than the *Odyssey*. In the later poem the Phoenicians are mostly rogues and slave-traders, but in the one written earlier they appear only as clever craftsmen and artists, whose products made highly desirable prizes for contests. In the twenty-third book of the epic a vessel of 'chased silver' is praised and we are told that 'it held six pints and surpassed in beauty everything in the wide world, for the skilled artists of Sidon made it ingeniously, Phoenician men brought it over the dark waves'.

Such expressions of admiration only turned to hate when the Dorian Greeks ventured forth on the high seas themselves and could not fail to see that the blue realm had already been appropriated—by the Phoenicians. But before the Hellenes reached this stage, in about the eighth century BC, they did in fact borrow liberally from the people of the Lebanon, adopting many of their ideas about life and also importing some of their principal gods.

The most famous Phoenician who was promoted to the Greek Olympus, was probably Aphrodite, the goddess of love, of womanly beauty—and also of prostitutes.

Aphrodite's birth is described by the Boeotian rhapsodist

Hesiod in a magnificent scene in his otherwise rather tortuous and convoluted *Theogony*. Uranus, the lord of heaven, he says, begot' her, although in a very painful way as far as he was concerned. One night, while he was sleeping with the earth-mother Gaia, his own son Kronos surprised him in the act of making love, fell upon them and castrated his father with a sickle. Then he threw the severed member into the sea, where it floated for a long time. But as it was not of mortal flesh, it was able to carry out its proper function even there. A cloud of white foam formed round the immortal part, and from it grew a woman who was driven by the waves towards Cyprus.

She came ashore at Paphos, near present-day Ktima. There are gigantic rocks there, which rise like natural breakwaters from the shallow water. The sea licks the stones with its white, foaming tongues. The scene is completely deserted, with only the blue of the Mediterranean sky above, the perfect setting for the appearance of a god.

When I was there, the ancient scene seemed to be repeating itself. A naked, red-haired beauty rose from the water and pranced demurely towards the shore. I thought I was the victim of an hallucination. Then I saw the camera, a bit farther off, and heard the yelled commands of a producer. Hesiod was being re-enacted on film.

Whatever foundation the Boeotian's story may have had in fact, we can be sure of one thing: he was groping his way along the outlines of an actual historical event. Paphos lies directly opposite the Phoenician coast. The cult of the beautiful goddess was brought to Cyprus from the east. It fell on fruitful ground. Mother goddesses had been worshipped on the copper island at the beginning of the sixth millennium BC. Small pottery female idols were found in Stone-Age graves, with babies in their arms, staring out at the world with large, glowering eyes. Later finds have large triangles marked across the pubic area.

The Phoenicians, who arrived in about 1,200 BC, can thus have had little difficulty in adapting the native cults to the Asherat-Astarte rites and so creating from an amalgamation of their own and foreign material the goddess whom the Greeks were later to call Aphrodite.

Herodotus anyway never doubted that the beautiful temptress was a near relation of the heavenly mother from the Lebanon and the Babylonian Ishtar. In his *Lydian Logos* he writes that the Phoenicians built her shrine in Cyrpus. But it was because of this that the Hellenes did not find it very easy to treat Aphrodite with the proper reverence. She had never, understandably, seemed entirely otherworldly.

As in Byblos, she was worshipped in Cyprus, and also on Cythera, the other island which claims to have first received her, with temple prostitutes and orgiastic ceremonies. Again Herodotus is our source, and we also find the information in fragmentary reports of the so-called 'Aphrodisia', the pilgrim festivals which were held every year in April at Paphos.

On the appointed days, white-clad pilgrims, both men and women, streamed there from every direction. From the harbour in Paphos they went singing, dancing and praying to the precinct which lay fifteen kilometres away, near present-day Kouklia. There markets were held, whose special attraction was the Cypriot slave-girls famed for their skill in the art of love. There were also contests, torch-races, bathing in the sea at night, feasting, poetry readings and, in the temple itself, ceremonial defloration ceremonies for young girls. But the young men received their first practical lessons in love from experienced priestesses and temple prostitutes. When they came out from behind the curtain, a small phallus and a lump of salt were pressed into their hands, as a 'confirmation present'—to remind them that the goddess was originally fathered in the sea.

Married women were less well served than the single. They were content to anoint the white stone which was held to be the image of Astarte-Aphrodite and which was famous throughout the Mediterranean.

As famous as this ancient fetish was the 'temple of a hundred rooms' of the Aphrodite of Paphos. Homer refers to it, and the Emperor Augustus was the last to have it restored. The building has not yet been entirely excavated. The remains of pillars which British archaeologists uncovered near Kouklia are only part of a small adjoining building which belonged to the vast temple. But we do know that it was 132 by 73 metres in area.

This all indicates that the eastern goddess and her priests were a powerful force. Their way of celebrating sexuality and being concerned with all the problems resulting from it, influenced the masses. Aphrodite could not therefore be simply dismissed by intellectuals who did not like her eastern earthiness. She had to become an accepted part of their Olympus, but never fitted in very successfully there. Although she belonged among the twelve great gods in the Greek hierarchy, she remained the pretty little trollop, who seduces every man, who gives pleasure and often causes great harm. She was also called 'Porne', the whore, and this enabled her to be divided into (at least) two different personalities. As Aphrodite-Urania she was the great stern mother goddess, which she had originally been. Flowers and incense were offered to her; the priestesses who served her had probably made a vow of chastity. But male animals were sacrificed to the vulgar Aphrodite; at her altars priestesses coupled with young adepts, and honourable women gave themselves to the pilgrims.

Phoenicia, where some of these customs originated, cannot have appeared to the Greeks as a model of morality and propriety. The younger nation was more concerned with discipline at the beginning of its colonizing era, and cultivated those repressions which lead to greater efficiency (and brutality); whereas the people of the Lebanon seemed to have discarded this principle— if they ever had it—long before the time when they came in contact with the Hellenes, earning the reputation of being a rather dissolute nation. They were also famed for their beautiful, sensual women. Jezebel was an example, as were also Europa and Aphrodite, the two symbolic figures.

The story of the maiden who gave our continent its name (and the Greeks their ideology) possibly only represents an attempt to illustrate the fact that the Near East provided Hellas with cults dedicated to womanly deities. Perhaps Europa was even a sister of the goddess of love.

The Greeks not only imported their prototype of feminine beauty from the east, but also at least one prototype of masculine beauty. Where Asherat-Astarte had found a way, her son, or lover as the case might be, was bound to follow: Adonis, the young fertility god, who embodies many of the attributes of the great god Baal. Yet even him the Greeks could not take quite seriously.

They said that he was a son of King Phoenix of Byblos and his daughter Smyrna. The latter, abetted by Aphrodite, had crept into her father's bed unrecognized, and conceived the youth there. When the old king realized with whom he had lain, he wanted to kill the girl. She fled from him and was changed by the goddess of love into a myrtle tree. When Phoenix struck the tree with his sword, his grandson and son Adonis tumbled out. Aphrodite, who had approached unseen, immediately hid the child in a coffer, gave him to Persephone, and became wildly jealous when the queen of the underworld opened the casket and at once fell in love with its beautiful contents. A feud between the two goddesses ensued, which was resolved when the Muses, ordered by Zeus to be the arbitrators, sentenced the much-coveted youth to a precisely measured term of amorous service with each of the lustful ladies, so that he was to spend a third of the year with Persephone, a second third in Aphrodite's bed, and to have the final hundred and twenty days free—a well-earned rest.

Moreover, this division of the year corresponded exactly with the cycle of the seasons in the Mediterranean. There is no real winter there, only the autumn which gradually becomes colder and then changes into a cool spring, which slowly grows warmer; then the dry summer. The old Phoenician legend is echoed by the decree of the Muses. When the harvest was ripe, the fertility god disappeared for a time to the underworld, to come to life in the world again in the spring. Baal-Adon also had to die in his Greek incarnation.

Ares, Aphrodite's wild lover, was the one who killed him—out of jealousy, naturally. He changed into a boar and gored the beautiful youth with his tusks. Only then—for the symbolically changing seasons could not be upset by this stupid murder—did Zeus bestow immortality on Adonis, reawaken him to life again and place him, in accordance with the old rule, once more in the service of his two mistresses. The cycle continued: a third of the year above ground, a third below, and four months of freedom. To what other use could he be put? He was beautiful and nothing else.

We too still say, as beautiful as Adonis, and in so doing imagine a slim, blond youth. But we are wrong. Adonis was a Semite, had a beaked nose, velvet eyes, the brown cheeks of a David and perhaps a small cheeky moustache. To see him you should go to Beirut; you can see his descendants there sitting in the cafés or lounging round the hotel swimming-pools. The women lie at his feet, as they have always done. I have even seen English icebergs melt at the sight of the gentle Lebanese *pappagalli*.

Although Aphrodite managed to penetrate the exclusive circle of the Olympian upper twelve, Adonis did not quite make it, remaining a subsidiary figure. We are not told exactly how his compatriot Dionysus fared.

Dionysus came with the wine, which was not discovered by the Greeks but by the people of Asia Minor and the Near East. The drink came from the Lebanon, where there are still excellent vintages today, via Crete to Hellas, whose inhabitants had until then only known the more homely headiness of beer. The first wine-bibbers must have been regarded with the same mistrust by the Greeks as are young hashish smokers today by solid spirit-drinking citizens. Wine was an exotic drug. They knew that the Canaanite priests had drunk it until they were 'high' enough to hear the voices of their gods and praise them in psychedelic ecstasy.

Dionysus, another exotic, who was only later adopted by Thebes and assimilated with the Lydian Bacchus (another god of wine) embodied and prefigured this type of ecstasy. Like Adonis, he was fashioned from the same rich source material from which the Phoenicians had created their Baal. Originally he was seen as just a horned creature, without any more specific attributes. The bull and the ram were among his heraldic creatures.

In a wild triumphal procession the oriental god stormed across the whole Mediterranean, stopped for a long while at Tyre, where the poet Nonnus mentions him as appearing, and even reached India. There he embodied a perpetual state of intoxication which some of his exponents saw as a kind of madness. He was a very demanding companion. Anyone who did not recognize him as their god met their downfall, or was torn to pieces and consumed by his female followers, the Maenads. He could only gain entry to Olympus by sheer muscle-power. The Greeks, or at any rate their intellectual leaders, therefore only rarely identified with him.

Dionysus was basically a stranger. He came from afar, from another heaven, and in so doing stirred up the lees of old myths, memories of ecstatic spring festivals which were held in pre-

Mycenaean Greece, of human sacrifices and dark mysteries. Yet he had to be recognized, if only because, like Aphrodite, he became the focus of tremendous religious energies, and thus represented a part of that dark madness against which the official marble gods, as it were, recognized by the state, could stand out all the more clearly.

The German Romantics, and following them, Nietzsche, later distilled a philosophic concept from his essential nature. They spoke of the Dionysian, irrational element in life and contrasted it with the rational Apollonian spirit, to illustrate the two different dimensions of the human soul.

Lastly, Dionysus, like Tammuz, Adonis and Baal, died temporarily and was resurrected. The pomegranate tree, which was also sacred to the Phoenician fertility gods, was said to have sprung from his blood.

Spring festivals were also started in Attica and Delphi, at which dancing, singing, piping priests invoked Semele, one of the personifications of the earth mother, and begged her to come forth from a mound of earth with the young Dionysus. The feast was derived from an old Canaanite rite, during which the worshippers 'hopped' and 'limped'. The word for this was 'Pesach'. The Jews still call their Easter this.

The Greeks treated the third hero who came to them from Phoenicia—Heracles, the Melqart of the Tyrians—with somewhat more respect than Adonis and Dionysus. This god, a near relation of Baal, possibly descended from the Sea Peoples of the north, had been the patron saint of the island-city for a long time, and had won increasing fame as the power and wealth of the island community grew. Phoenician ships carried his name as far as the 'Pillars of Heracles', which were possibly once called the Pillars of Melqart. It was inevitable that the Greeks should get to hear of him.

When they did so, they at once tried to find a place for him in the wild tangle of their heavenly family tree. It was not very difficult. According to Sanchuniathon Melqart's father was said to have been called Demarus. They replaced him with Zeus. But they gave him as his mother Alcmene, the wife of the King of Thebes. Then they let him go forth to carry out his proverbial twelve labours, and several more in addition. He slew the

Lernaean Hydra, cleaned the stables of Augeas, and carried the sky for a time for Atlas.

Yet strong as he was, a lionskin-clad and club-swinging muscle-man, he never lost one weak doltish trait. In his frenzy he killed his own six children and threw them in the fire—as a reminder that his Phoenician relations had demanded human sacrifices. And he was also said to have homosexual tendencies. And finally—reflecting a last echo of the old gods of the seasons —he too descended to the underworld, to seize the dog Cerberus in Tartarus, and to triumph over death once more, fighting for Alcmene, Admetus's wife.

Heracles was certainly the most active of the Greek demi-gods, and by no means always the shining hero. He suffered as well, committed serious crimes, was an acknowledged toper and finally died a miserable death. It is true he was afterwards pro-moted to Olympus. Whole generations of story-tellers and myth-makers must have contributed their part to the strong man's life history. His biography is a mixed bag of adventures, love affairs, warlike deeds and tragedies and he seems to have been cumbered with all the half-mythical, half forgotten tales of early Greek history. He willingly took them on his broad shoulders and personified them all.

That the Hellenes specifically adopted a Phoenician for this purpose, shows once again how much they were indebted to this people for being one of the creators of their civilization. Admittedly they later forgot, in the fervour of the Heracles cult, where the beloved giant had come from, but their travel writers rediscovered his origins.

Herodotus found the famous Melqart temple in Tyre and described its patron as the 'Thasian Heracles', because he was also worshipped on the Phoenician gold-island of Thasos. Lucian, however, recounted with mild surprise: 'There are temples in Syria which are not much more recent than those in Egypt. I have seen many myself, for example that of Heracles in Tyre. But this is not the Heracles of the Greek legends, but a Tyrian hero from the far more distant past.'

The fact-hungry Greek commentators were already trying to unravel the threads which their ancestors with their naïve story-telling had spun together. Diodorus Siculus discovered in the process that there had been at least three different heroes called

Heracles: an Egyptian-Phoenician, a Cretan and the son of Alcmene. Cicero then made six different heroes from this triad, and Varro, the most scholarly of all the scholarly Roman writers, discovered at least twenty-four Herculeses in the same great mythical frieze which depicts and animates with its powerful colours the whole Mediterranean scene from the Lebanon to the Strait of Gibraltar.

The Phoenician contribution to this giant fresco was perhaps only small if one considers the whole picture. But if one begins to peel away the surface, a basic outline begins to emerge from under the hundreds of layers of paint—the man with the lionskin and club, who was called both Baal and Melqart and who was later given a Greek name.

The Hellenes owed their rivals more than they cared to admit, and were never able to forget this. But a further Phoenician contribution to Greek culture completely surpassed this mythical heritage. As well as adopting Heracles and Aphrodite from the sea cities, the Hellenes also borrowed from them the basic tool of all written literature, the alphabet. Although from time to time they tried to hide the fact.

Greek mythologists said that it was the three Fates who had invented the five vowels, and the consonants B and T. Palamedes, the son of Nauplius, then added a further eleven consonants and left it to Hermes to create the appropriate letters for them. This incomplete phonetic system—the classical Greek alphabet had twenty-seven symbols—was taken to Egypt and was then brought back by the Phoenician Cadmus to Boeotia, where other scholars and priests completed it.

However, the story is only true in so much as the route which the letters took did in fact lead from Egypt via Phoenicia to Greece, and the Greeks did have their own script in Mycenaean times, the strongly Egyptian-influenced 'Linear B'. Knowledge of this, as has been seen, died out towards the end of the Bronze Age—which does not seem to have been any great loss: Linear B was a complicated, unwieldy affair. It consisted of nearly a hundred syllabic signs and a considerable number of ideograms and symbols, which represented certain concepts. Only professional scribes could cope with it; it was almost impossible for the average citizen to learn and master it. If the Greeks had stuck to it, they would possibly never have succeeded in creating a literature which was more than an esoteric diversion for a few initiates. A popular and influential literature presupposes an easily learnt alphabet.

The Phoenicians invented such an alphabet. It was probably their greatest and most important contribution to our cultural heritage. Without the ingeniously simple phonetic system, which first the Greeks, then the Romans and finally all the other European races took over from them, we would perhaps still have to learn from two to four hundred different characters, as Japanese or Chinese schoolchildren do, in order to be able to read our daily papers.

The history of writing is probably as old as that of human civilization itself. It seems always to have answered a particular need to set out what one knew, and also to convey messages to posterity. Many peoples and countless generations have strived to realize this dream—a long and arduous process.

The simplest method for conveying news is by means of picture writing. Certain facts are graphically represented in a simplified form. The Indians and Eskimoes do this, for instance. The next step is to have definite signs for definite statements, sentence writing. And from this developed word writing, which has a definite symbol for each object and each idea. The early Egyptians used this, and also the Sumerians and the Aztecs.

True hieroglyphic script represents the next logical step. The single signs no longer correspond to a thing, but to the word for the thing, to a number of sounds therefore. They could also be used for words which sound the same as the original one, but mean something quite different. From this the syllabic scripts then developed, to which category 'Linear B' belonged. They had of course to have at least as many characters as there were syllables in each language. Both the Egyptians and the Babylonians reached this stage, but still used word symbols as well as the syllabic signs.

Then the people of the Nile advanced a further step forward, by introducing signs for single consonants. They therefore understood that all words are made up of a limited number of sounds. The time was now ripe for the next step: the invention of letters.

In 1904 Flinders Petrie discovered an old Egyptian mining

centre near Sarabît el Khâdim in Sinai. Among the finds which his workers dug out of the sand were some stone tablets, inscribed with the signs of an as yet unknown script—single symbols joined together as if they were letters.

Extremely excited by the discovery, Petrie had the tablets carefully packed and took them back to England. There the brilliant Sir Alan Gardiner succeeded in deciphering the text ten years later. A sign shaped like a shepherd's crook, which constantly recurred, enabled him to see that the single signs were not word or syllable symbols but in fact phonetic symbols. Four of these, which appeared as B-'-l-t, he eventually interpreted as the name Baalat.

This was also an indication as to the people who must have carved the word on the stone. For Baalat was the chief god of the Giblites. Their town, the old Byblos, carried on a regular trade with Egypt, exchanging cedarwood among other things for turquoise and copper from the Sinai mines. What could be more likely, as Dimitri Baramki points out, than that Giblite kings or merchants employed representatives down there to oversee the ordering and transportation of the metal and semi-precious stones. It must have been these men who dedicated the stone inscription to their heavenly queen.

Whether this theory is correct or not, the experts now universally believe that the Sinaitic script is the oldest known example of the applied use of the alphabet; it dates back to about 1,500 BC. The authors, however, were really Canaanites, or Proto-Phoenicians from the Lebanese-Palestinian area.

Canaanites also further developed the phonetic script. Archaeologists found an entire spelling-book at Ugarit, dating from before 1,200 BC and containing all the letters of a complete alphabet. The people of the city which was destroyed by the Sea Peoples seem to have reduced the number of possible characters from the original thirty to twenty-two, and to have considerably simplified them compared with the Sinaitic symbols.

From the sign like an ox's head with which the Phoenician alphabet begins, a letter had developed which looks very like our A; H grew from a fence-like sign; K from a similar sign facing to the left. A little later, around 1,000 BC, in Byblos, twenty-three signs for consonants from B to W, some of which are not known in present-day languages, were used. If one made these symbols into words, the omitted vowels could be deduced from the sense.

Contemporaneously with the letters, or a little later, names were invented for them, descriptions which, however, did not correspond to the sound they made, but were probably used as mnemonic keys. Thus the first was *aleph*, the ox's head, the second *beth*, the house, the third *daleth*, the door. From these the Greek alpha, beta, delta later evolved, and our a, b, d—the Phoenicians had no c.

The beautiful cursive script which adorns the coffin of King Ahiram, and which can be seen on fourteen other stone documents, also developed around the year 1,000 BC from the variants of the primitive Sinaitic symbols. Only these fifteen examples have come down to us. But they are enough, with the finds from Ugarit, to show that it was Canaanites and Phoenicians who adapted from the complicated systems of the Egyptians and Mesopotamians the greatly simplified instrument which must then have been almost like shorthand writing. On this point scholars today agree that their greatest achievement of all was to put these sound symbols into an alphabetical sequence, from a to z, from alpha to omega.

But a shorthand system was exactly what the people of Byblos needed. They were merchants, to whom it was important to be able to note down what they needed to know quickly and unobtrusively, and who also had to keep books and carry on a world-wide correspondence. One cannot escape the conclusion that the first documents in the Phoenician script must in fact have been business letters. But as they were not inscribed on stone, like the dedicatory texts, they have not survived.

How and when the Greeks got to know the Phoenician alphabet and adopted it, is another of the things we do not know. Herodotus, who believed the legends, thought it had come to Boeotia with Cadmus and from there had gone to Athens. He also stated, however, that the Ionians of the islands and coast learnt the alphabetic script 'by instruction'. In fact it is now thought that this kind of 'class' took place principally on Melos, Thera and Crete—islands which were partly occupied by Phoenicians and which were all in close contact with them.

Intelligent as they were, the Greeks at any rate soon saw the

(Diagram of) the development of letters

	Sinai 1500 BC	Canaan 1000 BC	Phoenicia 750 BC	Greece 750 BC	Europe Today
Oxhead	𓃾	𐤀	𐤀	𐌀	A
Fence	𐤄	𐤄	𐤄	𐤄	H
Water	〰	𐤌	𐤌	𐤌	M
Human Head	𓁶	𐤓	𐤓	𐤓	R
Bow	〰	𐤔	𐤔	𐤔	S

advantages of the new system, and also realized that it depended on a logical analysis of sounds. They never forgot where it had originated, however, and for a long time even called their alphabet '*phoinikia grammata*', the Phoenician characters.

Of course they had to alter the series of letters from Byblos considerably before they could use them for their own language, so rich in vowels. They could not manage with the Semitic consonants alone. So they made two symbols which did not correspond with any sound they used into their alpha and omicron, one of the two Semitic hs into their epsilon and the Phoenician iot into their iota, i. Whatever was still lacking, they invented—their phi, chi, psi and the great open o, omega.

The advantages of the new system were enormous. Children could learn to read and write within a year, illiteracy almost disappeared, and the script was also being used for literary purposes by the eighth century BC. Although the travelling rhapsodists of the day used to recite their poems from memory, they always carried copies with them.

The great epic poems could hardly have been conceived without the alphabet. But above all (and this was almost more important), there was now no need for professional scribes in Greece. Intellectual education lost its professional and monopolistic character. Anyone who was not a complete fool could take part in cultural life and so begin to learn who he was, namely a member of a people with their own particular spiritual character.

Without writing, the Greeks would probably have been unable to develop either a national consciousness or that anti-Asian pro-European ideology which inspired all their great ventures. In this too we are their heirs—thanks to the Phoenicians.

The cultural influence of the people of the Lebanon proved to be disadvantageous to themselves, however. The literate spokesmen of the new Hellas brandmarked the Phoenicians as one of the enemies from the east, and the Greek politicians strove as best they could to drive the people thus reviled out of the Mediterranean zone. They would possibly have succeeded in doing so, if they had only had the old sea cities as their opponents. But these had had for some time now an ally in North Africa who was rich, strong and mighty enough to challenge the Athenians, Thebans and Corinthians. The Hellenes met their match in Carthage.

CHAPTER XIII

The Rise of Carthage

'THE CARTHAGINIANS,' PLUTARCH, the Greek friend of Roman emperors, writes, 'are a hard and sinister people, cowardly in times of danger, terrible when they are victorious. They hold on grimly to their own opinions, are stern with themselves and have no feeling for the pleasures of life.'

If we were not aware that this kind of overstatement seldom contains more than a kernel of truth, we would imagine the people thus described to have been a kind of spartan race of Scrooges, aliens in the civilized Mediterranean, deadly robots with but one will and purpose. But this is hardly likely to have been the case, if only because people are seldom as their enemies see them. Yet this is how they have gone down in history. The name Carthage has a sinister aura; it has no friendly associations for us and we still regard the town as it was regarded then by its enemies the Greeks and Romans. The former hated, cursed, fought and defamed it; the latter followed their example and then wiped the town from the face of the earth. In doing so they showed more brutality than towards any other community that stood in the way of their onward march. Nothing should be left of Carthage but a broken memory. And so it was.

This net result was not really modified by a later attempt at justification undertaken by Virgil, the most renowned of all Roman poets. He made the title hero of his epic poem the *Aeneid* come to the North African town and meet its queen. He rhapsodizes about the fabulous Dido, speaking of her 'matchless beauty' and how she towered 'above all the goddesses in stature'. Aeneas, the leader of the Dardani who had fled from the sacked Troy, fell in love with her and only left her when the gods commanded him to continue his journey and fulfil his historic mission in Italy: to pave the way for the founding of Rome.

Thus the Carthaginians, who appeared so sinister to Plutarch, were to Virgil the bearers of an old culture, surrounded by a mythical glory, blessed with beautiful women, interfused with the ancient history of their own state. The way the Romans saw them hovered between these two extremes, but the negative portrait was usually uppermost in their minds. Their memory of the old enmity was stronger than a pallid literary product. The Roman writer was no Homer.

But his poem is an epilogue to the history of an ancient city and a reminder that its inhabitants came from Phoenicia. Dido is for Virgil the one for whom Zeus had reserved the honour 'to found a new Tyre, to tame proud peoples to law and order'. She lives on in myth and literature as the founder of Carthage.

The historical Dido, if Josephus is correct, was a grand-daughter of King Mattan of Tyre, who must have died in about 814 BC, and a great-niece of Jezebel. Her compatriots did not call her by the name Virgil later used, but Elisha or, Graecized, Elissa. The story of which she is the central character is, however, not Phoenician but Greek in origin.

When Mattan died, its authors said, his son Pygmalion followed him on the throne, but had to share his sovereign power with Elissa. But this joint rule was particularly advantageous to a third party, namely Elissa's husband, the priest of Astarte called Acharbas. His had been the deciding voice in quarrels between brother and sister and he had thus become the real power in the island city. Even more importantly, Acharbas had appropriated the inherited wealth of his wife, a part of the capital of the Tyrian enterprise, in order to lend it out and thus limit even further the sphere of influence of his brother-in-law. The latter, unwilling to be made a pawn of in this way, had his opponent murdered.

Naturally the feud now became even more bitter. Some Tyrian nobles cast in their lot with the bereaved widow and decided to leave the sea city with her and the hidden treasure. As they had no ships—Pygmalion seems to have had command of the fleet— they thought of a clever deception. Elissa, who clearly lived on the mainland, sent to Pygmalion to request an interview. This was immediately granted. The island king obviously hoped his sister would return to him, together with her capital. He sent ships and men across to her. This was exactly what the fugitives had hoped for. They carried the gold secretly on board, hid it, and then placed sacks filled with sand on the upper deck, looking as if they contained the treasure which Pygmalion so urgently desired.

Once at sea, that is, in the channel between Usu and Tyre, Elissa began with much ado to bewail her dead husband. She begged him to take back the gold he had saved for her, as it was spotted with his blood. Her servants, who had only been waiting for these words, immediately threw the prepared sacks into the water. Pygmalion's sailors were rigid with horror. They had come because of the loot, and now it lay at the bottom of the channel. How would they ever face their sovereign again? In their despair they decided to flee, again reacting exactly as Elissa and her followers had foreseen they would. The sails were hoisted, the course set, and the boats sailed past the walls of the island fortress into the open sea, in the direction of Cyprus.

There the crews promptly blundered into the next trap. Eighty maidens, about to offer their virginity in the temple of Astarte at Paphos, stood on the shore and threw themselves into the arms of the fleeing men. They were prepared to forgo the ceremony and instead go with the men wherever they wanted. The offer appears to have been irresistible. And as the mutineers had meanwhile also learnt that the gold was still on board, they considered they were now sufficiently well equipped to continue their flight in earnest. The Carthaginian venture was under way.

It is impossible to tell how much historical substance there is in this tale of intrigue and adventure. The Greeks derived it from too many different sources. But there may well be some truth in it.

A Pygmalion is also the hero of the story of the beautiful Galatea. There he is a Cypriot king, who is so deeply in love with Aphrodite that he makes a statue of her and tries to sleep with it, which impresses the goddess of love so much that she slips inside the ivory idol and gives herself to him. As Galatea she later bore him two sons.

In fact the historical Pygmalion—whatever his real name may have been—seems to have been the husband of a Cypriot priestess of Astarte, and to have secured the famous white fetish of Paphos in order to ensure his power over the precinct. There are points of similarity with his namesake in Tyre. For one thing the latter had also had difficulties with a representative of the established church, his brother-in-law Acharbas; and secondly he was involved, like the Cypriot, in similar machinations. Only in his case the stolen symbol of power was not a fetish, but a part of the royal treasure.

It is possible that to throw light on a dark subject the Greeks included facts pertaining to Cyprus in a confused story from Tyre, or *vice versa*. They could very easily have made the existing Pummayyaton into a Pygmalion, and the existing Elisha into Elissa. The rest may have been compiled from current rumours about a quarrel, or even a revolt, in Tyre, which led to the emigration or flight of a part of the population.

The idea is not too far-fetched, because Carthage was not founded as part of the great Phoenician colonization programme, but from the beginning had a special position in regard to the existing ports. And its inhabitants were far more rigid devotees of the old gods of the Lebanon than their countrymen who had remained behind.

Arrived in Africa, they made no attempt to become integrated into one of the older cities, but looked for a site where they could start afresh. They also immediately had trouble with Utica, the nearest Phoenician settlement. The myth-makers have left a highly dramatic story about that too.

The King of Utica, the story goes, fell in love with Elissa and threatened to destroy the young colony if she did not marry him. The princess, who wanted to remain true to her murdered husband, replied to his blackmail by throwing herself into a flaming pyre, as Dido later does in Virgil, although there it is for unrequited love of Aeneas.

In plain words this could mean that Utica was ordered by Tyre to drive out the fugitive thieves, rebels, heretics or whatever they were, but failed to do so. The new settlers remained, and Elissa was held by them to be holy. They seem therefore really to have emigrated in order to be able to live according to their religious convictions in North Africa, rather like the Quakers, who left England for similar reasons and helped to found the United States in America.

The place which the settlers had chosen fulfilled all the requirements which the Phoenicians sought for their colonies.

To the north-east of present-day Tunis there is an arrowhead-shaped peninsula which projects sixteen kilometres into the sea. At the eastern end of this, flat hills rise from the shore, and to the south of them lie two large lagoons, one behind the other, one of which is joined to the sea.

Carthage was built on this promontory, surrounded on three sides by water. It was the perfect 'Punic landscape': a flat beach, sheltered bays, a narrow strip of land which could easily be defended joining it to the mainland, and behind it a wide, fertile hinterland.

The harbour was in the heart of the new settlement. It consisted of two artificial ports, the first roughly rectangular, and the other, behind it, round. An artificial canal about thirty metres wide, which could be barred by an iron chain when necessary, connected both to the sea. The outer half of the harbour—the rectangular port—was the dock for the merchant ships, the round inner port being for the warships.

Anyone looking at the flat ponds which are all that is left of the two harbours, will be amazed at how small they are. I have not measured them, but would estimate that the remains of the merchant port are about fifty metres wide and 150 metres long, and that the port for the warships is just over 100 metres in diameter. One wonders how a sea power the size of Carthage could contain its whole fleet in this fishpond.

However, the historians tell us that it was the Phoenician custom to keep only those ships in the docks which had to be unloaded or loaded. All the rest, at any rate during calm weather, remained outside in the shallow coastal waters, where they were anchored or drawn up with their prows on the beach. Moreover, there was also a jetty, which stretched far out into the Bay of Le Kram, and during the winter, anyway, navigation practically came to a halt.

The war harbour, nevertheless, in spite of its small size, could hold more than two hundred ships. They lay round the small island in the centre of the port and were tended and guarded by the port authorities stationed there.

The town itself was overlooked by the so-called Byrsa, a small hill near the coast. It was surrounded by a strong wall, so that it could serve as a fortress when necessary, but was otherwise used as a place to store state treasure such as the archives. It is usual to compare the Byrsa with the acropolis in Greek towns.

The equivalent of the Greek *agora*, the great market- and meeting-place was between Byrsa and the port area. Not far off lay the building in which the Carthaginian senate used to meet, and the area where law courts were held in the open air.

South of these lay the topheth, the place of sacrifice, and farther inland was a large residential area with gardens and even fields. The Carthaginians had plenty of room within the walls of their city, but in spite of this built many of their houses six storeys high, because this was what they were used to in the cramped confines of Tyre. All in all their city must have been much like one of those sleepy little, dust-ridden Mediterranean ports which you still see today on the Turkish, Syrian and Lebanese coasts, untouched by modern civilization. The buildings were closed to the outside world, with whitewashed, windowless walls. Their life revolved round the shady inner courtyards.

The temples too, of which there must have been several, were not very different from those in the homeland, being usually precincts surrounded by walls in which the holy images or stone pillars stood. But there were also more elaborate temples, such as that of Baal-Eshmun on the Byrsa, which was approached by a flight of sixty steps.

The whole community was surrounded by a ring of strong fortifications. The most vulnerable spot was the narrow neck of land, only five kilometres across, between the peninsula and the mainland. The fortifications must have been over fifteen metres high here, and ten metres thick. On the inside were great two-storeyed stables, which could hold three hundred elephants and four thousand horses, and also storehouses, arsenals and barracks.

But all this applied to Carthage at the height of her power, to the capital of a far-flung trade empire. The settlement which Elissa's men built was only a small village in a well-protected location. We do not know if the first settlers had any inkling of what their colony would become, but they may have done so. The name Qart-Hadasht, which the Greeks altered to Carchedon and the Romans to Carthage, can be translated as 'New City' but also as 'New Capital City'. Which may have indicated the programme they set themselves.

The political events which led to the emergence of the Carthaginian sea empire were preponderantly influenced by one major factor: Greek expansion.

Towards the end of the eighth century BC a society had developed in Greece whose leading members had reached the state when they wanted pleasures which their own country could not offer them—foreign wines, materials, women, jewels—and in far greater quantities than before. They therefore launched their own overseas trade programme, and their ships also went in for less costly piratical ventures. As they became increasingly involved in this new undertaking, however, they were speedily forced to accept its rules, the most important provision being the need to expand. Increased sales necessitate greater home production, greater home production makes a larger supply of raw materials essential, and as the rocks of their own country contained hardly any minerals, Greek ships were soon out to get copper from the same sources as the Phoenicians.

They realized, however, that the sea routes of the Tyrians and Sidonians were mainly oriented on an East-West axis, which cut diagonally across the Mediterranean. The Greeks could thus easily avoid confrontations if they kept to the north of the line Gibraltar-Sicily-Cyprus, and this they did for a long time. The first bases which they created were mainly on the northern coasts of the Mediterranean. And as they also found it necessary to go to Africa, they carefully chose a spot on the Libyan coast which their rivals had avoided. There they built Cyrene.

This cautiousness gradually gave way to greater daring, however, when the Hellenes discovered what riches the world had to offer and how much pleasanter it was in the fertile plains of southern Italy and Sicily than in their arid homeland. Colonists followed the merchants. They built Cumae in the Bay of Naples, a large centre for Etrurian copper, and then purely residential towns such as Catane (Catania), Messana (Messina) and finally the most important of the Greek towns in Sicily, Syracuse.

It is true that at the time when these colonies were founded it was not merely acquisitiveness which motivated the settlers, but also sheer necessity. The narrow valleys of their native land were too small and younger sons had to leave their father's homesteads. Where could they go, except abroad? They went first of all, naturally, to the existing Greek colonies, but when these also threatened to grow too large, new settlements had to

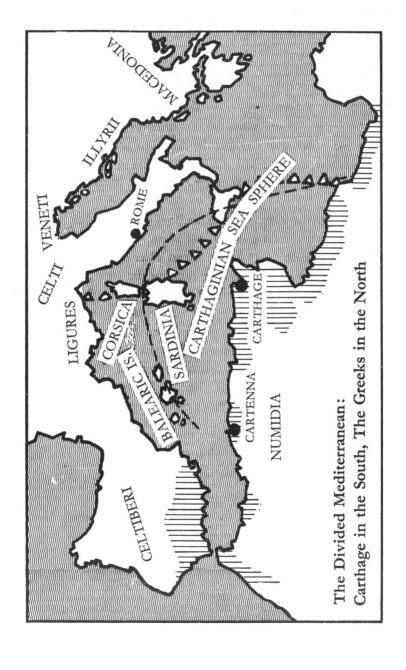

The Divided Mediterranean:
Carthage in the South, The Greeks in the North

be created. So there grew up in quick succession in Sicily, the dream country of the Greeks, Gela, Himera, Selinus (Selinunte) and Acragas (Agrigentum), besides many smaller, less important places. The Phoenicians on the island saw their position threatened.

Nor were they any longer the unchallenged kings of the sea. The people of the town of Phocaea in Asia Minor, who were held to be the best Greek sailors of that time, had now sailed as far as Spain in warships of fifty oars, and were greeted there by the native races as price-cutting rivals of the Phoenician monopolists. They dealt an even more drastic blow to the copper merchants from Tyre, when, in about 600 BC, they succeeded in founding the town of Messalia (Marseilles) on the south coast of France. With this base they had command of the Rhône valley and had won an important foothold on the way from Spain to the east. The attempt to prevent them building this town was hopelessly crushed in a naval battle.

Altogether it became increasingly clear in the years which followed that the Phoenicians were not, or were hardly, in a position to check the aggressive young newcomers. There were few soldiers at their bases, which were only suited for trade, and their supremacy at sea had seemed so secure that they had increasingly neglected to provide any military safeguards. This the Hellenes also realized only too quickly.

In about 580 BC they were already making their first attempts to drive their rivals out of Sicily. A man called Pentathlos attacked the Phoenician base of Lilybaeum on the western tip of the island and was only repelled with the help of the native Elymians. This ever-present threat was all the more serious for the merchants from the Lebanon because at that time they could hope for no support from the homeland. Tyre was being besieged by Nebuchadnezzar and had problems enough of her own.

Carthage's hour had come. The town, by now two and a half centuries old, had never depended like the other colonies on help from the Lebanon, but had methodically built up her own forces. She was now strong enough to take over the role of Tyre and Sidon, at least in the western Mediterranean. She seems to have kept out of the struggle for Lilybaeum, but it was already clear that she would not allow any further Greek attempts to conquer the whole of Sicily. This island, lying almost in the middle of the Mediterranean, was a strategic keypoint of immense importance. Whoever possessed it also had complete control of the Mediterranean.

The Carthaginians were not the only ones to regard the Greek advance to the west with displeasure. The Etruscans, who ruled the major part of the leg of Italy, suffered equally. It was the obvious thing for the two peoples to form an alliance.

When the Phocaeans in Messalia called to their Ionian country-men living under the Persian yoke to make a break for the west and settle in Sardinia, and then advanced on this important Phoenician base from their town of Alalia in Corsica, their sixty ships were met by a fleet of fifty Etruscan and fifty Carthaginian vessels. There is no exact record as to the outcome of the battle between the two fleets. The Phocaeans were alleged to have fought better than their opponents, but as they lost over forty boats, they were no longer in a position to carry out the pro-jected campaign. They even gave up Alalia; it was occupied by the Etruscans.

The first joint campaign by the two non-Greek Mediterranean peoples had therefore been successful. On the basis of this a close, almost friendly relationship could develop, which, however, must have had deeper roots than their common interests. Both the races concerned originally came from the east; both had a far older civilization than the Greek newcomers; and both were the arch enemies of the latter.

It has recently been established that the Etruscans most probably did come from Asia Minor, as the Roman texts state. In February 1972 the Bulgarian Indo-Germanic scholar V. I. Georgiev published an article in which he traced a close relation-ship between the language of the mysterious Apennine race and that of the Hittites. This also proved that Aeneas's flight after the Fall of Troy was not merely a poetic invention by Virgil and Livy. On the contrary: both had reproduced the historical facts. The Etruscans are Trojans; the Trojans Hittites. In about 1,150 BC the Sea Peoples, and therefore the Mycenaeans, had overrun their territory and had destroyed among other places the important port at the entrance to the Dardanelles. Its inhabitants had to flee. They packed their remaining possessions on ships and sailed to the west. The first of them reached the leg of Italy shortly afterwards and settled there. But they never forgot from whence they had come.

Near Veii, one of their most important cities, excavators have found some figurines which portray the flight of Aeneas and are much too old to have been influenced by Roman ideas. And in North Africa the French scholar Heurgon found five boundary stones on which is written in their language: 'Heed the Dardanian brought safely from afar!' A new proof of what Homer tells us. The Dardanians appear in his poem as the allies of the Trojans; their leader was Aeneas; he fled to Carthage.

It only remains to ask why the author of the *Iliad*, who names countless races of Asia Minor, does not mention one with a name resembling that of the later settlers in Italy. Georgiev gives a startling answer to that too. The Greek name for the Trojans, he says, was Troes. This word again goes back to an earlier Troses, just as Troy was derived from Trosia. A place of the same name is frequently mentioned in Hittite and Egyptian documents of the fourteenth and fifteenth centuries as Turush and Trusya. If, the Bulgarian continues, one takes the essential components of all these names, one is left with the syllable Tros or Trus. And this is also the main part of E-trus-ci or E-trus-ia. Therefore: when Homer said Troes, he was calling the Trojans by their correct name, because they themselves probably said Tros (or Trus), and only added the preceding E later in Italy, by a similar process as that in which the Latin word status, the state, became the Spanish Estado.

An answer at last to an old riddle? It would seem so.

But scholars would have spared themselves a lot of trouble if they had been prepared to accept Homer and Virgil as commentators to be taken seriously instead of merely dismissing them as storytellers.

Heinrich Schliemann had already shown that that was by no means the case. Georgiev only confirmed it. It is sad that there was no poet who recreated poetically the alliance between the Etruscans and Carthaginians. We would then perhaps know a little more about it. But we do know that the descendants in Italy of the people from Asia Minor who were driven out of their homeland joined up with the Phoenician Carthaginians—two races, thus, whose history was decisively influenced by the invasion of the Sea Peoples—and that there was an excellent relationship between them. Archaeologists have also re-confirmed this. In 1964 they found in Santa Severa, the old Pyrgi, in Sardinia, an inscription in the Etruscan and Carthaginian languages, in which a ruler Tiberie Velianas or Veliunas announces he has dedicated a temple to Astarte, so that 'the goddess's hand might raise him up'.

It is not known who this Velianas was. He may have been an Etruscan, who allied himself with the sea city and adopted its gods. If this was so, one could conclude further that the Carthaginians were the leaders in the European-African effort. They probably allotted specific zones to their allies and kept others, especially the sea routes, for themselves. This cannot have been altogether disadvantageous to the Etruscans, who needed a race that they could trust as far as trade was concerned, being themselves farmers and cattle-breeders rather than merchants and shipowners.

But this was only one of the results the bond must have had. The other was more important. Besides gaining a powerful ally in the Etruscans, Carthage succeeded in meeting the Greek invaders with an allied opposition force which covered the entire Mediterranean. For not only Tyre, Sidon and Byblos must certainly have joined the eastern bloc but also their Persian overlords. Which meant that from now on all Greek-Carthaginian engagements were no longer just local affairs but campaigns within the framework of a Mediterranean world war. This is in fact how the Greek authors described the position.

Carthage prepared for future hostilities against the Hellenes in a way which was typical of a merchant race. The town rulers totted up their resources and came to the hard-headed conclusion that a people with a population as small as theirs could not simultaneously control a vast trade network and support an effective army of their own men. So they disarmed their town militia except for a small élite corps of approximately three thousand men, and hired mercenaries instead. They relied principally on the native Libyan inhabitants of Tunis, Berber warriors, who provided an outstanding light infantry. Besides which they hired cavalrymen from Numidia and Mauretania; Celtic Iberian Spaniards, born guerrillas; and finally the famous slingshots of the Balearic Islands, who were the best light

A picture for every syllable: Egyptian hieroglyphs

Phoenician inscription of Abibaal (third century BC)

Two steps on the way to the alphabet: cuneiform script
and Linear B

artillery known before the invention of gunpowder. They also enlisted Sicilian or Hellenic Greeks as officers. They put no value on patriotic fervour, and only wanted the most effective war machine they could buy with good money, above all an army which could be disbanded as soon as hostilities came to an end and which did not have to be supported at great expense during the years of peace.

It was understandable that this rational method of recruitment did not encourage militaristic tendencies. A soldier was not worth much in old Carthage, and even a general was not a person of consequence. If he won a war, he was praised and pensioned off; if he lost it, he was crucified. But, naturally, all this only worked as long as they were successful in holding off the enemy at the cost of foreign lives.

Nevertheless, the attempt of a Spartan prince called Doriaeus to gain a foothold in Africa was thwarted by the Carthaginian army after a three-year struggle. They also stormed the massive *nuraghe* fortresses of the local princes who ruled the hinterland behind the Phoenician settlements in Sardinia. And in Sicily they were even successful in holding the rapacious Greeks in check to some extent.

But the position radically altered when the Greeks did away with their kings and replaced them with more or less democratically elected dictators. Nothing is more dangerous for this type of ruler than a too stable peace. They must continually boost their political position at home with foreign victories, otherwise they do not last long.

In 498 BC Hippocrates, one of these early Mussolini types, came to power in Gela. He formed an alliance with his counterpart Theron in Acragas, and together they seized the rich city of Syracuse. They thus became the most powerful Greek rulers on the island. But they were not seen as the uniters of the nation. On the contrary, the Greek tyrants of Selinus, Himera and Rhegium decided not to join forces with them, but with the Carthaginians instead, who were averse to all dangerous ventures. It was well known that they only waged wars when business made it necessary. But business soon forced them to do so.

The laws by which Hippocrates and his successor Gelon had come to power also demanded the propagation of the idea that western Sicily must be 'freed' from the Carthaginians. In Carthage they had foreseen this. The trading town commissioned its general Hamilcar to recruit an army that would be capable of repelling the Greek attacks.

The commander marshalled his forces, which Greek authors described as three hundred thousand strong. But as the Hellenes were never very accurate when it was a case of assessing the numbers of their opponents, one can take this as a gross exaggeration. Even thirty thousand men would have been a gigantic army for those days. Let us take it that this was in fact their number, and that they had been transported not in three thousand ships as reported, but in three hundred, from North Africa to Sicily, where they promptly became a part of world history.

Herodotus and his colleague Ephorus tell us that their advance in the year 480 BC exactly coincided with that of Xerxes on Greece; the battle of Himera, in which the island-Greek and Carthaginian armies fell upon each other, taking place on the same day as that of Salamis.

They would probably not have mentioned this if both battles had not ended with a Greek victory. At Salamis, Themistocles was triumphant. In Sicily, Gelon succeeded in capturing one of Hamilcar's messengers who was sent to brief the cavalry at the town of Selinus, and in making a surprise attack on this garrison. After defeating them he set the Carthaginian ships on fire, and also killed the Carthaginian commander in the onslaught, which gave him the day. The leaderless army was no match for him. He completely routed them and extorted a settlement which cost Carthage two thousand talents, more than fifty tons of silver.

Herodotus relates the outcome in a rather more fanciful way. According to his version Hamilcar remained in the camp while his soldiers fought. He wanted 'to win favourable omens by making a sacrifice, and burnt whole animals on a mighty pyre. But when he saw his own people fleeing, he threw himself into the fire. Thus he was burnt and vanished from sight.'

In a word, he behaved exactly as Greeks would expect a Carthaginian barbarian to. Nevertheless, his death in battle may have saved him from a much more shameful execution at home. Hamilcar belonged to the powerful Magonid family, but had caused his town to suffer the worst defeat it had yet experienced.

The Carthaginians, cool-headed even in despair, strove to learn from it. After Himera they also finally convinced the other

Phoenician colonies in the western Mediterranean that they were the only ones who could effectively represent their common interests and therefore take on the role of leader. These other colonies were in no position to object, because a few decades later their Etruscan allies were also taken from them. In 510 BC the ruling family of the latter, the Tarquins, were overthrown and Latin Rome took command in Italy.

CHAPTER XIV

The Punic Empire of the Phoenicians

THE CARTHAGINIANS MUST have realized by the end of the fifth century BC at the latest that they had only themselves to depend on in future conflicts. But how strong were they in fact? They were certainly said to be very rich. But what did that mean? The Greek Sicilian towns were also rich. Syracuse with its population of nearly five hundred thousand and its vast harbour was like an antique New York. In Acragas, present-day Agrigentum, huge stone figures of almost eight metres in height supported the roofs of gigantic temples. Dense crowds surged along the fine geometrically-laid-out boulevards of Selinus. Each of these Greek metropolises was far more splendid than their Phoenician counterpart in Africa, and they were all teeming with people, thanks to regular reinforcements from home.

Carthage on the other hand had developed only slowly, was excessively conservative, still used the barter system in trade while its rivals had long since switched to coins. Materially they were on the whole probably not very much in advance of the Greeks. But material wealth was not the only decisive factor in the disputes which were to follow. The trader city had to mobilize other resources in order to survive.

They probably consciously tried to do this. The result was that sinister mask which they presented to all outsiders, and a rigidly organized state system, constructed on the basis of a carefully preserved religious tradition. The founders of the town had been considered pious; now their successors were even more pious.

Prominent Carthaginian men and women were called Hasdrubal (Baal has aided), Hannibal (beloved of Baal), Hamilcar (servant of Melqart), or Batbaal (daughter of Baal). These names appear to reflect a somewhat pietistic religious fervour, as Hasdrubal could equally well be translated as 'god help',

Hannibal as 'god love' or 'god grace' (Theophilus), and Batbaal by Dorothea—'gift of the gods'. At the same time they clearly show that most of the eastern Phoenician gods lived on in North Africa. However, they began to show marked changes there: the life-renewing Baal-Melqart became the stern, solemn Baal-Hammon and the Astarte modelled on Aphrodite became the much more lofty Tanit, who was also called Tanit Pene Baal, Tanit the face of Baal.

Whether these changes were merely the fruit of a desire for innovation is doubtful. They seem much more likely to have been attributable to a harking back to long-lost traditions and possibly to a heightened spirituality. Baal-Hammon resembled the old El, the almost faceless primeval god of the people of the Lebanon, and Tanit too seems to have recollected that she had once been a rather sinister earth and sea mother. The tendency was away from the frivolous externals and back to the essence.

Besides Tanit and Baal-Hammon, there were of course many other gods who were worshipped in Carthage, Melqart in particular. But the West Phoenicians probably only took really seriously the august trinity of Baal-Hammon, Eshmun and Tanit, the same committee of three which had presided over the Lebanese Olympus. To them was dedicated the central rite of the Carthaginian cult, sacrifice.

The immolation of offerings seems to have been the most vital, indeed almost the only possible, means of communication with their heavenly superiors for the North African merchants. And sacrifices to them meant not only gifts of meal, oil, milk or meat, but also primarily human beings. The people chosen, both children and adults, were burnt alive in the topheths, either on simple pyres, or if a much-disputed report by Diodorus Siculus is true, by a process in which those destined to die were laid on the outstretched hands of a great bronze statue, from which they were then slid into the fire.

The principle of *molchomor*—by which a living animal could be substituted for a human—applied to this terrible ritual, but not in every case. From time to time the gods needed human flesh and human blood if they were to remain favourably disposed towards their followers. If this highest mark of respect was not accorded to them regularly enough, they could become extremely unpleasant.

However, in spite of this the mass human sacrifices in Carthage only became numerous when the town was in danger or when they had to give thanks for great victories. Thus two hundred children from the best families were said to have been sacrificed in 310 BC, when the Sicilian Agathocles lay before the walls of the West Phoenician capital and the town was sorely pressed, while on another occasion, after a victory over the Sicilians, three thousand prisoners of war had to 'go through the fire'.

What makes the description of these ceremonies even worse is that the relations of the person sacrificed were strictly forbidden to give expression to their grief at the altar. One tear, or sigh, would have diminished the value of the offering. Baal-Hammon and Tanit required that one should give them one's dearest possessions, but with a happy and impassive face. The Carthaginian ceremonies were the schools of a spine-chilling, inhuman discipline, a harshness which the East Phoenicians, who had grown rich and negligent, appear seldom to have known. The terrible fate of being a man had to be borne imperturbably. It was no wonder that the Greeks considered a people who managed to do this sinister and dangerous.

The Romans would have more easily been able to understand their later enemies. They practised human sacrifice themselves, and after the battle of Cannae buried two Celts and two Greeks alive in the Forum. However, it is not their town, but Carthage which has gone down in history as the symbol of an archaic piety. Its inhabitants did not believe that one was given life and well-being by loving and forgiving gods. Their sense of reality allowed few illusions. They rarely even referred to a life after death. The dead were buried with votive offerings, but seem nevertheless to have been consigned to a nether world about which no one had any very precise ideas.

Whether the Carthaginians allowed an occasional relapse into orgiastic ecstasies before the altars of Tanit-Astarte, is not known, but they very probably did. It would have at least provided an outlet for their suppressed anxieties.

We have more precise information about the priesthood in charge of the Carthaginian temples than about possible defloration ceremonies and temple prostitution. The priests worked according to fixed rules and with precisely laid down tariffs. In a document which was found near Marseilles it states: 'Temple of Baal-Saphon. Account of the dues which the thirty controllers of dues have fixed: . . . for each ox, whether it is a sin offering, a peace offering or a burnt offering, the priest shall be given ten pieces of silver.' The writ also lays down what must be paid for other animals or for gifts of vegetable produce. It was all very orderly.

The hierarchy of the priesthood was also governed by strict rules. A chief priest and two deputies were in charge of each of the large temples. They in turn led an administrative staff which included sextons, bookkeepers, musicians and barbers, the last of which were given the task of shaving the heads of mourners.

To be a chief priest or the high priest of a whole town was a highly respected office. It was often handed down from generation to generation within certain families, generally belonging to the patriciate. It is not likely, however, that the clergy also had a political role. In Carthage power was already somewhat mistrusted.

Towards the end of the third century BC Eratosthenes of Cyrene, a famous mathematician and geographer, head of the Library of Alexandria, stated rather angrily that the Greeks were wrong to describe all non-Greeks as barbarians. The description, he said, did not apply to at least two Mediterranean races besides themselves, the Romans and the Carthaginians, because they both had a constitution.

Admittedly Eratosthenes was not saying anything very new. By this time the Greeks had discovered how the stronghold of their rivals was governed, and discussed this with some amazement. Aristotle also knew and wrote about the Carthaginian constitution. Unfortunately, he included it in the part of his collected works which was later lost. So we have no exact description of it and can only piece together what it was like from different accounts.

The following points emerge: those with the highest power in the trader city were the *suffetes*. The title is usually—like the Hebrew *shophetim*—translated as 'judges', which is probably not quite accurate. We should talk rather of consuls or doges, who embodied the monarchical power and were originally perhaps Tyrian viceroys whom the rebellious founding fathers, in the course of the further history of their city, had deigned to recognize—just as the office of the Venetian city governor developed from the Byzantine viceroy. The suffetes were naturally chosen from the ranks of the rich patricians. But that was not solely on bourgeois capitalistic grounds: it was very necessary. To carry out the duties of the highest office in the state required a considerable private income, and expense allowances had not yet been invented. The suffete was the head of the community for a year—possibly two—and then he had to abdicate or be reinstated. It is not clear what powers he had. We only know that he could neither declare wars, nor control the state treasury, nor lay down regulations for moral conduct. There were special ministries for all these things. The Carthaginian doges were called to office either through the senate, a kind of upper house, whose members were also patricians, or through the public assembly, to which all adult citizens belonged. But this last body had the least authority.

The aristocratic club of senators—or more exactly a 'committee of a hundred' to which, in spite of its name, 104 notables belonged—was the main political body. The upper house of several hundred members could only discuss, turn down or accept the resolutions it put forward. If there were differences of opinion between the patrician assembly and the suffetes, then the public assembly had the last word.

On the whole it seems that it was an almost watertight parliamentary system, leavened with purely democratic elements. The suffetes probably had control of the judicature and a limited executive, while senate and public assembly shared the legislative and the rest of the executive powers. This arrangement had come about, if the accounts we have are not misleading, mainly from fear of the power of the army, of which they had had unhappy experiences.

Thus the Roman historiographer Justin recounts that in 550 BC a Carthaginian general, whom he calls Malchus, after a defeat in Sardinia marched against his own home town and besieged it, to avenge himself because he had been punished for the disaster by banishment. It is true, Justin continues, that they were then able to capture the rebels and execute them, but another commander of the same ilk as Malchus soon appeared on the scene. He—Magon—succeeded in making the post of commander of the army hereditary in his family, and thus in giving it considerable influence over the regime. 'Finally,' he continues, 'such a numerous clan [as the Magonid family] were so dangerous to the public safety that a committee was set up, which demanded a full report from the generals after their return from war, so that from fear of punishment and respect for the laws their duties on the field were justly carried out.' With the passing of the edict the power of the Magon family was broken, and the parliamentary constitution could be established.

But the question still remained as to whether the danger of a military dynasty had been averted for ever. The Carthaginian strategists came mainly from the same houses as those from which the state drew its suffetes and senators. They were at the centre of power, were used to commanding, and must have sometimes been tempted to enforce their own ideas with the help of the army which had been entrusted to them.

The Magonids were not the last to attempt this. Later the Barcids, the clan to which the great Hannibal belonged (great, that is, compared to various other Carthaginian generals of the same name) tried the same thing. It was inevitable. Military skill was concentrated in a few families. Fathers who had led an army handed on their experience to their own sons in preference, and Carthage was dependent on this experience.

Although they would have liked their generals to have been intellectual morons, in the long run the city businessmen could not prevent the ironsides from having political ideas occasionally, or from having to have them if they wanted to be successful. The choice between dumb swordsmen who would possibly fail in the field and clever strategists who could become dangerous to the state, had to be made continually. It was in order to keep the latter tendency in check as much as possible that they formed their constitution, thus revealing a typically bourgeois trait in their character. The Carthaginian merchant distrusted the Carthaginian soldier, even despised him. But he needed him. He had too much to lose.

Sailors must have been more popular than soldiers in Carthage. The navy was more useful than the army; it was the instrument which safeguarded their wealth. It had to be kept up, was continually modernized and was used for commercial as well as military purposes.

In the years following the foundation of the North African

city, the small skiffs of the Phoenicians had developed into far bigger ships. They were no longer open, but had a deck running along the length of the vessel, with a pointed ram at the prow, at water level. They now also had two banks of oars instead of one.

The boats of Tyre and Sidon had had fifty oars at the most, but even the smallest of the new Carthaginian vessels had twice as many blades. Each man had his own oar. Those in the upper bank sat farther away from the side of the boat than their mates on the lower deck. The armed guard which accompanied every boat marched noisily to and fro above their heads.

These new types of ship, which the Greeks called 'diere' and the Romans 'biremi', or 'double-banked', were naturally considerably faster than the old kind, because they had more muscle power per yard. They may have reached a speed of about five to six knots, and even more before the wind.

The Carthaginians did not at first advance beyond the two-bank ship. The trireme, with three banks of oars and up to 170 oarsmen, was invented by the Greeks, and only copied in North Africa, while the quinqueremes, with five men to an oar, were a Roman development. They were the fastest ships in the ancient world. Five men rowed each oar and thus propelled the boat at an incredible speed. Yet even they were not the largest ships at that date. Towards the end of the third century ships with twenty and thirty oarsmen to an oar were being built in the East Phoenician docks. The largest war galley of all time, however, was the ship of forty men to an oar which Ptolemy IV of Egypt had built in Tyre or Sidon.

We know less about the Carthaginian merchant ships than about these warships, but they must have also been fairly large. At all events they were larger than the boats in which the English settlers went to America in the seventeenth century. The *Mayflower* had a displacement of 180 tons, whereas Roman corn freighters in the third century BC carried well over a thousand tons, and the Carthaginian ships cannot have been much smaller.

These ships had a large rectangular yard sail, a triangular topsail forward and a mizzen sail astern, but these smaller sails were used for manœuvring rather than speed. In harbours the up-to-thirty-metre-long freighters had also to be towed by auxiliary

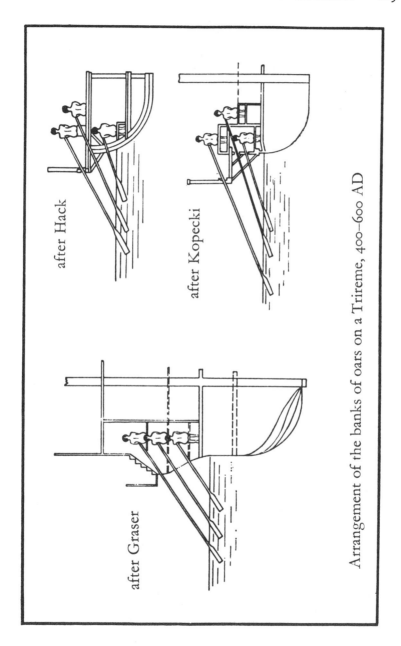

after Hack

after Kopecki

after Graser

Arrangement of the banks of oars on a Trireme, 400–600 AD

vessels, like the ocean giants of today, only the tugs were of course rowing boats.

If the ships needed repairing, they were brought—again exactly as they are today—into dry dock, another Phoenician invention. A classical writer describes this in the following manner: 'The Phoenician dug a trench under the ship, which was exactly the same length. He gave the trench a base of solid stone, and erected a row of stocks which reached right across it, with space below. Then he let water flow into the trench through a lock gate, until it was full. He towed the ship in with the help of unskilled labourers. When the gate which had been opened to begin with was then shut, they pumped the water out. When this had been done the boat rested securely on the aforementioned stocks.' It was then easy for the engineers to get at the hull from below.

The routes which the Carthaginian ships followed were essentially the same as those which the East Phoenicians had chosen. Above all they linked Tartessos, the land rich in minerals, to the colonized countries of the east, including Greece. But where was Tartessos?

One can only say with certainty that this mysterious place was an area in southern Spain. Strabo thought it was a river 'with springs rich in silver', whereas Herodotus told of a king who ruled over Tartessos, and so must have thought it was a country. If one pieces together everything which the classical authors wrote about it, one gets the picture of a large community which took its name from a river, the present-day Guadalquivir, and which lay on an island between the two arms of its estuary. It was rich, because the river came from the 'silver mountains' and brought great quantities of the different noble and non-ferrous metals with it, especially tin, copper, gold and silver.

If this description is approximately accurate, the Iberian El Dorado must have been situated near the sherry town of Jerez de la Frontera, between the Guadalquivir and the Rio Guadalete, because the first of these two rivers does not have two mouths. The silver mountains, however, were identical with the Sierra Morena, a mountain range in which there are in fact rich deposits of copper and also smaller quantities of silver and gold. But there is, at any rate now, no tin there.

In 500 BC Tartessos disappeared from sight so mysteriously that Plato was inspired—or so one imagines—to base his Atlantis myth on it. The facts which remain are: from their old base of Cadiz (which lies opposite the mouth of the Rio Guadalete) the Carthaginians traded with an Iberian people, who must already have had skilled miners, and then transported the ore back to the Mediterranean. In addition they appear to have also bought or occupied land there, because an old chronicle, based on Greek texts, the *De ora maritima* of the Latin poet Avienus, speaks of many 'peoples and towns', beyond the Pillars of Hercules, which were ruled by the Carthaginians. Modern historians have even suggested that more than twenty ports of varying sizes on the Atlantic coast of Spain and Portugal owe their origins to West Phoenician activities and that the North African town ruled almost half Spain. The limits of the Carthaginian sphere of influence are generally indicated today by a line from the mouth of the Ebro to that of the Tagus. Hannibal later advanced as far as Helmantiké, present-day Salamanca. Cartagena (New Carthage), Saguntum and possibly Malaga were built by his countrymen.

Among other things, these and later settlements in Iberia gave rise to a strange rumour, which claims that the many Spanish Jews who, until their banishment in the late fifteenth century had played such an important and splendid role in the commercial and spiritual life of the Christian territory between Gibraltar and the Pyrenees, were in fact not genuine descendants of the people of Israel but, for the most part, the descendants of the Phoenicians, whom they so much resembled. To support this thesis it is claimed that their great number—around 1490 there were in Spain more than 300,000 Jews—cannot even be explained by assuming that large numbers of them immigrated together with the Moors. And further, so say the supporters of this theory, after the Reconquista, no one could really tell the difference between semitic-looking people of Jewish, Islamic or Christian belief. Whoever looked like a Jew or a 'Marrano' (literally: pig), a baptized Jew, was considered to be one. And since the Phoenicians or their descendants were not very different from genuine Jews or their descendants, the suspicion gains in probability that there were perhaps many many great-grandnephews of Carthaginian merchants among the Sephardim who were banished by the Grand Inquisitor Torquemada to North Africa, Turkey or to South America and who there established their impressive money dynasties. Some of these are still to be found in America. We seem, then, to have a parallel with the development that began in the silver market of Tartessos. For even then the silver had been only the trigger, the occasion, for much greater undertakings.

By now the Carthaginians had discovered that there was gold and tin across the sea from Spain in West Africa, and also in Britain, as well as in the Sierra Morena. And as the mineral trade was the basis of their wealth, they tried to reach both these places.

In about 450 BC a Carthaginian captain called Himilco set out from the Portuguese coast towards the north-west. He reached Brittany and from there went across to Cornwall, where he tried to make contact with the natives who worked the tin mines. Whether he succeeded and whether a direct business relationship developed between Carthage and Britain as a result of these first contacts, is neither proved nor disproved. Archaeologists have so far found nothing to show such ties existed. But Strabo tells the story of a Roman attempt to discover whether, and in what way, their North African rivals obtained tin from England. To find out, he says, they commissioned one of their ships to follow a Carthaginian merchantman which sailed from Cadiz in a northerly direction. When the latter noticed the snooper, however, he immediately ran his ship aground and travelled back to Carthage by land, where the senate reimbursed him for the loss of the vessel and also gave him compensation for loss of profits. The suffetes seem therefore to have known very well what their monopoly on the British tin trade was worth, and this in turn would indicate that such a trade did in fact exist. It is known that the coveted metal from Britain had already reached the Continent in the Bronze Age and that the Tartessians played a part in obtaining it. It is very likely that they were later superseded by the Carthaginians or that they braved the October storms of the Bay of Biscay on their behalf. It was technically possible. The North African captains had crossed far vaster oceans.

About twenty-five years after Himilco, the leader of another expedition, Hanno, sailed along the Atlantic coast of Morocco to the south and dedicated to Baal a precise account of the voyage, which has fortunately come down to us in a Greek version.

In his first paragraph Hanno describes how he travelled through the Strait of Gibraltar with sixty ships and a company of thirty thousand people, both men and women. But here the riddle begins. Sixty ships? Thirty thousand people? It sounds more like a migration than an expedition and has therefore often been strenuously queried. Yet, as B. H. Warmington points out, these details need not necessarily be completely untrue. Hanno could have been describing a larger colonizing expedition, of which he was the advance guard and which later took place with more ships. There were already several Phoenician bases on the West Coast of Africa; perhaps they wanted to build them up, provide them with larger garrisons and build new towns there.

In fact he says in the next paragraph that on the second day of his journey he founded the colony of Thymiaterion, and on the fifth and sixth days Karikon, Teichos, Gytte, Akra, Melitta and Arambys (we need not take his estimate of the time too literally). Then he came to the mouth of the River Lixus, where he took interpreters on board, probably from among the existing Phoenician settlers. He had now reached the area below Rabat, the furthermost outpost of his people, at the edge of the unknown. Here the adventure began.

'We sailed,' he writes, 'for two days to the south, parallel with a desert shore, and then eastwards again and found a small island of about five stades [a kilometre] in circumference at the far end of a bay. We founded a settlement there and called it Cerne. . . . Then we sailed up a river called Chretes and reached a lake, in which three islands, bigger than Cerne, lay. We sailed on for another day and reached the end of the lake. Some very high mountains towered over it, which were inhabited by savages wearing wild-animal skins, who threw stones at us and prevented us from disembarking.' This too is a rather confusing description. An island off the coast, a river which led to a large lake— where could they have been?

Most commentators take Cerne to be the island of Hern off the coast of the Spanish Sahara and believe that Hanno's colony there was a gold-trading post, because the metal is found in the

Rio de Oro in the southern part of the Spanish territory, as its name indicates. However, Warmington believes the River Chretes was the Senegal, which in fact passes two lakes, Lac Rkiz and Lac de Guiers; it is true they have no 'very high mountains' round them, but lie in a rather barren wilderness.

Up to this point Hanno's notes are still fairly clear, but after that they become more difficult. The Carthaginian reached a 'high tree-clad mountain' and beyond it 'a vast gulf, with plains on either side of it, where at night we saw large and small fires flicker up and then go out again'. The landmark could be Cape Verde, the gulf the Bay of Bijagos in Guinea; the fires were probably forest fires.

The company took more water on board here, voyaged on and reached another island, on which only huge woods could be seen by day. 'But at night there were many fires, and we heard the sound of flutes and cymbals and wild voices. We were seized with fear and our interpreters bade us sail away.'

But their fears remained with them. During the following days they saw great streams of lava which flowed into the sea, and could not land because of the heat. Finally a mighty volcano reared up before them, which Hanno learnt was called the 'Chariot of the Gods'. He does not say who told him this and it is not clear where this mountain would be on our maps. However, some commentators have made the striking suggestion that the Carthaginians saw Mount Cameroon, which rises from flat swampy land and can be clearly seen from some distance away.

If that is the case, we could guess on and say: now we know what they were looking for. A large stretch of the Gulf of Guinea was not without reason later called the Gold Coast, a second stretch the Slave Coast and the third the Ivory Coast. It is possible that the Carthaginians traded for the same goods in this area, because the men who had commissioned the expedition were as interested in ivory and slaves as in the yellow metal. Hanno is silent about this, or suppresses the information, giving us instead a strange and dreadful story.

They had seen men, he says, whom their interpreters called 'gorillas'. Then he continues: 'We chased some of them, but could catch none of the men, because they were used to climbing the rocks and pelted us with stones from there. But we caught three of the women. They bit and scratched those who carried them off, because they had no desire to come with us. So we killed them, and skinned them and brought the skins back to Carthage. We sailed no farther, because our supplies had come to an end.'

A parting shot—one which testifies to a brutal curiosity. But one detail is very interesting. Where did Hanno get the word 'gorilla' from? Linguists have tried to discover if there is a similar expression in the dialects of the Negro tribes of Guinea, but have found nothing to confirm this. So we do not know whether the creatures described were man-apes, who are found there, or whether the Carthaginians killed Pygmy women. Zoologists avoid the subject. When they listed the apes, the largest African anthropoids, they gave them the name which had first been written by Hanno in his report. A Carthaginian thus became the gorillas' godfather.

The Carthaginian records nothing about the journey home. It seems to have run according to plan—which perhaps went without saying as far as he was concerned, because it is quite possible that the expedition was not such a great adventure after all, but only a tour of inspection to territory which was already well-known. Two points suggest this. The first is that the people from his country had already sailed round Africa two hundred years earlier. They may have left accounts in archives, and may have been followed by others who added to their fund of experience. Secondly, who else can Hanno's interpreters have been, knowing names and places as they did, but Phoenicians from the West Moroccan colonies, who already knew this stretch of land?

It means little that the captain did not mention this. For one thing his employers, to whom the report was addressed, would certainly have known why and under what conditions he was making his southerly voyage, and for another he would not have wanted to give information about Carthage's interests in Africa to outsiders. Their Greek rivals must be left undisturbed in their belief that beyond the Strait of Gibraltar the world they could travel came to an end—a belief which the lyric poet Pindar, a contemporary of Hanno, firmly held. The Carthaginians were better informed. They dealt in West African gold until well into the second century BC, but maintained a deathly silence about their activities. It was only after the downfall of Carthage that

Africa once more became the dark, unknown continent, which new explorers would have to rediscover. The East Phoenicians buried their knowledge with them.

Their trade in noble metals was a great pillar of Carthaginian commerce, but not their only commercial activity. Everything which could be marketed somehow or somewhere was bought and sold in the North African port. Plautus, the Roman playwright, in his play *Peonulus* (*The Little Carthaginian*)—the Romans called their rivals *Poeni*, which later became our Punic—introduces a Carthaginian merchant who sells among other things: shoelaces, whistles, nuts—and panthers. His audience found this highly amusing.

We can conclude from this that their contemporaries did not always regard the East Phoenicians as kingly traders, but as hucksters, pedlars, sellers of gewgaws, charlatans, and cheapjacks as well—which is not surprising if one remembers their history.

The people of the Lebanon were more or less the pioneers of trade. They took their products to places where even a glass bead was an object of value, and so lived largely by selling cheap goods at low prices. The Carthaginians also used these methods for a long time. They were, and remained, primarily specialists in trading with underdeveloped races, with whom they bartered goods. This also explains why they only began to mint their own coins in the fourth century BC, three hundred years later than the Greeks (and their Phoenician brothers).

Then too they seem to have found it difficult to become part of the Mediterranean trade network, to deal with other civilized states, and the principle of *laissez faire*, *laissez aller* was always rather suspect in their eyes. It was as easy for foreign merchants to do business in Carthage as for the locals themselves, but they had to accept that the goods they sold could only be re-exported in Carthaginian ships. The Punic traders had a monopoly on transport in the western Mediterranean and wanted to keep it that way. This was the underlying principle in most of the contracts which they forced on their weaker partners, such as the Etruscans, and equally importantly the reason for the far-flung and comprehensive system of bases which they maintained. The markets they had won were vigorously defended. A stranger who encroached on them must expect to be driven off or have his ship sunk. But this did not prevent the Carthaginians from encroaching on foreign markets in their turn. Their ships transported Corinthian pottery and Etruscan *bucchero* vases. They had agents in Syracuse and probably in other Sicilian towns. And of course they also had their own industries, which mainly manufactured cheap mass-produced goods and *Kitsch*.

Carthage exported coloured materials, carpets, cheap jewellery, amulets, painted ostrich-eggs, glass, weapons, pottery, scents; but none of these products seem to have had a reputation for being quality goods. For more expensive and better-made things people turned to the Greeks, who had better taste and practised more careful workmanship. The time when Homer had praised Phoenician goods so highly was long since past.

But fancy goods brought in money. In the fourth century, after Alexander's Indian campaign, people in the Mediterranean were flooded with so many new stylistic trends that they lost their own inborn sense of style and anything was acclaimed which was bright and exotic or even just pleasing. The Punic craftsmen, who had never developed an individual style themselves, seem to have been past masters at filling this need. Hellenistic *nouveaux riches* in Ptolemaic Egypt and Seleucid Syria made it worth their while. They considered these trumpery goods to be art.

However, Carthage imported mainly those things which she needed urgently herself, preferably from her own colonies because they supplied them cheaply. So she got corn from Sardinia, wine and oil from Sicily and fish from western Morocco, but gave considerable benefits in return for what she took. In Sardinia the Carthaginians encouraged the planting of olives and flax and possibly also introduced the palm there and built large glass factories. Under their regime Malta blossomed into a trading centre which was rich enough to build and extend its own colonies.

In general they seem to have been good household managers, with a surprising bent for husbandry. The seafarers and traders liked to dream of their own little plots.

A Carthaginian who perhaps had a shipping-business or was a partner in a glass-works or had won fame and riches in some other way liked to put his savings into property. He bought an estate in the fertile plains south of present-day Tunis and built a large house there. On his land he cultivated olives, fruit, dates and vines, and he bred cattle or horses in his pasture-land. It seems to have answered a need felt by many entrepreneurs who have exhausted themselves in the cut and thrust of business. To own land ennobles capital, makes aristocrats of rootless adventurers, and offers safety, security, peace and the chance to recover.

The Carthaginians realized this ideal systematically and very efficiently. Their upper echelons were not content to wander aimlessly through the fields, patting horses on the neck as they passed; they built model farms and developed agriculture into a systematic science. This can be seen from another of the rare texts which we have inherited from them, although it is not in the original, and by no means complete. A man named Mago wrote it and it is a treatise on agriculture with romantic undertones.

'If you have bought a farm,' he writes, 'you must sell your town house, so that you are not tempted to honour the household gods of the city more than those of the countryside. Whoever likes it better in the town than outside, has no need of a farm.' This sounds a bit like Rousseau, a dream of the sane natural world as opposed to the miseries of civilization. It is possible that as well as being a writer of treatises, Mago was also a fashionable writer, who fawned on a rather snobbish society.

In other passages, however, he becomes completely factual, as when for instance he is writing on cattle. He says oxen must be 'thick-set with firm limbs and long, blackish, strong horns; the brow must be broad, covered with curly hair, the ears shaggy, the eyes and lips dark, the nostrils curled-back and open, the neck long and muscular'. In fact he seems to have known a bit about his subject, and was clearly even considered an authority, as his remarks on cattle were copied or quoted by many classical authors.

One wonders if he gleaned his knowledge purely from the sphere of amateur farming, or whether (which seems more likely) he had systematically tackled a subject that was as vital for Carthage as knowledge of sea currents and mineral sources. The town always had to be prepared to be cut off from its overseas suppliers, and was therefore forced to have a reserve of agricultural land in the near vicinity, with produce which would feed the citizens in times of need. Their hinterland was certainly adequate in this respect, and was later used for hundreds of years as a granary by the Romans. It was the Carthaginians who made it into one.

Diodorus Siculus describes the little paradise. 'It was divided into vegetable gardens and orchards, with streams and canals running through them, which irrigated each bit of land. There were splendidly laid-out country houses everywhere, with stucco façades which demonstrated the wealth of their owners. The barns were filled with everything one could need for a luxurious life. Parts of the land were planted with vines, others with olives or other useful trees. Beyond, cattle and sheep pastured in lush meadows, and there were fields with horses out to grass. These were the visible signs of wealth in the region where the leading Carthaginians had their estates.'

But the citizens of the trading port probably only occupied land which was not farther than a day's journey from the gates of Carthage; anything more distant was left to the native Libyan inhabitants, who admittedly were duty-bound to supply them.

However, that was not the limit of the Carthaginians' activity. They gave regular economic aid to the Numidians in eastern Algeria, to the Berber tribes and to the natives of the adjoining districts. They probably not only introduced vines and olives, but also figs, pomegranates, which the Romans called *mala punica*, and also almonds, walnuts and pear-trees. In addition they gave them instruction in planting and cultivating these crops. They taught them that olive trees must have at least twenty-two metres between them—one can still measure out these distances in Tunisian orchards—how vines are planted, harvested and sweetened, and also introduced threshing machines, one of which, the *plostellum punicum*, is mentioned by Varro. It was a wooden sledge which ran on notched rollers and was also known in the Near East.

Altogether they seem to have built up a solid means of supply. That they not only fed off their own land but still imported Sardinian and Sicilian corn as before may have been because of trade agreements which could not suddenly be given up, or possibly because the population of Carthage grew more quickly than the amount by which they could increase the agricultural yield in the hinterland.

At the height of their power, in the early third century, there must have been about four hundred thousand people living in the town and its immediate neighbourhood, the cape on which it lay. But these were by no means all pure-blooded Carthaginians of Phoenician origin. Most were slaves, either born there or from abroad. Possibly another hundred thousand Carthaginians lived outside the town on African soil between Lixus and the capital. Together with the garrisons of the islands and outposts this gave a population of less than half a million people.

This means that a people who would not have filled the town of Düsseldorf, ruled an empire which linked the West African coast to southern Europe and Anterior Asia. Was it any wonder that the Carthaginians found little time for reflection, philosophy, or writing poems and plays? All hands were needed to keep their state ship on course; they could only find time for the practical sciences and yet continually had to do the one thing they liked least, because it seemed to them such a pointless waste of time and effort—wage wars.

They were seldom defending their very existence, but usually their possessions. And often they attacked in order not to be attacked. The laws by which they had started out drove them to continual expansion. Every step forward which was not taken might be a step backwards. The Greeks, who had understood this well themselves, taught them this in the fifth, fourth and third centuries.

Between 409 and 215 BC some of the most fascinating and colourful figures of Greek history (which was so rich in great heroic figures) attempted to bring down the Carthaginians, while in the east their countryman Alexander was dealing the death-blow to Phoenician splendour.

CHAPTER XV

No Empire for Carthage

'THE TOWN OF ACRAGAS,' writes Polybius, 'differs in various ways from many other towns, particularly because it is so strongly fortified . . . its walls are built at the edge of a steep cliff . . . its citadel is protected on one side by an impassable ravine and can only be entered at one point from the city.'

The learned Greek's description can be verified on the spot today. If you visit present-day Agrigento, you will see, above an almost perpendicular rock-face, golden temple pillars which tower up into the blue Sicilian sky, with the ruins of a Cyclopean wall at their feet. It is hard to imagine how any army could ever succeed in taking this boldly conceived mountain stronghold—without powerful guns.

Yet the Carthaginians succeeded, although they had no cannon. In the hot, dry summer of the year 405 BC one of the largest armies they had ever raised lay outside the rich Greek city. Diodorus Siculus says it was 120,000 strong, which is certainly an exaggeration. Even if it were only a quarter of this size, it was still an overwhelmingly large force, and a dangerous one, because its commander was Hannibal. This Carthaginian general, who had military brilliance as well as a name in common with the Hannibal who crossed the Alps, could at that time already look back on considerable success in his campaigns. Five years previously he had taken the mighty Selinus, leaving only those melancholy ruins which today still stand on the flat south-Sicilian coast. Then he marched across to the north side of the island and meted out the same fate to the equally well-fortified Himera. Now it was the turn of Acragas.

Hannibal's recipe for taking strongholds was simple, but highly effective. He relied less on the valour of his men than on technical expertise. He usually brought huge attacking towers, of the kind the Phoenicians had seen the Assyrians use, up to the walls, and posted archers and slingshots there to sweep the walls clean of anything which dared to show itself. The Greeks had no weapons then with which to counteract these travelling fortresses, and were usually so horrified at the sight of the monsters that— as in Himera—they simply left the town by the rear gates and sailed off.

At Acragas, however, Hannibal's recipe seemed to be ineffectual. The land beneath the walls of the stronghold was too clefted for the towers to be ranged there. The general lost two of them in a first attempt on the western side of the fortress.

He then tried the south side. To fill the bed of the river Hyspas, which flows there, he ordered his soldiers to tear up the gravestones of a nearby cemetery and throw them into the water. His troops obeyed, but unwillingly. They did not think the gods would let such sacrilege to the dead pass unnoticed. In fact their fears seemed to be justified shortly afterwards. A fork of lightning from the pitchy sky shattered one of the stolen stelae. A little later an epidemic broke out in the camp, from which hundreds died.

We do not know how Hannibal reacted to these blows, but we are told that he himself succumbed fatally to the sickness. His comet-like career was at its zenith. In the blinding light of the ominous storm he becomes momentarily visible as a tragic figure whom Fate prevented from completing his course. The question is just how his career would have developed. It had begun in the twilight of complicated political intrigue.

Hannibal belonged to the powerful Magonid family, who had been prevented from seizing power in the state in the middle of the fifth century by the introduction of constitutional government. The suffetes had confiscated the privileges of his father Gisgo and his uncle Hanno, and driven them out of the country. Both had gone to Sicily and settled in the Greek town of Selinus, which their son and nephew later destroyed. It is not known if Hannibal went with them and returned later, or if he left his family straight away. One fact seems to point to the former case, in that he had a friend called Empedion in Selinus, who was later the only person whom he allowed to continue living in the sacked town.

But all this is of minor importance. The important thing was that he must have become successful very quickly in Carthage in order to have reinstated the family name. Which meant that either he had been able to mobilize a sufficient number of supporters or that the anti-Magonid feeling had quickly died down after Gisgo's expulsion. If the latter was the case, it also follows that the 'merchants only' policy of being involved in nothing but business, was not nearly so generally accepted as one might suppose from the controversy over the constitution. And furthermore, there were now more than enough citizens in Carthage who thought it was high time to give the Punic commonwealth, that relatively loose confederation of cities and bases, a firm political shape, that is, to consolidate it into a state.

It is equally obvious that this concept, once formulated, must have deeply worried the tradition-loving Carthaginians. The conservatives must not only have feared that it might lead to a military coup, but also hardly have found acceptable the divergence from the approved Phoenician methods which was involved. A loosely woven network of shipping routes, linked only by the occasional trading station or base, was an elastic affair, which could be inexpensively maintained and easily repaired if damaged. A tightly knit state, on the other hand, with extensive territorial possessions, demanded the permanent presence of military and government forces and sapped vital energy.

But Hannibal appears to have thought along different lines from the old men. The chroniclers of the young general are agreed that one of the motives for his first Sicilian campaign was the wish to avenge himself on the Greeks for the defeat they had inflicted on his grandfather Hamilcar in 480 BC at Himera. He abhorred the Greeks. In addition he also embodied a conviction which—quoting Marx freely—leads to the leap from capitalism to imperialism. The sons of the rich Punic entrepreneurs wanted to be more than rich entrepreneurs themselves. They already had their aristocratic estates; now they wanted an empire to rule.

As a result of these trends the Magonid succeeded in making the 104 sanction something of which at heart they possibly did not at all approve. Taking a cry for help from Segesta, their ally and also the ally of Athens, as an excuse, they ordered an attack on Sparta's ally Selinus, which was threatening Segesta. Thus they entered the Peloponnesian War, which had by then split the entire Greek world into an Athenian and a Spartan camp.

Hannibal used the permission he had been granted to attack Himera after Selinus, to quench his thirst for revenge. His political argument for the action was the safeguarding of the old Phoenician bases in western Sicily. But in this he was concealing rather than revealing his true motives, because after his victory he added the allied territories, until then partially independent, together with the Greek towns he had annexed, to the mother state as 'epicrataia', or permanent provinces. This re-confirmed the same point: powerful Carthaginian factions wanted to break with custom and create an imperialistic state.

That they went about it in a way which would ultimately lead straight to disaster was not foreseen by the Hannibals of the Magonid era. It was only a hundred years later that the engagement of Carthage in Sicily provoked her deadly battle with Rome. This had to be fought not by Gisgo's son, but by his namesake from the house of Barca. Hannibal the elder died at Acragas.

The epidemic that broke out in his camp cost the hero of Selinus and Himera his life. He died after a short but terrible struggle. His deputy Himilco, now his successor, drew the only possible conclusion a Carthaginian could draw from this fatal blow. He sacrificed a child to the visibly angry Baal-Hammon and then proceeded with the siege.

But it seemed that the god could not be appeased so easily. Baal-Hammon had other grave blows in store for his followers. First he sent a Syracusan supplementary army, which completely routed a part of Himilco's army, then a naval unit from the same town, which disrupted his supply lines. Finally he also enabled the Syracusans to join up with the garrison which had broken out at Acragas. And the epidemic took further victims.

It was not until a Punic squadron broke through the Greek blockade that the tide turned in Himilco's favour once more. Now the citizens of Acragas began to run out of foodstuffs, and as they were renowned for their liking for luxury and good-living, nothing could seem more terrible to them than to go hungry, and they decided quite simply to hand over the town. In a magnificently planned manœuvre the besieged succeeded in getting all the inhabitants to the nearby harbour, the present-day Porto Empedocle, unseen by Himilco, and from there they sailed to safety. When the Carthaginians climbed over the walls the next day, they found themselves in an empty ghost town. Doors banged in the wind, which blows almost continuously over the high ground of the settlement, and their clattering steps were answered only by a hollow echo.

However, the soldiers' state of shock was greatly alleviated by plenty of booty. The fleeing men had been able to save their lives, but not their possessions, and Acragas was one of the richest of the rich Greek towns in Sicily. The works of art alone, which Himilco had transported, filled his ships to capacity, but turned out to have a hidden sting on arrival in Carthage. The men who unloaded them there were far more impressed by the beauty of the cargo than the value it represented. At the sight of these stolen statues, vases and friezes the Carthaginians seem to have understood for the first time how far superior culturally the Greeks were to themselves, and they took it to heart. Henceforward, anyone who prided himself on his status in the best Carthaginian circles dressed like a Greek, behaved like one, and placed a statue of Zeus or Artemis beside the bare stones which symbolized his own gods at his household shrine. This makes one wonder who really won at Acragas—Punic soldiers or Greek artists.

The episode also throws light on the situation in which the Carthaginians now found themselves. They were not only fighting against soldiers but also against a whole civilization and the people who had created it. Which meant that while the war was for them a more or less coolly calculated bid for acquisitions, for the Greeks it was a fight for survival. The Greeks thus never had to consider its cost or usefulness, but could freely invest all the men and money they could. Then too they never surrendered until they were completely beaten. The Carthaginians never took matters to such extremes. Every time the reckonings of the Punic leaders turned out to be false, they had to stop and break off, while the Greeks renewed their strength and consolidated their position.

Since the Carthaginians never quite took Sicily, but always only almost took it, and their calculations never quite worked out, each of their thrusts set off an Hellenic counter-thrust. Hannibal's second campaign triggered off a war of nearly a hundred years, of which the single campaigns always followed the same pattern: Punic advance as far as Syracuse, withdrawal from there, counter-attack by the Greeks, further Punic attacks, another abortive attempt to storm the walls of the port, and so back to square one. It was a wearisome see-saw, which led to pointless loss of strength on both sides, and only ended when both were thoroughly tired of the attempt. The battle for Sicily, as it turned out, benefited neither the Hellenes nor the Carthaginians.

But as has been seen, nearly a hundred years of futile endeavour would have to pass after the siege of Acragas before this bitter truth would dawn. Himilco must have still believed that he could realize the dream of his predecessor.

The Carthaginian army had one success after another on the battlefield. Hannibal's successor marched against Gela on the south coast of Sicily, defeated a Syracusan supplementary force there, took the town, and also occupied the neighbouring Camarina, then turned towards Syracuse, the last large Greek settlement which could dispute possession of the island with Carthage. It seemed to be only a question of weeks before it too would fall.

But here the fatal cycle began to run its course for the first time. Syracuse did not fall. Instead of siege machines Himilco unexpectedly sent a truce party to the walls to make a peace offer to the ruling dictator Dionysius I. We do not know what caused him to do so. There are reports of rumours which held that the anger of the gods struck the Carthaginians a second time, and that they once more fell prey to an epidemic.

Dionysius at all events was saved from catastrophe and the loss of his office. So he accepted the offer of the Punic commander without too much parleying and allowed a treaty to be dictated which guaranteed Carthage possession of nearly all the towns she had taken and thus of the major part of Sicily. She was to have Acragas, Selinus and Himera, and the people of Gela and Camarina were to pay tribute to the North Africans.

At first sight the treaty looked like an excellent arrangement, but in reality it contained the seeds of the next war.

The saved city of Syracuse was not just any Greek town, but the most powerful of all the Greek communities at that date, its ruler Dionysius no ordinary local politician, but one of the most gifted and unpredictable demagogues of ancient European history. He had risen from simple town scribe to town ruler. After the various defeats which he had suffered, his people would probably have got rid of him, but now a paragraph of his treaty with

Himilco named him as the rightful ruler of the port and made him almost unassailable.

It was precisely these words which cost the Carthaginians so much blood, sweat and money. Dionysius was not at all inclined to accept the safeguarding of his position by Carthage. On the contrary he wanted to clear his tarnished reputation. He set about it in the speediest way he could find. In a propaganda campaign in the approved style, his envoys branded the Carthaginians as Greece's enemy number one, and made their banishment from the island the prime national goal. At the same time, completely disregarding all existing treaties, he prepared to win back the lost territory.

In the year 398 BC the dictator struck. He captured Motya (Mozia) on the west coast of the island, a city which, like Tyre, stood surrounded by walls on a small island; for which reason it, like the secret metropolis of the East Phoenicians, had to be conquered by means of large scale dam-building operations. Dionysius here used the *ballistae*, possibly invented by himself: enormous catapults which, with their barrage, so completely destroyed the island town that it could never be rebuilt. Shortly after this spectacular success, however, Himilco drove him back in a series of quick thrusts. A little later he found himself besieged in his own town once more.

It once again looked as if Syracuse must succumb, but again the angry gods intervened. The epidemic, probably malaria or typhus, broke out a third time. Himilco's Libyan soldiers suffered in turn from 'a catarrh, which made their throats swell up, fever and unbearable pains in the back, heaviness in the legs, and finally diarrhoea and pustules. Some,' continues Diodorus, 'also became deranged, lost their memory and wandered delirious through the camp hitting everyone they met on the way.' The Greek thought that the illness was caused 'by the smell of the unburied corpses and the miasma from the swamps' in which the Carthaginian camp was pitched.

However accurate or otherwise this diagnosis may have been, Dionysius seized the chance which the bacteria offered him, attacked the Carthaginians while they were at their lowest ebb, and put them to flight. Among the few who were able to save their skins was Himilco—but he was not at all happy about it. When he got home he starved himself systematically to death, and his reaction clearly shows how oppressed this Semitic people were by their ideas of an incalculable, inhuman deity. The brilliant general felt he had been condemned by his gods, and therefore saw no further point in his life.

But on the island the fight against Dionysius continued for years, as already explained, and the end result was more or less a *status quo ante*. The Carthaginians kept about a third of Sicily, and the dictator of Syracuse controlled a larger area, since the gods clearly preferred him to his sombrely old-fashioned opponent.

The Carthaginians must have interpreted events in this way too, because they turned even more towards the Olympians. They built a temple in their town to Demeter, the goddess of fertility, and hired Greek priests, so that she would be worshipped in the correct manner. They were very punctilious in such matters and tried now in their methodical way to become part of the new era, without ever really understanding it.

Brilliant soldiers and strategists as they proved themselves to be in the battle for Sicily, the picture one gets of the Carthaginians in these encounters is unflattering and unsympathetic. A few details will illustrate this point.

Firstly: they were brutal. At Himera Hannibal had three thousand Greek prisoners executed, and his successor Himilco was guilty of similar bloody acts. Yet these massacres seem to have been less the expression of an inborn bloodthirstiness than of a (to us) inaccessible, but none the less primitive, religious feeling. The victims of battle were offered to Baal-Hammon for having made victory possible. Following the archaic custom, the blood of the dead must seal the bond between him and his true servants and sanction further conquests. That their god nevertheless remained hostile and sent the epidemics which prevented them occupying the entire island must have been harder to bear for the Carthaginians than their failure itself. Baal had turned his face from them or no longer possessed the power to help.

The Greek gods were mightier.

Of course one can regard the fevers in a more prosaic light than the pious Carthaginians did; one is then forced to the equally unflattering conclusion as far as they are concerned, that —point two—they did not much hold with cleanliness. They could probably have avoided the epidemics in their camps if they had followed the most primitive rules of public hygiene, because there are no reports of the Greeks, who were much cleaner, having been similarly affected by fevers.

And finally a third point: militarily too, in the last part of their struggle with Dionysius the Carthaginians seem to have been no longer quite at the height of their power. Himilco used to use a type of weapon in his campaigns which was about as old-fashioned then as cavalry is now—the horse-drawn chariot. When he set out on his second Sicilian campaign, four hundred of these vehicles were loaded onto his ships in Carthage. It was no wonder that he was in no position to counter with equivalent tactical manœuvres the heavily armed Greek foot-soldiers, the so-called hoplites, who advanced in massed phalanges in close formation. Compared with these (at the time) modern formations his motley army must have seemed like a troop of medieval mercenaries faced with a Prussian army of the time of Frederick the Great. That in spite of this the Carthaginians defeated Dionysius's troops again and again can only have been the result of an almost suicidal bravery or of the greater experience in action which regular soldiers have compared to a conscript army.

Only at sea were the Punic sailors clearly superior, both technically and tactically, as they had been before. Their small but easily steered and well-controlled ships sank the heavy quadriremes and quinqueremes of Dionysius at each encounter, and finally at Catania. In the biggest naval battle which had ever been fought in the Mediterranean, Himilco succeeded in sinking or. boarding a hundred Syracusan vessels and taking twenty thousand prisoners.

If an expert had had to form an opinion of the Punic chances in the fight for Sicily on the basis of these facts, he would, in spite of their victories at sea, probably have given them very poor odds. It was not only that many of their methods and techniques were outmoded, but they were also hopelessly inferior in number to the island Greeks.

So they were unsuccessful in their attempt to prevent the clever demagogue of Syracuse from building an empire which stretched as far as Corsica. On the other hand Dionysius too was unable to realize his ambitious nationalistic plans for Sicily. When, after forty years of war with the Carthaginians, he died in 366 BC, they still owned, as well as their original territory, the Greek towns of Selinus, Heraclea, Minoa and Himera and large parts of Acragas.

More important than this strategic failure, however, was the fact that the Carthaginians were now trying to learn from their mistakes. They were trying to shake off their reputation for being brutal, bloodthirsty savages, and their efforts succeeded.

During the years which followed, the people of the Sicilian city states, who had meanwhile grown rather tired of their loud-mouthed, demanding tyrants, began to co-operate on a more friendly basis with Carthage than had been possible hitherto. In fact the ties between Gela, Camarina, Acragas and the Carthaginians became so close that Plato even feared that sooner or later the Greek language would be supplanted in Sicily by the Phoenician. But this at least never happened. Although Socrates' pupil never succeeded in conveying his strict ideas of the republican ethos to the life- and pleasure-loving Siceliots or Greek Sicilians (he tried for a while to realize his idea of a Utopian state in Syracuse), the Carthaginians never finally succeeded in ruling their hard-won island colony in peace and imposing their culture on it. There was always something happening at home or abroad to prevent this.

While they were forcibly putting down the attempt to usurp power by Hanno the Great, one of their military dynasts, in about 340 BC (the general was crucified) a new conflict broke out in Syracuse over the throne of the deceased Dionysius, and this, it soon became clear, would queer their pitch too. The victor in the Syracusan quarrel was the Corinthian Timoleon. He was a fervent democrat, who had 'In Tyrannos' written on his banners, referring to the Carthaginians amongst others. This led to further trouble.

A general called Mago sailed over to Syracuse and took his fleet into the harbour of the port to drive out the troublesome usurper. When he failed, he committed suicide, in order to forestall a court martial at home. After him, two other officers called Hasdrubal and Hamilcar tried to drive the tyrant and Punic enemy from the island, but lost a battle against him at Segesta— on their own territory. Hasdrubal was executed. Gisgo, a son of the crucified Hanno, and the third man to be sent to Sicily by

Ruins of Carthage from the time of Antoninus Pius (*c.* AD 150)

Ahiram's sarcophagus

Forester from the cedar forests of the Lebanon: the Phoenicians probably looked like this

the suffetes, was no longer told to overthrow Timoleon but only to save what could be saved and then make an acceptable peace treaty. He did so. The result: Carthage kept her previous possessions; the river Halycus which runs into the sea at Himera and is now called the Plátani was henceforward the dividing line between the Greek and Punic territories. Timoleon, more honourable than Dionysius, contented himself with banishing the Greek city tyrants to the eastern sector of the island, and finally went blind and gave up his office.

In the years of peace which followed his abdication, the island Greeks and Carthaginians worked happily together as they had tried to do before the war. The country flourished, and the ruling oligarchs on both sides of the Sicilian Channel saw no reason to jeopardize their profitable business relationships because of further nationalistic experiments. Besides which the Hellenes now had new rivals in southern Italy: the Oscan tribes. The Greeks found their primitive ways so terrifying that the Carthaginians seemed almost like members of their own race in comparison. Then, however, all these Sicilian happenings faded in importance beside an event which came to pass in Greece at about this time. Alexander the Great set out to conquer Persia. Thus the Hellenistic age began, a time in which there would no longer be a place for the Phoenicians, a people whose history had begun far back in biblical times.

The Macedonian had announced this fact himself, in that very speech which he made in 332 BC in his camp outside Tyre. The decisive sentence was: 'They still laugh at us, because they live on an island, but I will show them that they too belong to the mainland!' Alexander was not only referring to the dam which he would build across to Tyre: he also meant that there must now be an end to the position of maritime exclusiveness in which the descendants of the Canaanites and the Sea Peoples had taken refuge and from which they had operated so long and so successfully. And in fact he was uttering Carthage's death sentence too, because Carthage was only a larger Tyre.

Twenty-two years later it would see itself threatened in the same way as the mother city, but would escape a like fate, only to be conquered after another 164 years by a general who likewise cut it off with a man-made dam from its vital element, the sea.

The man who succeeded in doing so, was Scipio Aemilianus

and came from Rome; the one who had attempted it before him was a Sicilian Greek called Agathocles. But it was the young leader from Macedonia who had opened the door to the angel of death.

He stood on the shore at Usu and looked across at the island fortress. His staff were gathered round him. Alexander said: 'My friends! As long as the Persians [or more precisely: their Phoenician squadrons] rule the sea, I cannot march to Egypt undisturbed. And it is not practicable to pursue Darius as long as the city of Tyre, of whose allegiances we know nothing, lies behind us. There is also the danger that the coastal towns [Aradus, Byblos and Sidon who had surrendered to him] will be reconquered if we march towards Babylon with our whole army. And finally Darius might think of taking a larger army to Greece where we are in conflict with the Spartans and where the Athenians are refraining from fighting us more out of fear than conviction. But if we can take Tyre, we can hold Phoenicia and get the best, the strongest part of the Persian fleet, the Phoenician units, on our side.'

This speech, which Flavius Arrianus recorded, describes with terse succinctness the situation in which the Macedonian found himself, when he lay outside the island stronghold. He believed he had to take it, for reasons which did not admittedly seem very valid to most of his later interpreters. To leave Tyre behind unvanquished, would not, they feel, have been very dangerous. But Alexander obviously had too high an opinion of the Persian-Phoenician fleet to begin to consider the alternative. He did not think it was possible to conquer the Orient without getting control of its most active maritime race, a people who moreover appeared so sinister to the Greeks. Besides which he was naturally deeply offended at the contemptuous refusal of his request to be allowed to make a sacrifice to the Tyrian Melqart, even though the petition had only been a politely expressed demand to capitulate.

So the spectacular work of building the dam began, with an evaluation of the situation about which historians disagree. The Macedonian had no illusions about the technical difficulties which would be involved. He let his soldiers know this, in the cryptic manner of the day. Heracles, he announced, had appeared to him in a dream and had pointed with outstretched hand to the sea city. Any Greek who was at all educated knew what this meant. The outstretched arm signified victory, but the man to whom it belonged was, among other things, symbolic of hard and dangerous endeavours.

In fact reality very soon confirmed the royal dream. In the shallow water near the shore, Arrianus reports, it was easy to construct the dam, 'but then, when they [the soldiers] approached the middle of the channel and were thus also nearer to the town, the problems began. From their walls the Tyrians assailed them with a hail of missiles, which were all the more dangerous to the Macedonians because they were carrying work tools and not armour. Besides which the Phoenicians, who still ruled the sea, sent in their triremes to disturb the work where they could. The Macedonians finally tried to counter these attacks with two vast towers at the end of the mole. They posted their catapults there and covered the scaffolding with skins as protection against burning arrows.'

But the Tyrians were not discouraged by these defences. They filled a great horse transport with flammable material, installed two crane-like erections on its deck and fastened huge vessels filled with tar and sulphur to its arms. They filled the stern of the ship with sand and stones, so that the prow reared up out of the water. Then they waited for favourable winds, towed the vessel up to the mole and let it run at full speed towards the wooden towers, after they had set light to its combustible cargo. As expected, the raised bow reared up on the dam and so reached the towers, while at the same time the tar-filled containers, also burning, were flung into the scaffolding by the shock of the collision. The whole thing burst into flames. Troops hurrying to put out the fire were fired at by sharpshooters in the crow's nests of the towships alongside. The destruction was completed by a raiding party. 'Jumping ashore from small boats, it shattered all the catapults which the fire had not reached,' Arrianus reports, and then says that the next day the islanders rowed up to the dam and laughed at Alexander and his soldiers.

The besieged citizens, as Diodorus also confirms, still seemed at that time completely convinced that their town could not be taken. When a delegation from Carthage arrived at the port to make the customary sacrifices to Melqart, they happily celebrated the yearly feast of the god with them. They believed they had good cause for their optimism. Their friends in North Africa had assured them that their senators would never allow Alexander to triumph over Tyre. This promise carried as much weight as that which the Americans made during the Second World War to Britain, when she was cut off from Europe. But the Americans kept their word, and the Carthaginians did not.

Soon the Tyrians had to fight not only Macedonians, but also Phoenicians. The rulers of Aradus and Byblos, who like the King of Tyre, were serving in the Persian fleet, had learnt that their towns were held by the Greeks— surrendered by their representatives there—and immediately sailed for home. There they did not hurry to the aid of their hard-pressed neighbour Tyre, but placed their total of eighty ships at Alexander's disposal. The (Phoenician) regents of Cyprus, who meanwhile had also learnt that Darius, their protector, had been beaten at Issus, now saw fit to follow the example of their mainland colleagues, and offered the leader of the siege a contingent of a further 120 units, which he naturally accepted. The position became untenable for Tyre. Alexander could now attack the town from several sides at once and also counter the continual attacks on his advance parties more successfully. The Tyrians were unable to leave their harbours because the entrances were blocked, and so they were cut off from the outside world.

The next blow was even harder to bear. The Macedonian mobilized Phoenician engineers against the island. These loaded a number of ships with heavy siege machines and with them tried to approach the sea walls which were, Arrianus says, 'about thirty metres high, correspondingly strong and made of heavy blocks of stone'.

At the same time the dam was advancing farther out into the channel. The Tyrians' salvoes of stones and arrows from the walls were no longer any use against the threat on this side. They had to take the offensive. They risked it, cut the anchor cables of the ships loaded with catapults and let them be blown out to sea by the wind. In a second raid they even succeeded in surprising the Cypriot ships which were blockading their harbours and drove them off, sinking some of them. But even while they were engaged in doing so, a Macedonian squadron approached (manned by Phoenicians, naturally) and sank several of their swiftest and strongest boats in return. The crews saved themselves by swimming ashore. Meanwhile the dam was almost finished. Alexander's rams began to pound at the walls—with minimal success. Not the smallest crack appeared, certainly no breach through which they could enter. The King therefore repeated the manœuvre with the help of ships against the fortifications of the so-called Egyptian harbour to the south of the town. Here the walls gave, but the Macedonians trying to scale them from unstable bridges had no chance against the Tyrians fighting on firm ground. They were thrown into the sea.

In spite of these successes it gradually became clear to the Tyrians at about this time that sooner or later their town must fall. These fearful misgivings manifested themselves in sinister rumours. Apollo, they said, wanted to desert Tyre. But pious as they were, this time they did not let themselves be scared by the threat from on high. To prevent him leaving them, they bound the statue of the god to its socle with golden chains, and anchored it to the altar of their Melqart, in whose patriotism they obviously placed greater trust than in that of the imported Greek. The ancient historiographers saw such significance in this fact that four different accounts of it have come down to us—one being by the Greek priest of Apollo, Plutarch. Indeed he makes it strikingly clear that the Tyrians took their decision to defend themselves to the last with deadly seriousness. What made them feel like this, we cannot tell. Was it only pride, or did they still hope for relief from a Carthaginian fleet? The delegation from North Africa was still within the city walls.

But the Carthaginian fleet remained far away, and Alexander was getting nearer and nearer. His soldiers erected attacking towers at the end of the dam and tried to throw bridges across from there to the tops of the walls. The Tyrians thwarted this plan also. They threw fishing nets over the Macedonians who were trying to fight perched between earth and sky, and toppled them off the narrow bridges. They filled bronze shields with hot sand and threw it over their attackers, so that it fell between their armour and skin and burnt them. The attackers had to give up.

The Macedonian King had already had to decide on a massed attack, which would be made both from land and sea simultaneously and would deal the death-blow to the city. To take the tiny sea stronghold, he would have to deploy his entire strike-force. Sheer weight of numbers was the last resource remaining to him.

It was only this superior strength which at last defeated the Tyrians. The entrances to both harbours were simultaneously breached, the walls by the dam scaled; the Macedonians were suddenly everywhere.

At the head of his bodyguard, the King advanced to the so-called Agenor shrine, where those who still remained alive had taken refuge. The last act of the bloody drama thus took place in the sanctuary of the legendary father of the Tyrian princess Europa. Orientals defended it, Europeans attacked it. The orientals were all hewn down. In all, Alexander's final attack was said to have cost eight thousand Tyrians their lives. He himself reputedly only lost four hundred men.

With the taking of Tyre by the Macedonians, the history of Phoenicia came to an end. The boldest and finest creation of the Semitic seafarers, the city in the sea, the man-made island, was joined to the land by a dam for evermore and thus robbed of its uniqueness. It blossomed once again under the Romans, and today boasts mighty ruins from Imperial times, but these columns and triumphal arches reflect nothing of that older glory, of which Ezekiel once sang: 'Thou has been in Eden the garden of God; every precious stone was thy covering . . . and gold: the workmanship of thy tabrets and of thy pipes was prepared in thee in the day that thou wast created.' Alexander had silenced these instruments for ever.

'Tyre,' the Roman Quintus Curtius wrote four hundred years later, 'was taken in the seventh month after the beginning of the siege, a town which merits to live on in the memory of those who come after, both because of its honourable origins and because of its eventful story.'

The envoys from Carthage, who were not molested by Alexander but sent home in their own ships, sailed away sadly into a world which had suddenly become empty. The mother city of the Phoenicians had been destroyed, the daughter now stood alone against those new forces embodied by the Macedonian. When would he come to North Africa?

Everyone knows that Carthage was never attacked by Alexander, but he does in fact seem to have planned an advance into the

Punic territory. This is confirmed by Flavius Arrianus, who even speaks of a Macedonian declaration of war which was sent to Carthage after the conquest of Tyre. We do not know if his statement is completely true, but it cannot have been entirely fabricated.

Carthage, nominally still a colony of Tyre, was even more nominally a vassal state of Persia. The vast Asiatic empire of Darius would thus only be completely conquered when Alexander's standards also gleamed above the Byrsa. That this never happened may have been primarily because the young king died too early. If he had lived longer, he would probably also have sailed westwards, to add the Sicilian Greeks and their Punic rivals to his empire and thus safeguard its exposed flank.

The Carthaginians thought he would do so. They sent a man called Hamilcar to his court. He gave out that he had been banished by the suffetes, and for many years sent the latter information about Alexander's plans.

The successors of the Macedonian King, the Diadochi, seem to have worried little at first about what went on to the west of their frontiers, in Tunis. It was not until 310 BC that Ophellas, an officer of King Ptolemy of Egypt made an attempt to penetrate the Carthaginian zone. The one-time bodyguard of Alexander of Cyrene marched with ten thousand men to Tunis—a good two thousand kilometres straight through the Libyan desert—and covered the distance in only three months. But he left no details of the number of men who were left behind on the way, dying of thirst or sunstroke. The sand probably still covers their bones.

In Tunis Ophellas's troops joined up with the army of the Sicilian Agathocles, who had asked him for help and who was in fact the instigator of the whole plan. Agathocles is, however, the man who, twenty-two years after the fall of Tyre, threatened the Carthaginians for the first time in their history on their own home territory and almost conquered the Punic capital. That makes him the hero of his own turbulent story.

Agathocles came from Syracuse. He began his career, in a typically Syracusan way, as a political agitator. The ruling oligarchs banished him twice for his seditious activities, and in so doing helped him on his way to success. In exile he succeeded in winning so many followers that they soon became a threat to his home town. When things had got this far, Hamilcar, the Punic governor in Sicily, thought it wise to intervene by diplomatic means. He arranged an agreement between Agathocles and his political opponents. The result: the rebel was taken back into favour and made military commander of the port. It was hoped that this would satisfy his ambition.

But their hopes were not fulfilled. Agathocles, by no means prepared to vegetate in this post, followed in the footsteps of the dead Timoleon and seized power in the city state. Then, following almost automatically on this first step, he tried to oust the other East-Sicilian tyrants from their thrones. Messana, present-day Messina, fell, and he was soon threatening Acragas and even advanced westwards across the Halycus, into Punic territory.

Carthage, which after the final battles with Timoleon had disbanded almost its entire army, was shocked out of its happy state of peace on learning this and began, reluctantly, to beat up for recruits; it mobilized its fleet and looked around for a general to take command. The senators finally decided upon a grandson of the crucified usurper Hanno, who, like the over-diplomatic governor, was also called Hamilcar. (When things went badly, the Carthaginians always turned to the younger members of their rebellious officer families.)

At the beginning of the year 310 BC the newly appointed general crossed the Sicilian Channel with four thousand men, marched to north Sicily and met Agathocles's army at the mouth of the river Himera, near present-day Términi. He utterly defeated it. The Greek had to flee, lost town after town to the hotly pursuing Carthaginians and finally found himself, like Dionysius before him, thrown back on Syracuse.

Here the parallel with the earlier battles for the island ended. This time the Punic gods made no attempt to send their followers an epidemic. Agathocles had to try to get himself out of the uncomfortable position in which he found himself under his own steam. After racking his brains feverishly he finally came up with one of the most reckless plans that was ever hatched up by a general. He decided to leave the town which Hamilcar was besieging to the protection of its strong defences, and to sail to North Africa with his remaining ships and attack Carthage. He would outdo the enemy at his own game, and risky as the ploy sounds, he succeeded.

Unnoticed by the Carthaginians, his fleet left the blockaded harbour, sailed southwards for six days and landed, again unnoticed, west of Cap Bon, and thus very near the promontory on which Carthage lies. Agathocles burnt his ships behind him and marched without delay on the enemy city. The Carthaginians, who were entirely unprepared for such a manœuvre, must have hardly been able to believe their eyes when they saw the Sicilian army camped outside their walls next morning. In frantic haste they appointed two commanders, the younger of whom, Bomilcar, was again a member of one of the outlawed military families. They sent them with forty thousand foot soldiers, a thousand cavalrymen and two thousand war chariots to meet the invading army, which was fourteen thousand strong at most.

No one with any sense would have laid any money on a victorious outcome for the Greeks, but a rational man would have lost his bet. At the end of the first day of fighting, three thousand Carthaginians lay dead on the battlefield, while Agathocles was triumphant.

Overwhelming and magnificent as this victory was, it was of little use to the Sicilian. He could, it is true, now occupy the whole hinterland of Carthage, but he soon saw that he would never breach the strong fortifications on the neck of land between the headland and the mainland, and that he could not cut the port off from its sources of overseas supply; he had no fleet.

But possibly Agathocles had nothing of the sort in mind. His whole manœuvre could have simply been an attempt to force Hamilcar to give up the siege of Syracuse. The latter had no intention of obliging his opponent by doing so, however, and so both forces continued in a kind of strategic clinch. It was a case of keeping their cool.

The Carthaginian citizens lost theirs. As always when in difficulties, they immediately thought the gods were angry, tried to discover the reasons for this and decided it was their fault. Baal and Tanit, it appeared, had not received enough, and particularly not enough noble, victims in recent years. The rich patricians had given them slaves instead of their own children. This mistake must be rectified at once, and was indeed rectified. Two hundred innocent youngsters from the best families had to 'go through the fire', and three hundred more were freely offered by their parents. The pseudo-Greek façade which Carthage had adopted cracked in a matter of days; the dark primeval substance of which her people were made became visible once more, as did the archaic fear of poor desert nomads which still haunted them in their rich, comfortable and civilized city.

Outside the walls, meanwhile, Agathocles's strength increased from month to month. He made allies of native princes, built a large, well fortified camp and soon possessed the whole of east Tunisia and some of its towns. Then he made his pact with Ophellas from Egypt, who brought him his ten thousand men. (In gratitude for this he was perfidiously killed after a quarrel with the Sicilian.)

But in Carthage there were now bloody internal feuds. Bomilcar tried to make himself tyrant. He was defeated and, according to the rigid laws of the community to which he belonged, tortured to death.

Agathocles had now been on Carthaginian soil for over a year. He had his bit of territory so completely under control that he thought he could leave it for a while and sail back to Syracuse in a newly built fleet with two thousand men, to see to things there. But he overestimated the possibilities and his own strength, and the move lost him the game. The Carthaginians took advantage of his absence, attacked the leaderless army which had remained behind and practically wiped it out. When the Sicilian returned immediately with reinforcements, it was clear that the situation was now hopeless. His troops had lost faith in him, felt they had been done out of the booty he had promised them and flocked over to the Punic side in large numbers. He had to leave the camp secretly in order to save at least his life and his position in his homeland.

He had nevertheless achieved one thing: Syracuse escaped once more from falling into Carthaginian hands. The suffetes made a peace offer to Agathocles, which he accepted. And the war on two continents came to nothing, ending as the ones before had done. The border between the Punic and Greek sectors of Sicily remained the Halycus, that meagre stream which can with justice be called one of the most fought-over rivers in history—though this means nothing to the poor Sicilian farmers who water their sheep there today.

The Halycus border was thus the only result of the ambitious undertaking that a young general called Hannibal had begun about a century before. The Carthaginian empire in Sicily he had dreamt about had not come to pass. He had overburdened his countrymen by suggesting it. It had very soon become clear to them once more that wars are not business undertakings, especially for a community which could not recruit soldiers from among its own citizens but had to rely on expensive mercenary armies. And Carthage would not have had enough people to occupy a large compact territory and Punicize it. Basically the Carthaginians were still a small nomad race, who must be content with having a few secure places here and there in their vast territory which could offer shelter, protection, food and help to its members before they pressed on to the next stopping place at which to market their wares. They could not really have coped with the larger tracts of land which lay between.

It was this fact which finally defeated all the Carthaginian military dynasts, from Mago to Bomilcar. They strove for the power which is based on colonial possessions, but both the power and the imperialistic schemes were mistrusted by their fellow citizens, particularly the power. The Carthaginian gods were terrible enough; they did not need tyrants as well.

In spite of this the Carthaginians did have an empire in the last century of their history. It was even larger than the whole of Sicily. But that this could happen was symptomatic of their approaching downfall.

CHAPTER XVI

Then Came Rome

CARTHAGE SLUMBERS IN the sunshine. From above on the Byrsa the view is of a prosperous city with oriental features. In the roads before the two harbours, the round and the rectangular, lie ship after ship. The narrow streets of the inner city teem with people. Dignitaries in black caftans, the traditional conical fur caps on their blue-dyed hair, push through the crowds of dock workers, ropemakers, coppersmiths, clothiers, fruiterers. Blond Celts, brown-skinned Moroccans, statuesque Egyptians mingle with the original inhabitants, who are still representative of the Semitic type. In the cypress groves of the temple, barefoot, white-clad priests carry out their duties. In the green fields, beyond the great walls, gleam the cupolas of the country houses of the rich. Light is reflected from well-filled cisterns. Farther to the south lies the next sea of houses, the town of Tunis.

At the end of the fourth century BC, the Carthaginians could feel pleased with what they had. It seems that they had escaped from the mainstream of history for a while. The major events and state manœuvres were not taking place in North Africa but over in the east. There the Diadochi had formed three large empires from the land inherited from Alexander: Macedonia under the Antigonids, Seleucid Anterior Asia and Ptolemaic Egypt. All three were really only different from modern industrial states in that man- and animal-power could not yet be replaced by motors. Their trading houses got tin from Cornwall and iron from China. There was so much maritime traffic that within three days a traveller could find a ship to take him to any place he fancied in the Mediterranean. The entrance to the harbour at Alexandria, the first metropolis of antiquity, had the 120-metre-high Pharos lighthouse towering above it, the one at Rhodes a statue of the sun god, through whose spread legs the ships entered the harbour. They were among the seven wonders of the world. Naturally the East Phoenicians, who now belonged to the Seleucid state, participated a great deal in the trade and traffic of the Hellenistic states. King Antigonus built great dockyards in Sidon, Byblos and Tripolis. 'He gathered together woodcutters, lumbermen and carpenters from the whole country and had the wood from the Lebanon taken to the coast,' writes Diodorus. 'Eight thousand men were occupied in felling and cutting the wood alone, then a thousand ox teams transported it farther, for the mountain is covered with the finest cedars and cypresses.'

But the maritime monopoly which the people of the city states had still had in Persian times was theirs no longer, and when Ptolemy Philadelphus, King of Egypt, opened the old Suez canal again, they also lost their Southern Arabian trade. The Egyptian ships sailed direct from the newly built harbour of Berenike on the Red Sea to Alexandria. The route from Eilat to Tyre via Petra which had been opened in Babylonian times, was no longer used. However, this did not ruin the city states. Shipbuilding and Mediterranean trade were still profitable enough, and their political situation was bearable.

Seleucid rulers seldom interfered in the affairs of the regents of the rebuilt Tyre. There were once more kings (or suffetes), who were called Adonibaal and Bodmelqart, and a council of a hundred on the Carthaginian pattern. Apart from this the city states must have by now become thoroughly Hellenized. Within their walls, gymnastic contests were held, and sacrifices made to Greek gods in the Greek manner, and there were also a kind of Olympic Games, which were held every five instead of every four years, in Tyre. The only things reminiscent of the old days were the contacts with Carthage which had been quickly re-established after Alexander's death, and the admiration which the Tyrians felt for the successful daughter city.

For the Carthaginians, on the other hand, the ties with the mother colony and through it with the Seleucid empire were of considerable importance. They still mainly delivered gold from Spain and also found there a welcome market for their home-made *kitsch* articles. They were also on good terms with Egypt, their nearest neighbour on the North African coast, importing elements of Hellenistic culture as well, in return for their products. For the rest, compared to the kingdoms of the

Diadochi, they remained only a second-class political and commercial power, which did not worry them. They flourished in the shadow of the giants, were still the leaders of fashion in Sicily, and all in all were still rich enough to awaken envy occasionally in their neighbours.

Their prosperity was particularly irking to a nation which was then just beginning to take shape. The North African town had come up against its most dangerous opponent.

That Rome of all places should become a threat to them would have seemed almost unthinkable to a Carthaginian at the time when Hannibal sacked Selinus. What was Rome anyway? An insignificant town on the Tiber, which was slowly and surely getting bigger, which had overpowered its Etruscan allies in the fifth century and which in 400 BC ruled a territory reaching approximately from present-day Cervéteri to Monte Circeo in the south and Avezzano in the east. But it still could not be compared with the Greek city states of southern Italy or Sicily.

However, the suffetes were cautious. In order to obviate future difficulties and to guarantee the safety of their merchants in the Roman zone, they signed three treaties in all with the young republic, the first in 510 BC, the second 162 years later and the third in 306 BC. In all three documents the parties agreed on their spheres of influence, the Romans being forbidden to found towns in Sardinia or raid the Spanish coasts. In return they could shelter in Carthaginian ports if the need arose and do everything and anything in Carthage itself which her own citizens were allowed to do. The stronger power dictated to the weaker as to the limits within which it was allowed to move, and offered in return 'Friendship between the Romans and her allies and the Carthaginians, Tyrians, people of Utica and their allies'.

The friendship lasted for about two hundred years. Undisturbed by the Carthaginians, the Romans, in a series of bloody wars against the Samnites, Latins and the remaining Etruscan principalities, spread out over the whole of Apulia and, long before they got anywhere near the Carthaginian sphere of interest, came into conflict with the south-Italian Greeks. Tarentum, the richest trading port in the leg of Italy—then still called Taras—thought it wise to check the invaders from the north. When the Roman fleet seized their harbour in 303 BC they turned first of all to that old enemy of Carthage, Agathocles of Syracuse, and then, on his sudden death, to King Pyrrhus of Epirus, a relation of Alexander the Great, to ask him for help. Thus on the one hand Rome was dragged into the Hellenistic sphere, and on the other Carthage also felt herself challenged. Pyrrhus had no intention of fighting a small inter-city war; he wanted, as so many had done before him, to realize the dream of a Greek empire in southern Italy, to which naturally, as the Carthaginians well knew, Sicily would also belong.

The landing of the Epirote in Tarentum was a spectacle in the best Hollywood tradition. Twenty-five thousand soldiers came pouring out of the holds of his ships, greaves clanking and aigrettes nodding, as he marched at their head, enveloped in iron, victoriously resplendent like a second Alexander, and— if his portrait bust in the National Museum of Naples is correct— as good-looking. But the chief attraction in this first act of a drama which promised to be spectacular, were twenty elephants, tanks of flesh and tough skin. The Macedonians had discovered them in India. Since then the trunked beasts had been part of the basic equipment of every Greek army.

The glorious prelude was in fact followed by glorious victories. The Epirote defeated the Romans wherever he encountered them, but paid for this each time with such heavy losses that in memory of this we still speak of 'Pyrrhic victories'. In spite of this the Romans began discussing peace terms with him—which led to the involvement of Carthage.

At this point the North African town was once again at war with Syracuse. Its leaders wanted at all costs to prevent Pyrrhus from becoming free in Italy and able to hurry to the aid of their opponents. So a Punic ambassador sailed with 120 ships to Rome and tried to persuade the senate not to give in to the young king. He spared neither silver nor other presents, but could get only an agreement by which the Romans promised to come to the aid of the Carthaginians if they were attacked, and *vice versa*, although the latter would supply the ships in either case.

As would soon emerge, this was not enough. The Romans did in fact make a peace treaty and Pyrrhus did come to Sicily. There he meted out the same fate to the Punic armies that they had been accustomed to dealing out to the Siceliots. He drove them from the island. Only the strongly fortified Lilybaeum (present-day

Marsala) held out against him. However, the capricious hero then lost interest. He returned to southern Italy, where the Romans had meanwhile descended on his allies. But at this point luck seemed to desert him. His decimated troops—the Carthaginians had attacked him on the way over and sunk seventy of the 110 ships which he possessed—were no longer in a position to deal with the attackers. So he decided against the venture and left like a star performer who refuses to appear on a provincial stage. A little later he was killed in a street fight in Argos.

Two victorious parties remained behind on the southern Italian stage, however, who had worked together successfully if in different spheres: the Carthaginians and the Romans. Eight years later they came to blows—in Sicily.

The First Punic War began with a strange prologue. The scene was Messana. The town in the straits was occupied at that time by Campanian mercenaries, one-time auxiliaries of Agathocles, who called themselves Mamertines, or sons of Mars. Their perpetual raids made the whole of eastern Sicily unsafe and they were constantly fighting with the Syracusans.

In the spring of the year 265 BC Hieron, the ruler of Syracuse, began to grow tired of their antics. After he had dealt them several severe blows, the ex-mercenaries asked Carthage for help and were sent a Punic garrison. Another section of the Mamertines had simultaneously turned to Rome, however. And as the senators in the town on the Tiber saw no advantage in Syracuse possibly gaining possession of Messana and the straits, they also sent two legions, led by two consuls.

A conflict between the Latin Republic and Carthage seemed inevitable, but the commander of the Punic garrison in Messana did not at first allow things to get this far. When he heard of the arrival of the Roman fleet, he simply vacated his post. This cost him his head later, but seemed at the time to be in keeping with Punic policy. Rome and Carthage were as good as allies.

Then their friendship changed almost overnight into something quite the reverse. When the two legions not only arrived in Messana but also seemed to have every intention of staying there, Carthage joined up with Syracuse and made a vain attempt to drive the Romans out. They were shamefully defeated. The Syracusans left their joint camp when Rome sent four more legions.

Thus the prologue ended and the First Punic War began. When the Romans withdrew the major part of their army after their success in Messana, obviously thinking nothing had happened to upset the Carthaginians, the latter were furiously angry. They said Rome had broken a treaty which required one party—the Romans—not to establish themselves in Sicily, and the other— the Carthaginians—not to set up camp in Italy, and now the former were sitting in Messana. Rome at once said she knew nothing of such an arrangement, and it is difficult to know which of the two was in the right. B. H. Warmington is of the opinion that the Carthaginians had in fact worded the contract which they made with the Romans in Pyrrhus's day too generously, and were horrified that a power which had now become so strong controlled the Strait of Messina, which was so vital to them. One way or the other, it came to war.

Carthage landed a vast army at Acragas, and at the same time began to attack the Roman ports on the west coast of Italy. Rome for its part sent troops which captured Acragas and beat the Punic soldiers back onto their own territory. Two years later the state of the parties was still undecided, with a slight advantage for Carthage. But it would not remain thus for long.

Until 261 BC the Romans had hardly been able to deploy their full strength because they had no ships and the Carthaginians had unchallenged control of the sea. The latter seem to have become a little careless. Their usually hawk-like spies apparently did not notice that the citizens of the town on the Tiber were making vast efforts to make up for this lack.

Using a captured Punic ship as their model, they (reputedly) built in the shortest possible time no less than a hundred quinque- remes, giant vessels, with twenty-five to thirty oars on each side, each rowed by five men. At that date ships of this size were only known in the Hellenic east and in Carthage. As, however, battleships need to be not only large and swift, but also skilfully manœuvred and as the Romans could not produce a hundred experienced captains at a moment's notice, they thought of an addition to the vessels which would make up for their lack of dexterity. It was a simple but ingenious affair: bridges ten metres long and about a metre wide were lashed to the masts, hanging at an angle of forty-five degrees over the ships' sides. As they came alongside an enemy ship these boarding planks came slamming down and bored into the deck of the enemy ship with their sharp spikes, thus making a firm bridge for the soldiers waiting to attack.

This Roman invention revolutionized the sea warfare of the day and at the same time robbed it of some of its nautical elegance. Until then a tactical expert could put enemy ships out of action by ramming them, smashing their oars and perhaps entering them. Now, however, the methods of infantry warfare were introduced at sea, and as footsoldiers the Romans were far superior to the Carthaginians.

This was demonstrated for the first time in 260 BC. Off Mylae (Milazzo in Sicily) a Roman fleet of 143 ships met an equally strong Carthaginian fleet. The Carthaginians, as always on the sea, thought it would be a walkover. Their commander, a man called Hannibal, did not even take the trouble to range his vessels in proper battle order. He advanced on the enemy in loose formation, and so to disaster. The grappling-planks of the Romans suddenly crashed down on the Punic decks, heavily armed naval infantrymen stormed across the narrow bridges and took thirty ships before the Carthaginian had realized what was happening. Hannibal signalled a withdrawal at once, but this was of little avail. He was defeated and the Punic reputation for being invincible in their own blue realm was so badly damaged that it could not be restored even after the Battle of Thermae (Términi in Sicily) which was fought a little later, and which ended victoriously for them.

The Romans made good use of their advantage. At the end of the seventh year of the war, in the winter of 257 BC, they built a huge armada of (reputedly) 350 ships, and sailed to North Africa. Considering the rather inexperienced captains whom they could employ, it was no less hazardous an undertaking than that which Agathocles had attempted along the same route. But it succeeded. The consuls Manlius Vulso and Atilius Regulus beat an enemy fleet which was in fact somewhat larger than theirs off Gela and landed a little later east of Cap Bon, opposite Carthage.

Once again, just as when the reckless Sicilian had surprised them, the Carthaginians immediately lost their heads. They were simply not used to fighting on their own ground. Luckily for them the two Romans were not particularly inspired strategists.

It is true they took Tunis and were said to have reduced Carthage to the point of begging for peace, but this is not known for certain. There is also no precise information as to the supposedly over-harsh demands which Regulus made. We only know that a Spartan officer called Xanthippus hurried to the aid of the oppressed citizens and was able to raise their morale. He drilled the Car-thaginian army according to the most modern methods and then challenged the Romans to a battle before the walls of the trading city. Regulus accepted. He would have done better not to have done so. The Numidian cavalry and particularly the Punic elephants—a weapon which the Carthaginians had got to know when fighting Pyrrhus—were too much for his legionaries. They were surrounded, trampled down and decimated, and Regulus was taken prisoner. Carthage was now able to gather her strength and reorganize herself. One of the men who was given this task was called Hamilcar Barca.

Barca went to Sicily to see what could still be saved for Carthage from this bloody battlefield. His first impressions must have been shattering. Only two of the Punic bases in western Sicily still held out against the Romans—Lilybaeum and Drepanum (Trapani); the rest of the island was in enemy hands. The general did not think the situation could be saved by a battle. He there-fore contented himself with reorganizing the completely de-moralized Carthaginian troops on the island, then took a massive rock west of the already captured Punic base of Panormus (Palermo) and from there led a guerrilla-like war against the Roman lines of communication. He later changed his head-quarters, occupied the Eryx near Drepanum, the present-day Monte San Giuliano, which rises steeply from the plain, and tried for three years longer to wear down his opponents from this lair. He might even have succeeded if the politicians at home had sent him reinforcements and if the Romans, who had mean-while built a new fleet, had not once more used their grappling-planks successfully against Carthaginian ships. They won a brilliant victory off the Aegates Islands, to the west of Sicily.

Hamilcar was now cut off from his North African supply bases. The Punic cause in the Mediterranean and in Sicily was finally lost. A mere land power had driven the Queen of the Sea from her throne. She gave up.

Hamilcar was ordered to make a truce. He asked to be allowed to leave freely with all his troops, but in return had to agree that from now on the island would be Roman. In addition to which his adversaries demanded an indemnity of three thousand two hundred talents (8,320 kg) of silver, payable in ten yearly instalments. Numb with shock, the Carthaginians sat in their walled city and reckoned up what their objections to the presumed Roman breach of faith had cost them. It was a depressing total. Countless lives lost, their whole hard-won Sicilian territory lost, and—bitterest of all—their reputation for being the leading seapower in the western Mediterranean lost.

Nor can the Romans have been completely happy. They were now well on the way to becoming a great power, but at what price? A census undertaken in the year 247 BC, showed that the number of their adult male citizens had decreased by fifty thousand during the twenty-three years of the First Punic War. This even spoilt their pleasure in their victorious fleet. During the following years they almost entirely refrained from using it in action.

Both sides however tried to learn from their experience won at the cost of so much blood, and the Carthaginians came to a surprising conclusion. They realized they also had the ability to become a strong land power, that moreover they needed a substitute for their lost Sicily, and finally that Rome was an enemy which one only had a hope of beating, if at all, if one fought her on her own land, that is in Italy.

It was Hamilcar Barca, the father of the great Hannibal, who put these theories to the test once more. But before doing so he had to win power for himself at home.

According to all we know about him, Hamilcar was a representative product of those Carthaginian military families who tried from time to time to wrest the ship of state out of the hands of the ruling oligarchs. Among his political ancestors were Mago, Gisco, Hanno the Great and Bomilcar, yet he differed from them n various externals which made him a product of the Hellenistic age. The most significant of these details is his second name, or more precisely his nickname. We do not know exactly what Barca meant, but it probably corresponded to those titles which Ptolemaic and Seleucid kings gave themselves at that time. They called themselves 'Epiphanes', he who visibly brings help, or

'Philadelphus', he who is filled with brotherly love. The Carthaginians had adopted and somewhat simplified their bombastic practice and now used the name Barca, which is usually translated by 'Lightning', or 'Monomachus', the single combatant, or 'Saunites' the Samnite. But this was more than just a fashion, it was a claim to individual respect, and, politically speaking, a claim to individual power. People wanted to be more than just another link in the chain of Theophiluses, which stretched back into a communal past. The first Carthaginian whom we know to have had more than a single name, was a traitor. He lives on in history as 'Hanno the Great', although it is not certain if Greek historiographers have translated the Punic word correctly.

We know practically nothing about the family from which Hamilcar came. The legend that he was directly descended from one of the old Tyrian city kings is certainly no more than that. It may have been disseminated in order to further his dynastic plans. The marriages which he arranged certainly worked to this end. He married two of his four daughters to influential members of the senate, and the other two to Numidian princes, who supplied the Punic cavalry contingents. Thus he seems to have purposely built up his dynastic power.

Another of his fellow citizens was simultaneously trying to do the same. He was a Hanno, who was called 'the Great', which leads one to suppose that he was from that old and tried rebel family who had already seen one of their members crucified. Hanno had been clever enough to enlarge Carthage's North African territory considerably during the time Hamilcar was in Sicily. This had naturally gained him a better reputation with the Punic citizens than Hamilcar could hope to have. He returned as a conqueror from his campaign, while his rival returned vanquished. Sooner or later it would have to be established which of them would finally win the fight for power in the state, since it was quite clear that they both wanted to get to the top.

Hanno, as has been seen, at first had all the advantages on his side. He was a rising star in the political heaven, whereas Hamilcar, according to custom, was cashiered and sent to his country estate, and could think himself lucky that he had not been brought to trial. But then, in Carthage itself, that dark and dire civil war broke out which inspired Flaubert to write his novel *Salammbô*.

'It was in Megara, the suburb of Carthage . . .' Thus the Frenchman sets the scene. 'Men of all nations were gathered together
here. Ligurians and Lusitanians, Balearics, Negroes and fugitives
from Rome. Next to the heavy Doric dialect one heard Celtic
syllables which sounded like war chariots, and the Ionic endings
rolled against the consonants of the desert, harsh as the jackal's
bark. One could recognize the Greek by his graceful build, the
Egyptian by his high shoulders and the Cantabrian by his broad
calves. The Carians bore feathers proudly in their helmets, the
Cappadocian bowmen had painted great flowers on their bodies
and some of the Lydians were eating, dressed in women's clothes,
with slippers on their feet and earrings in their ears. Others, who
had painted themselves with cinnabar for the occasion, looked
like coral statues.'

The reality must have been less extraordinary and far less
decorative. Hamilcar's troops, certainly a very mixed crew, made
up of Iberians, Celts, Ligurians and Greeks, about twenty
thousand men in all, had come back from Sicily and demanded
their arrears of pay and also bonuses for their pains. But the senate
was niggardly. It offered less than they had expected, and they
began to rebel. They went with their bags and baggage, women,
children, camp followers and waggoners to Sicca, which was
about two hundred kilometres west of Carthage, and made a fortified camp there. Their leaders were an Oscan slave called Spendius and a Libyan cavalry soldier, Matho. Some were angry that
they had not been paid, others were also aggrieved at the fact
that Hanno was brutally oppressing the people and levying
heavy taxes. Neither party would have broken out, however, if
a general they respected, such as Hamilcar, had still been in
command. But Hamilcar was sitting in his villa.

It seems to have been the Libyan who finally turned the mutiny
into a revolution. He brought twenty thousand of his countrymen
into the rebel camp. Then he attacked Hippo Acra, a town near
Carthage, while Spendius besieged Utica.

The suffetes gave Hanno orders to round up the rebels. The
victor of Numidia mobilized the so-called 'Holy Troop', a
guard of young middle-class citizens, and also enlisted mercenaries
and finally advanced into battle with fifteen thousand men and a
hundred elephants. But he had no success. He could not relieve

Utica or prevent Spendius's troops marching on Tunis. The Carthaginians began to fear for their lives.

At this juncture the suffetes remembered Hamilcar and threw him into the fray as well. The 'Lightning', who had at least lived with his soldiers for several years, knew his troops better than Hanno, whose experience was obviously more in the line of political intrigue. After he had slain some of Spendius's men, he asked the survivors if they wanted to join his force. But when their leaders, seeing through this psychological ploy, tried to keep their men by letting them participate in an execution of captured Carthaginian officers, he also switched to brutality and let the next lot of prisoners be trampled to death by elephants.

In spite of these in the long run quite successful campaigns, the civil war lasted a good four years. It began in 241 BC and it was not until 237 BC that Matho was captured and, as Flaubert writes, sacrificed, after running the gauntlet, to Moloch. 'A child,' the Frenchman has it, 'tore off his ear. A young girl, with the point of a spindle hidden in the sleeve of her gown, slit his cheek open; his hair was torn out in handfuls, his flesh was ripped from his body in strips . . . a wild howling filled Carthage and continued relentlessly.'

The Carthaginians were cruel, certainly, but we know only that Matho was crucified—nothing more.

For Hamilcar, however, the death of the rebel mercenary was something like the keystone in the edifice of power which he had carefully constructed. His son-in-law Hasdrubal led one of the strongest parties in the senate; two of his other daughters' husbands controlled the Libyan hinterland; he himself was now regarded by both the general populace and the rich merchants as the saviour of his country.

Nothing which Hanno the Great could offer could match up to this combination of political factors. He faded into the background, while Barca was named generalissimo of all the Carthaginian forces, and thus achieved the position which so many before him had striven for. The military dynastic principle seemed to have been realized after more than two centuries. A Carthaginian of the Greek stamp had become almost an unofficial king in a still democratic republic. And he had every intention of taking advantage of the fact.

At the time when he first reached the peak of his career, Hamilcar's plans had long been laid. He wanted above all to do two things: to wipe out the humiliation he had suffered at the hands of the Romans, and to find a substitute for Sicily, which his city had lost, and for Sardinia, since in the meantime this island had also been annexed by his Latin opponents. If the emotion behind his policy was really, as the legends say, hatred for Rome, then this feeling was compounded of wounded pride, patriotism, and ambition. And as he knew very well that one lifetime would not be long enough to realize the lengthy plans thus involved, he supposedly, again according to historical legend, took the precaution of inspiring his three sons with the same hatred. Hannibal, one of them, at any rate later told the Seleucid ruler Antiochus III, that Hamilcar had made him swear that he would never live in friendship with Rome. Whatever the case may have been, it sounds as if the Lightning was a man of grim determination.

The man who later crossed the Alps, then nine or ten years old, went with his father in 237 BC to Spain, the jumping-off ground later for his famous march into the heart of Italy.

Most modern historians speak of Hamilcar's Spanish campaign as just one of many military actions, which were undertaken in the course of Carthaginian history. But few of them seem to be really convinced that this was so. Sabatino Moscati, for instance, writes that the Carthaginians had now 'gone beyond their usual kind of primitive expansion towards a true policy of annexation'. This is stated even more clearly by Professor Wilhelm Hoffmann of Giessen, who attributes to Hamilcar the decision to make 'a Carthaginian empire in Spain'. But scholars seldom go beyond such intimations, for reasons, one imagines, of academic scrupulousness. This is a pity, because it seems so obvious to compare the expedition from Carthage to Gades with that other expedition which was begun just six hundred years earlier in Tyre and which led to North Africa. At that time a group of patently dissatisfied citizens sailed to the Phoenician colonial zone, to found a community which was very different from the mother city. Now a Carthaginian aristocrat was setting out to an extensively settled Punic colony, firstly to find a replacement there for the territories the mother city had lost, and secondly

to found a kind of army kingdom on foreign soil, with an auto-
cratic central government.

This was precisely what Hamilcar achieved. He annexed a
carefully planned third of the Iberian peninsula, advanced to the
Ebro and almost to present-day Toledo, subjugating peoples
such as the Turdetani, Bastetani and Oretani, and would have
probably done even more, if he had not been killed at Elice
(Elche) in 228 BC. After him, his son-in-law Hasdrubal took the
step which immediately makes clear what these military dynasts
were probably aiming at. Hasdrubal founded a town in a fairly
typical Punic landscape, in a bay flanked by high hills, and called
it Cartagena, which the Romans translated as Carthago Nova, or
New Carthage. It was like a new Tyre, lying on a peninsula
reached by a narrow causeway from the mainland. Was it just
another overseas base, like the many others they already had, or
was it to be the capital of a new Carthaginian empire in Spain?
We do not know, but, as I have said, it is very tempting to think
that Hasdrubal and his predecessors intended the latter.

In the following years too, Hamilcar's son-in-law pursued
a course of action which showed that he saw himself as a ruler
in his own right rather than as a governor. Thus he married,
probably after the death of his first wife, the daughter of a Spanish
prince and also arranged for his brother-in-law, Hannibal, to
marry a native-born princess. He obviously wanted his family
to put down roots in Iberian soil, which again clearly meant that
he wanted to be more independent of the mother country. He
finally let himself be appointed king by the Spanish princes, and
thenceforward held court in his sea citadel like some Greek
autocrat, surrounded by bodyguards, luxury and informers.
He is shown on coins with a worthy expression on his face and a
diadem on his head. The fact that he had them minted is further
proof of his un-Punic royal aspirations; especially as, for the
Semitic people to whom he belonged, it was not considered
good taste to have one's portrait executed.

But however much they talked and grumbled about Hasdrubal
over in Carthage, particularly in the circle round Hanno, they
could not remonstrate about his methods, because his native
country was becoming increasingly dependent on the silver
which his Spanish mines supplied.

Hamilcar had once told a Roman delegation the following: he

had to amass Spanish riches, he said, so that his people at home could pay their huge debts from the First Punic War to the senate in the Tiber city. The Romans appeared to believe him, but in fact their mistrust grew in proportion as the Punic hold on Spain tightened. In 226 BC they came a second time to find out what the Lightning's son-in-law was really up to. This time Hasdrubal managed to fob them off with the assurance that he had no intention of advancing northwards across the Ebro into territory which the Romans already considered as their own sphere of influence.

This must have given Hannibal his first opportunity of seeing his future enemies in the flesh. Five years later he sat on Hasdrubal's throne himself. His brother-in-law had been murdered by an Iberian.

The young Barcid furthered the cause of his family with energy, vigilance and increasing daring. Summer after summer he penetrated farther westwards with his Numidian and Celtic horsemen, reaching the area round present-day Salamanca and bringing other large tracts of central Spain under his sway. The Douro, which forms the northernmost end of the Spanish-Portuguese border, soon became the limit of his territory. This meant that the major part of the Iberian peninsula now belonged to him, a fact which soon stirred up the Romans again. When he returned from campaigning in the spring of 219 BC, one of their delegations was waiting for him in Cartagena, and acquainted him with a point of law which he must have found very confusing.

Like all republics, Rome always placed great importance on ratifying her political moves juridically, and so justifying them to her own conscience. For the senators of the city on the Tiber the world and history were a gigantic forum, round which countless critics thronged, ready to seize every opportunity of accusing the man on the rostrum (the speaker's platform) of lust for power, immorality and despicable greed. It is easier for dictatorial or oligarchic regimes. Within the narrow circle of like-minded colleagues or toadies one can occasionally confess one's crimes tongue in cheek, when it seems likely to prove profitable to do so. The representative of a democratic community, however, has to appear irreproachable to the outside world and must therefore dissemble or employ legal finesse, if he wants,

let us say, to start a war which is pragmatically justified but by
no means just. The Romans had found a solution to such situations in their excellent legal apparatus. Relations with all foreign
states were defined and regulated in a perfectly legal manner.
There were for instance different classes of allies, each with a
precisely graded right to call on Rome for support if they were in
need. The necessity to protect any ally thus justified any war.
Which consequently meant that if one wanted to start a war one
only had to find a friendly nation which felt itself to be threatened
by the enemy of the moment.

The delegation which visited Hannibal at the beginning of
219 BC was to let the Carthaginian know that Rome had just
found such a friend. It was the town of Saguntum, present-day
Sagunto in the province of Valencia. This colony, originally
founded by Greeks, had a strong pro-Roman and a less strong
pro-Carthaginian faction. The pro-Carthaginians had been driven
out by their opponents and had joined up with the Iberian
race of Torpoletae and now wanted to force their way back with
them into their old home. The friends of Rome immediately
appealed to Rome for help. Rome seized this favourable, possibly
even contrived, opportunity and sent its envoys to Hannibal to
demand that he should see that Saguntum was not molested.

We cannot of course know what the Punic leader replied, but
it probably caused him to raise his eyebrows. How is that? he
may have asked. Have we not been agreed since Hasdrubal's
time that Carthage has a free hand on this side of the Ebro? Now,
my lords, Saguntum lies a good 150 kilometres south of this
river, and therefore incontestably in Punic territory. You must
be mistaken in assessing the situation!

What the Romans replied is also not known. Modern historians,
however, think they must have been even more amazed than their
opposite numbers. Who is talking about the Ebro? (in Latin,
Iberus), they may have said; we never meant this northerly
river when we made the treaty with your honoured brother, but
the Jucar (present-day Rio Turia), which flows into the sea quite
a way below Saguntum. Hasdrubal must have misunderstood us,
wilfully perhaps, because he could never have thought that we
would allow him to include land in his *territorium* where our
confederates are settled.

However the dialogue may have ended, Hannibal was not

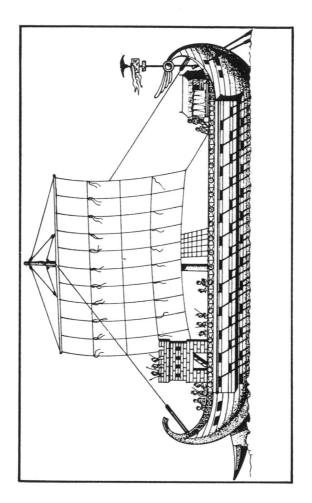

Drawing of a Roman battleship.

prepared to follow the Roman argument. He reiterated that the senate of the Tiber city should not interfere in the affairs of Saguntum, and showed their emissaries the door. The Roman delegation then sailed on to Carthage, repeated their warning there, and were told by the suffetes that their Iberian governor was finally responsible for such matters—in spite of Hanno's protests.

Thus a situation had arisen which could lead to war, but which need not necessarily lead to war. For Hannibal it also had another aspect. He could not allow the Roman senate to undermine his position in Spain with a policy of niggling pinpricks. Today it was Saguntum for which he was responsible, tomorrow it could be another Greek settlement. If he gave in, he would soon be ringed in by dozens of Roman dependencies on the Spanish coast, and his freedom of action would be limited. Hamilcar's son immediately thought in strategical terms, thus confirming the fears of Hanno, who years before had tried to prevent the young man being brought up as a soldier, and—according to Livy— had backed up his misgivings in the Carthaginian senate with the following proposal: 'He should be kept at home and taught to live a life of law and order like other people, so that later this small spark [the thirst for military power] does not set a great fire alight.'

In fact Hannibal never seems to have learnt to do just that— live a life of law and order. He grew up as a prince, in an army camp, in the shadow of autocrats; he was used to making decisions at lightning speed in dangerous situations, and to seeing that they were carried out. He was a soldier, and a good one. Livy writes of him: 'He possessed the greatest courage in braving dangers, the greatest presence of mind in seeing them through. No effort could tire his body or vanquish his spirit. He showed equal fortitude in heat or cold: in eating and drinking he was governed by what he needed rather than self-indulgence; what remained to him [of time] after he had completed his work, he devoted to sleep; but even this was not wooed with a soft bed or silence; many have often seen him sleep covered only by an army cloak, lying on the ground among soldiers in the outposts . . . he went first into battle, and was the last to leave the fight when it was over.'

Admittedly the Roman then added negative traits to this

glowing portrait, namely: 'inhuman savageness, more than Punic faithlessness [it was proverbial]; truth meant nothing to him, nothing was sacred to him; he did not fear god, recognized no oath and felt no religious commitment.'

Posterity has never quite agreed with Livy, whose prime purpose was always to praise and justify Roman greatness, in his attempt to decry the Carthaginian. It has remembered the tough, brave soldier and forgotten the faithless, savage Carthaginian. And how was it possible for a man from the Phoenician people to have no religious commitment? It was not Hannibal's fault his gods were so grim. Yet he always refrained from making large-scale human sacrifices in the style of his namesake, the Magonid, and is described by other witnesses as particularly humane. He is much the most attractive of all the Carthaginians whom we know about—which is perhaps because we know more about him than others.

What did he look like? One of the Barcid coins shows a young man with heavy eyebrows, saddle nose and obstinate chin. If this is a portrait of the Barcid, he was a well-built, energetic, very earnest young man.

So, after the incident of the Roman delegation, the young hero made one of those snap decisions for which he was famous with the soldiers. He besieged Saguntum, probably in order to find out how the Romans would react. They decided in May 218 BC for war. But by this time Saguntum had fallen and the son of the Lightning was already marching northwards. He had crossed the Ebro.

Hannibal's famous Italian campaign is, with Alexander's Persian campaign, probably the most perilous and daring feat of ancient military history, if not nearly as reckless as Agathocles's venture. The Carthaginian was playing for high stakes when he made his Rubicon-like decision on the banks of the Ebro, but he was well prepared for the gamble. The Barcids, as has been explained, had long since realized that they could only fatally wound their enemy if they could surprise him in his own camp, and had therefore methodically prepared to do so. When Hannibal set out, the Punic fleet was only half as strong as during the First Punic War, but he had over fifty thousand well-trained soldiers and a nine-thousand-strong first-rate cavalry corps. His thirty-seven African

elephants were not much by comparison, although of course
the terrifying rumours about them spread panic in advance. Nor
was the plan which he followed a rash improvisation. It was carefully worked out, checked and, where possible, prepared well
in advance with the help of spies and scouts who had inspected
the route.

Hannibal set out briskly, with the approval of the Carthaginian
senate. The Romans had thrown down the gauntlet to them shortly
before, almost literally. The consul Gaius Lutatius had made his
toga into a pouch in the parliament of the trading city, and had
said: 'We bring you peace or war; take which you will,' at which
the Carthaginians had replied, 'Let him give what he will. And
when he shook out his toga and said he gave them war, they all
replied that they accepted the challenge' (Livy). In this way the
war which historians, who like to set the scene correctly, call the
Second Punic War was officially declared.

Hannibal crossed the Pyrenees and the Rhône, followed this
river until it joined the Isère, followed this up into the mountains
and finally turned east down the Arc valley. Following this
mountain river he somehow got past Mont Cenis, over the summit
of the Alps and past Turin to the edge of the Upper Italian plain.
It was an achievement that deserves a place of honour in the
annals of sport as well as war. Except for wild hordes of Celts,
an army had never crossed the European central massif; men
used to the warmer regions of Europe and the heat of Africa
had never weathered the perils of glaciers and avalanches,
without even being suitably equipped. That they also had to
withstand the attacks of Gallic tribes at the same time makes
their achievement all the more impressive. However, the real
martyrs of the campaign were not the soldiers but the elephants.
Seventeen of them perished on the eighteen-day mountain trek.
But Hannibal's human retinue also suffered heavy losses. He
reached enemy terrain with only twenty thousand foot-soldiers
and six thousand horsemen. In order to be able to continue
with any hope of success, he had to enlist fourteen thousand
more soldiers from the ranks of the Upper Italian Gauls, who were
ill disposed towards the Romans.

There now followed the four great battles which won the
Carthaginian his reputation for being one of the great strategical
geniuses of all time. The first was on the Ticinus (Ticino), near

Pavia. There he defeated the consul Cornelius Scipio, who had already tried to intercept him at the Rhône. The next followed in December 218 BC on the Trebia, a tributary of the Po. Here he used his famous encircling technique for the first time. He immobilized the enemy in the centre and outflanked him. His opponent, the consul Sempronius Longus, was just able to save his own life. The rest of his army fled southwards through snow and fog.

Hannibal now had Rome by the throat, but not by any means at his feet. He knew this. If he wanted to defeat the enemy with his comparatively small army, he had above all to get the non-Roman populace of the country on his side, and make treaties with the local princes. Besides which he had to feed his troops entirely off the land, because there was no question of the Carthaginian fleet getting supplies through by sea.

He must have brooded on all this while he sat in Bologna during the winter of 218–17 and drilled his new mercenary recruits. His mood cannot have been made any happier by the fact that he went blind in one eye from the cold. And the news from other fronts was hardly cheering. The Romans, invading northern Spain, had given his deputy Hanno a severe beating. A Carthaginian naval squadron had been destroyed off Lilybaeum in Sicily. Malta, one of the oldest and richest Phoenician colonies, the last island base which Carthage still possessed in the central Mediterranean, was now Roman. This meant that the Carthaginians' only hope was Hannibal and his army, now completely cut off.

For Rome too there was little cause to feel optimistic as spring approached. They were feverishly re-arming on the Tiber. The consul Gaius Flaminius sent his commander-in-chief a newly equipped army. In June 217 BC they met the Carthaginians. It was the third of the four great battles, on Lake Trasimene. Hannibal, who had unexpectedly advanced towards Perusia (Perugia), lured the enemy into a trap. Charging down from wooded hillsides, he fell upon Flaminius's units in a narrow valley near the shore and almost completely destroyed them.

Now Italy lay open before him. He could march through it practically unchecked, because the new Roman commander-in-chief wanted to avoid a battle until he could hope to manœuvre the enemy into a tactically unfavourable position. As, however,

Hannibal also wanted to avoid losing the few good troops which remained to him in unnecessary encounters, they played a game of cat and mouse. They marched past Rome to southern Italy and only came face to face in August 216 beneath the spur of the Italian boot. The place was Cannae.

Here Hannibal won the last of his four great battles, and the most beautiful, if one can describe a battle thus. The encircling technique was carried out with almost parade-ground precision on a broad, level plain. The Punic troops waited for the Roman attack in half-moon formation, with Celtic and Spanish infantry in the centre, Africans in the rear and cavalry divisions on the flanks. As Hannibal had expected, the attack was heavy. But as his troops in the centre stood firm, the Numidian horsemen could encircle the west flank of the enemy and attack from the rear. The Romans were completely surrounded and literally mown down. They lost about thirty-five thousand men, two-thirds of whom were killed, one-third taken prisoner; their leader Terentius Varro narrowly escaped with his life.

Although the Carthaginian's star now seemed to shine so brightly, he was little better off. Cannae was a glorious, but Pyrrhic, victory. In the long run it would only have helped if the Samnites, Sabines, Umbrians, Lucans, and all the other Italian peoples had gone over to Hannibal in vast numbers, and if the Roman state had disintegrated. But this did not happen. Capua, it is true, a rich and prosperous city in the Campanian plain, originally an Etruscan town and eclipsed by the new city on the Tiber, and a few other small places welcomed him, but the majority of other Italians remained surprisingly loyal to Rome and announced themselves more than ready to pay high war taxes if the North Africans could only be driven out. Hannibal had lost his gamble.

The Latin Republic possessed something which the Carthaginians had never had: a people who identified with the state. It was not, like Carthage, a community almost entirely held together by its trading interests, which immediately threatened to go to pieces if it was attacked on its own ground. Hannibal could do nothing against it, but it was a long-drawn-out and painful struggle.

For thirteen years the one-eyed general marched up and down Italy. He managed to draw Philip V of Macedonia into the war, took Tarentum and had command of the toe of Italy for a while. But while this was happening, the Romans took Syracuse, which had allied itself with Carthage once more (and there murdered the brilliant mathematician Archimedes); conquered, together with several Greek towns, the Macedonian King Philip; defeated Hannibal's brother, who had advanced on Upper Italy; took Capua, although Hannibal was at the gates of their capital; advanced with the Numidian Prince Massinissa on Gades, thus annexing the whole Punic terrain in Spain; and finally, under Scipio Africanus the Elder, crossed to North Africa, where they took Tunis and began to set out their peace terms.

But before these were settled, the Carthaginians recalled their general from Italy—his younger brother Mago was killed in Upper Italy at about the same time—and gave him one last task. Their victorious leader must drive the Romans from the homeland. At Zama, south of Carthage, he tried to do so—and lost. Scipio completely routed the Punic forces. Then he dictated peace terms.

It was one of the harshest treaties ever inflicted on a defeated people: they had to waive all claims to Spain, and also to the Numidian territories in North Africa—which went to Massinissa —give up all their warships except for ten triremes, and pay an indemnity of ten thousand talents of silver in fifty yearly instalments; they were forbidden to wage any war outside Africa, or to undertake any military action in Africa without the consent of Rome. A high price to pay for the Barcid attempt to rebuild the Punic empire.

Yet the Carthaginians did not bring the son of the man who had started it all to trial. Instead they made him a suffete seven years later—a sure sign that their outlook had changed. Generals were no longer tiresome people employed to carry out political manœuvres, to be executed if they lost a battle; on the contrary they were recognized as national heroes—a luxury which hard-headed commercial nations do not usually allow themselves. The Carthaginians were tired of calculations. But there was a third act to the play.

In the few remaining years he spent in Carthage, Hannibal seems to have become something of a moral institution. Haggard, rigorous and stern, dressed in severe black, he towered above the rest of his countrymen. When they moaned about the size of the war indemnity, he was said to have laughed aloud, and then, when he was taken to task for this, to have said (according to Livy): 'If one could see the soul's mood as one can see the expression on a face, you would soon realize that this laughter comes not from a happy but from an almost mad heart; and yet it is not as false as your terrible and mawkish tears. . . . You wail and moan because you must pay the war indemnity out of your own private incomes. How sorely I fear that you will soon see you cried today over a very minor hardship.'

If his words are authentic, they were prophetic. And yet the man who spoke them did everything he could to prevent them coming true. He reformed the Carthaginian state, broke the power of the 104 by introducing a new method of election, saw that the indemnity was promptly paid to Rome, and at the same time carefully made contact with the Seleucid Antiochus III, who lived in Syria.

The Romans got wind of this. They had a nasty feeling in their bones that he was preparing their downfall, and demanded that Hannibal should be interned. But before his political enemies could carry out the order, the Barcid fled to Tyre, and from there to the Seleucid's court. He is said to have told him of the oath which his father once made him swear, and to have added: 'If you are thinking of making war on Rome, choose me as your adviser and I will serve you with all my might' (Livy). Antiochus was impressed, but it went no further. He could not nerve himself to make an attack on Italy as the Punic general had suggested. So, a few years later, the Romans surprised him in his own territory in Asia Minor and defeated him in the first battle.

When Hannibal learnt this, he left the Seleucid court. After many wanderings he turned up at the court of King Prusias I of Bithynia, the ruler of one of the smaller Hellenistic principalities on the Bosphorus. The King employed him as an admiral of the fleet and architect, reputedly let him draw up the plans for his capital Prusa, now Bursa in Turkey, and then finally betrayed him to the Romans. When Bithynian troops surrounded Hannibal's villa, to capture him and hand him over, he killed himself.

What his compatriots in Carthage thought about this, is not related. Many epitaphs have been written for him. One of the most succinct is by B. H. Warmington, who calls Hannibal 'the noblest failure in antiquity'. Fine and moving words, and also true.

At the date he was buried, probably in 183 BC, the Roman scene was dominated by the red-haired, blue-eyed super-moral senator who was described by a contemporary epigram as being so vicious that Proserpina would have even sent him back from Hell, if he had gone there. His compatriots called him Cato, because he not only had a sharp tongue, but was also *'catus'*, wise and intuitive. This description was certainly accurate, because his most famous utterance does show brilliant insight economically speaking. Plutarch describes it thus: 'At the end of a speech, Cato, it is said, on picking up his toga in the middle of the Senate let some African figs fall, and when people admired their size and beauty, he said, "The land where this fruit grows is only three days' journey from Rome." Even more striking, however, was the way in which, when he gave his opinion on any subject, he always finished with these words: "Moreover I am of the opinion that Carthage must be destroyed. *Ceterum censeo, Carthaginem esse delendam.*"'

Rome wanted to annex the Tunisian paradise which the Carthaginians had created, and which was the only thing they now possessed. Therefore they had to find an ally, in the approved manner, whom they could protect from the impoverished community. They found one.

It was Massinissa, the Numidian beneficiary of the Roman victory over the Barcids, who brought disaster to the Carthaginians. Encouraged by the Romans, he troubled the Carthaginians for so long with attacks and other minor irritations that they finally repaid him in his own coin and thus began a war which according to the peace treaty should have been sanctioned by Rome beforehand. The Romans arrived on the spot at once with two armies. The third Punic War had started. It was 149 BC.

The story can be quickly told. Carthage first asked humbly in Rome what it could do to be pardoned for its misdemeanour. The Romans demanded three hundred children as hostages and submission to their rule. Carthage agreed. But the hostages had hardly been handed over when the leaders of both armies made fresh demands. The Carthaginians must also hand over all their weapons. They complied. But the torture continued. They were to leave their town and settle elsewhere. This was too much. There was a sudden change of mood by the Byrsa. The Punic citizens decided to put up a resistance, although they must have known that this was tantamount to collective suicide. In a rush of pride and despair they began to forge swords, hammer out shields, build catapults and man their huge fortifications. They were now in the same mood as the Tyrians who had made their last stand at the Agenor shrine 153 years before. A people were preparing for their end. If Baal-Hammon demanded this sacrifice also, he would receive it, but he would have to take many Roman lives as well.

And he was given many Roman lives. A general called Hasdrubal had positioned a cavalry troop behind the town and harried the invaders untiringly and murderously. The best legions fell at the walls of the town. The besieged city held out for three whole years, although its harbours were blockaded by the Roman fleet.

To put an end to the costly business, the senate of the city on the Tiber eventually had to mobilize one of its best strategists. Scipio Aemilianus, adoptive son of the victor of Zama, the natural son of the consul who had lost the Battle of Cannae, a friend of Greek philosophers, then exactly forty years old, was given supreme command on the Carthaginian front. He came to North Africa, looked around and decided to adopt Alexander's technique. A dam across the neck of land between Tunis and Carthage would cut the town off from its hinterland, a second dam across the harbour mouth would cut it off from the sea.

The Carthaginians, remembering the fate of the mother city, at once realized what the Romans were up to. They gathered together all the wood they could find and built a fleet of fifty ships, with which they broke through the deadly contraption; however, they then became involved in a naval battle which they had no hope of winning. Scipio's soldiers occupied one of the moles by the harbour entrance and from there led their siege machines up to the walls. The ram's heads began their terrible bombardment, watched by a public half crazed with hunger and despair.

Despite this, when the walls eventually caved in, the Carthaginians turned every house round both harbours into a fortress, and countered the invaders during six days of gruesome street fighting. The historiographer Appian, who was probably cribbing from Polybius, an eyewitness of the butchery, describes it thus: 'From the six storeys of the tall houses which surrounded the market-place by the Byrsa, the defenders rained down a hail of arrows on the Romans. When the attackers succeeded in entering a building, the fighting continued on the roofs and narrow planks between the houses, during which many fell down or were killed by those who fought in the narrow streets. Scipio set fire to the whole [port] quarter . . . when that happened, many fell from the upper storeys, killed by the fire, or still alive and only singed by the flames. But Scipio had troops standing ready to clear the streets, and they threw dead and living into great graves all together, and often people who were still alive were trampled to death by the hooves of the cavalry horses.'

In the Maximilianeum in Munich there is a picture which shows the final stages of the battle for Carthage. In the foreground are iron-clad Roman legionaries, in the centre (one leg forward, the other stretched back), the young general Scipio Aemilianus, and at his feet a bowed man in bonds, regally dressed, bearded of course and also looking rather sinister. In the background a great flight of steps leads up to the smoke-wreathed pillars of a burning temple. On the top step stands a young woman, who holds two children by the hand and is about to throw herself into the flames.

I must admit that this historical extravaganza always succeeds in making an impression on me, because however little the operatic conception of the scene reflects the bare historical facts, it seems to capture a breath of vanished Carthage. The woman who is throwing herself into the flames is the wife of the general Hasdrubal. He himself lost his courage in the final moments of the battle and begged Scipio for mercy—kneeling before him here with his hands bound—but his wife tore herself free from him, called him a traitor and coward and ran up the steps to her death. Many others were said to have followed her. Fifty thousand gave themselves up.

The town burnt for seventeen days. Scipio, looking at the fire, quoted (his friend Polybius reports) the two most famous lines of the *Iliad*: 'Some day the time will come when holy Ilion will die, and Priam himself and the people of the warrior king.' Later he ordered that the town should be utterly destroyed, and the land ploughed over. Salt was scattered in the furrows, to make the soil unfruitful.

Yet Carthage rose from her ashes once more—as a Roman provincial town. The great ruins of its baths today provide a living for many an honest Tunisian guide, and the tourists who sit on the terrace of the neighbouring hotel *De la Reine Didon,* drinking coffee, can at least see that those who built the city chose one of the most beautiful spots on the North African coast. Carthage is the residential district of Tunis. Habib Bourguiba lives there.

CHAPTER XVII

The Phoenicians and Us

'A state can disintegrate, can be broken, a people will live on.' *Theodor Heuss,* valedictory speech to the German Bundestag, 1959.

DOES A TOWN like Carthage simply come to an end and die, and vanish from the face of the earth? Do her people disappear with her, who although never very numerous, influenced their contemporaries more than almost any other race? That we must ask the question, itself rules out an over-hasty 'yes'.

The Punic capital was indeed so completely destroyed that archaeologists today are thrilled if they find a single Carthaginian brick intact under the Roman remains, but it was not by any means erased from the memory of those who had caused its downfall. On the contrary, it experienced a Renaissance there, which began in effect on the day when Scipio stood on its smoking ruins. Appian recounts how the Roman shed tears and said to his friend, the historian Polybius: 'This is a great moment, Polybius, yet I am seized with dread and the fearful presentiment that one day my native city will suffer the same fate.' His quotation from Homer seems also to have been the expression of a deep emotion, not just a snobbish attempt to display his erudition.

Appian lived and wrote more than two hundred years after the bloody event. One might imagine that the subject of Carthage had long since lost its aura of novelty and fascination by his day. But nothing was farther from the truth. It was precisely at that time—and this was the reason for the prophetic words which the historian attributes to his hero—that the death of the city struck the Romans as a turning point in their own history. It suddenly occurred to them that before the Punic Wars, their state had been

a young, healthy, powerful community, as noble as any Rous-
seau-like wilderness which has not yet been contaminated by
civilization; afterwards it became fat, rotten and ostentatious,
grew accustomed to owning the world and gave free rein to
every kind of decadence. Naturally this was a mood of nostalgia,
such as we too are apt to experience at fairly regular intervals,
but it is, however, interesting that this kind of Romanticism
could centre on the phenomenon of Carthage. The Punic State
had become almost a symbol of their guilt to the Romans.

They knew all too well that the methods which their consuls
had used in the Third Punic War to blackmail Carthage had not
been very nice. Livy, much the most important Roman historian,
made pettifogging efforts to explain and justify their low trick
in retrospect, which he was only partly successful in doing by
painting the Carthaginians in the blackest possible colours, as
Plutarch does, and thus transmuting the shock which the Romans
had felt when Hannibal attacked them to pure hatred.

But his older contemporary Virgil had already begun carefully to correct this impression. Aeneas, the hero of his epic,
stands amazed before a radiant Carthage and its inhabitants. He
does not see sinister, avaricious merchants, but 'bees busy in
sunshine amid flowery fields. . . . Some dig here in the harbour,
others lay the foundations for a theatre and hew gigantic columns
from the rocks, the noble ornaments for the stage they will build.'

It was an attempt to reinterpret the past poetically, and the
beginning of a new concept of Carthage. It would have immense
significance.

At the time when Virgil was writing, in the reign of the
Emperor Augustus, Rome was beginning to welcome exotic,
particularly eastern, ideas. This soon led to gods such as Tanit
and Baal being worshipped at Roman altars. The Latins felt
particularly at home with the latter. He had long since become
assimilated with other gods in the great temple cities of the east,
particularly in Emesa (Homs in Syria), and in the process had
emerged as a radiant sun god.

Among those who helped to open the doors of the Roman
temples to him were Phoenicians—the philosopher from Tyre,
for instance, who was named Malchus and called himself Porphyrius, or 'the man from the purple land'. A pupil of the Neo-
platonist Plotinus, he developed a view of heaven in which eastern

and western gods could be effortlessly brought together and related to one another. In his day he influenced whole generations of religious (and sectarian) thinkers, but also unwittingly prepared the way for Christendom in a manner which would later hold particular meaning for intellectuals. He conceived of a great father god, who commanded saints, angels and other gods to rule the world, with suffering sons, like Baal, among their number.

Porphyrius not only influenced theosophists, but also some of the Roman emperors. Septimus Severus had the likeness of the Carthaginian Tanit engraved on Roman coins, and the mad Heliogabalus from Emesa worshipped his gods with orgies like those which were celebrated at the Asherat altars in Phoenician times, with defloration ceremonies, Bacchanalian dancing and drunken ecstasy.

As I have said, Punicisms and oriental cultic practices had become fashionable in the late Roman empire. The largest temple in the realm was not in the capital on the Tiber but in the mountains of the Lebanon. It was the gigantic and probably age-old sanctuary at Baalbek, whose great hewn stones today still conjure up visions of supernatural beings who came from the stars to bring the benefits of civilization to the earth.

All this means that Phoenicia, the land whose inhabitants were so scornfully dismissed as 'only merchants', was an amazing generator of spiritual activity long after the death of the nation, and influenced late antiquity in ways which we are only just beginning to discover. But our philosophy owes more to the sons of the Lebanon than the memory of a fantastic religious cult.

Thales of Miletus, the first great scientist we know—he is said to have forecast the solar eclipse of the year 585 BC—was half Phoenician, and one of the classical philosophers of the pre-Socratic age, Zeno of Citium, the darkly glowing star in the post-Socratic sky, was almost certainly pure Phoenician. Ridiculed in Athens for his Phoenician appearance—anti-Phoenicianism seems to have been a forerunner of anti-Semitism—he developed a doctrine whose basic concepts still serve as ethical and moral landmarks: stoicism.

He did not believe in a tangible, personal god, but only in a remote ruler of life and nature. It was pointless to beseech him, pointless to depend on him—he was immovable fate itself. The stoic therefore concludes that he will gain nothing by living according to godly precepts, but only according to those of the intellect. He also scorns instincts or desires, and withdraws into a state of unemotional detachment. Because he expects nothing, he cannot be disappointed, and because he is able to discipline himself completely, he is duty bound to help those who cannot. The stoic ideal is inhuman and of such stern grandeur that it arouses the suspicion that behind it lurks Baal, who demanded children as sacrifices and expected them to be smilingly offered. Stoic behaviour in the topheths? Gerhard Nebel scents 'a barbaric element in the extremeness with which the stoic ideal of life, the philosophic existence, is conceived and expounded'.

Zeno himself appears to have lived a consistently Phoenician life to the end. At the age of thirty-eight he reputedly starved himself to death.

Later, when Rome had been Christianized for some time, two men of a sternly spiritual character much like Zeno's again appeared on the scene: Tertullian and Augustine, both fathers of the church, both Carthaginians.

Tertullian is the more colourful, wild and extreme of the two, an elemental fanatic of the same type as the priests of Baal, the 'most difficult author in the Latin tongue'. An officer's son, he became a presbyter in the service of the church, but seems to have seen this organization principally as an anti-Roman underground movement. 'We are of yesterday,' he writes, 'but we have already spread through the whole world; towns, dwelling places, palaces, governments, academies, even the army.' He roars at his tormentors: 'Torment us, torture us, sentence us, trample on us; your maliciousness is the proof of our innocence.' It sounds as though he would proclaim the cause of his betrayed native city once more before the courts of posterity.

Tertullian was famous above all for his elegant, pungent antitheses. One of these was the sentence '*credo quia absurdum est*', 'I believe because it is absurd [to believe?]', but this is only attributed to him. What he actually said was that he was convinced of the bodily resurrection of Christ, because it appeared so impossible, '*certum est, quia impossibile est*'.

Tertullian was both spiritual and a materialist, a being of contradictions. Like the stoics, whom he despised, he expected nothing from the world and was therefore prepared to seek martyrdom instead of fleeing from it. In order to understand his God completely, he even made the '*sacrificium intellectus*', gave up attempting to comprehend inexplicable phenomena intellectually, and owned to complete irrationality, to unconditional trust in a being whom one could quibble over as little as—the comparison is again unavoidable—over the existence of the inscrutable Baal.

A more moderate and altogether greater and more important figure than Tertullian was his countryman Aurelius Augustinus from Thagaste near Carthage. As a young man, as he writes in his *Confessions*, he 'wallowed in the mire of the streets of Babylon, as if it were sweet-smelling water and precious balm'. He stole, drank, whored and then suddenly decided on the hermit-like life of a high priest in Carthage, and finally died as a greatly esteemed church father in Hippo, when it was besieged by vandals.

He left us, above all, the twenty-one books of his *De Civitate Dei, The City of God*, a Christian counterpart to Plato's *Laws*, the keystone of medieval European philosophy and for a long time virtually the basis of the Catholic Church.

Embedded in his work like a hidden time-bomb, however, was also one of the most explosive theological and philosophical concepts imaginable, the doctrine of predestination, or predetermination. St Paul had introduced it when he wrote (Romans 9:16) that it was not 'of him that willeth, nor of him that runneth, but of God that sheweth mercy' whether he was saved or not. Augustine, developing this theme, thought that not only salvation, but also every instinctive act, every revelation was by God's grace and that Adam had forfeited man's ability to be free from sin. It was a continuation of the age-old controversy as to the limits of man's free will. Luther later almost despaired over it, Melanchthon adroitly overcame the problem, but Calvin made it his central truth, calling it the 'terrible decree'. He taught that the principle of predestination was 'irresistible and inescapable', but that one could judge by one's success in life how much or little one stood in God's grace.

In this way he bridged the gulf between the teaching of

Augustine, nurtured by the Punic tradition, and modern economic ideology. Calvin's theory that everyone could determine from his own material conditions the measure of love God had apportioned to him gave the propulsion to the rocket which carried medieval Europe into the modern era. The 'protestant ethic of capitalism' was established, wealth and the striving for riches theologically justified, and the day was not far off when the 'invisible hand' would be glorified, which was believed by Adam Smith, the father of political economy, and also by modern neo-liberals, to regulate the equilibrium of markets. Its highest altars are in Manhattan. Was it chance, however, that this doctrine was founded by a descendant of precisely that merchant race, which had always been convinced that economic prosperity was the surest sign of godly grace? Our capitalistic ideas are not so very different from those of the Carthaginians.

Augustine was also a true descendant of Hamilcar and Hannibal in that he called his son Adeodatus, the god-given. In Phoenician it would have been Baalyaton, Baal has given him.

It seems therefore that races, especially if they are as gifted as the Carthaginians, do not vanish finally and irrevocably from history, when they are conquered. The Phoenicians did not do so. That can clearly be seen in the country from which they came.

Anyone who goes to the Lebanon can hardly help noticing that he is in one of the homes of world trade. This, the smallest, most beautiful and by far the most lively of Arab Mediterranean states, has as few natural resources as the old Phoenicia and yet has an economic capacity which neither the far richer Iraq nor Syria can rival.

The streets of Beirut, the old Berytus, which the Greeks called Berytos, are packed with traffic. In the Hamra, its main shopping and strolling boulevard, everything is sold which can be sold, from French perfume to Swiss watches and genuine Lebanese hashish. The currency is more stable than the dollar, and if there are occasionally major bank scandals, then they are (almost) on the American scale. The town is international, with French flair, Arab customs; you can even eat sauerkraut there.

The people who live in Beirut are the result of an incredible mixture of races. Persians, Greeks, Romans, Arabs, crusaders, Egyptians, Turks, Britons, Frenchmen have mingled down the centuries in the Lebanon and have produced a type which is not directly descended from the Phoenicians but is a very close match. Courteous, sly, shrewd, elegant, eloquent, they run hotels, antique shops—'Roman coins, sir, very original?'—shipping lines, airlines, breweries, wine businesses, warehouses, bishoprics and some of the most magical nightclubs in the world.

They are very conscious of their history. As the Lebanon is only about half Mohammedan, the other half Christian, the califs are not necessarily regarded as the universal historical prototype, and the people consequently try to relate to their original ancestors, the Phoenicians—indeed are very keen to do so. The largest hotel in Beirut, an atrocious luxury affair, is called 'Phoenicia', and others 'Cadmus' or 'Byblos'. The country's flag has a cedar on it, and the government pays out considerable sums for archaeological research into the age of Hiram, Shipitbaal and Co., and for reconstruction work. The beautiful and famous woods of Mount Lebanon have long since fallen a prey to the woodcutter's saws. Now they are being reforested.

Outside Beirut, where the prosperity which the metropolis displays so blatantly peters out in the dust of Arab villages, particularly in the remote valleys, you still meet people of almost pure Canaanite-Phoenician stock, with aquiline noses, a low hairline and rather slanting eyes. They are not as slippery as the smooth Levantines in the bank foyers, or as effeminate as the slim Adonises, who offer melting, long-lashed glances at the counters of the smart bars, but they are friendly, reserved, proud, immensely hospitable. Even the poorest of them will insist that he pays for the arrack which you have drunk with him.

Down on the coast, however—in Gebeil (Byblos), Tripoli (Tripolis), Saida (Sidon) or Sur (Tyre)—the sleepy orient has established itself. Confectioners' shops are brimming with poisonously bright sweetmeats, people doze in the shade of houses, bits of melon and fish rot in the market places, boats rock in the sluggish harbours and only the children seem to be alive, although a guide will always materialize to ask if one wants to see any 'antiquities'.

The modern Sidonians, moreover, appear to have little in common with their clever ancestors. Saida is regarded as the Gotham of the Lebanon. I have been unable to find out why.

Phoenicia has been absorbed by history; there is still the purple land, washed by the waters of the Mediterranean, where the *murex brandaris* and *murex trunculus* snails live on, spiky baroque creatures with their dye-secreting glands. No one catches them any longer, but in the Beirut souk the finest materials overflow from the traders' shelves just as they used to do: damask from Damascus and muslin from Mussolo. The forebears of many who sell them could have climbed from a ship in Africa or Greece two thousand years ago, and have praised them with the same loquacity with which they are now spread out before foreign tourists.

An archaeologist walks proudly past, having just unearthed another temple foundation or amulet from the sand somewhere with the aid of a European or American grant. He will faithfully hand over everything he finds to the National Ancient History Museum and so widen a little the small crack through which we look back from our present to the still mysterious Phoenician people, the great silent ones of antiquity, who must have been so voluble in their own day.

We are just discovering them for the second time and beginning to deepen the knowledge accumulated—often incorrectly—in the nineteenth century. Phoenician documents have become hot, avidly sought-after property for the museum directors of the western world. From which we may conclude that their authors are about to re-emerge, possibly not under the auspices of a new Phoenicio-mania, but certainly swimming on the crest of a fashionable archaeological wave, and bursting into our consciousness. They will still present us with many riddles to crack, but will offer many surprising revelations, not the least of which will be our growing certainty that they are a part of our own history.

Bibliography

Arrian, *Anabasis Alexandri*, London 1929
Baramki, D., *Phoenicia and the Phoenicians*, Beirut 1961
Barreca, F., *La civiltà di Cartagine*, Cagliari 1964
Baudissin, W. W., *Adonis und Esmun*, Leipzig 1911
Boeckmann, K. von, *Vom Kulturreich des Meeres*, Berlin 1924
Carcopino, J., *Le Maroc antique*, Paris 1948
Clemen, C., *Die phönikische Religion*, Leipzig 1939
Dimont, M., *Jews, God and History*, New York 1962
Dunand, M., *De l'Amanus au Sinaï*, Beirut 1953
Dunbabin, T. J., *The Greeks and their Eastern Neighbours*, London 1957
Eiselen, F. C., *Sidon*, New York 1907
Eissfeldt, O., *Philister und Phönizier*, Leipzig 1936
Eissfeldt, O., *Ras Schamra und Sanchunjaton*, Halle 1939
Flaubert, G., *Salammbô*, Paris 1862
Fleming, W. B., *History of Tyre*, New York 1915
Glueck, N., *The Other Side of Jordan*, New York 1940
Görlitz, W., *Hannibal*, Stuttgart 1970
Graves, Robert, *Greek Myths*, London 1958
Harden, D., *The Phoenicians*, London 1962
Herodotus, *Histories*
Hiltebrandt, Ph., *Der Kampf ums Mittelmeer*, Stuttgart 1953
Hitti, Ph., *Lebanon in History*, London 1957
Jidejian, N., *Byblos Through the Ages*, Beirut 1968
Jidejian, N., *Tyre Through the Ages*, Beirut 1969
Josephus, *Josephus I-III*, Cambridge 1957
Keller, W., *Denn sie entzündeten das Licht*, Munich 1970
Kenyon, K., *Amorites and Canaanites*, London 1966
Livy, *The War with Hannibal*
Lucian, *The Syrian Goddess*, London 1941
Marcuse, L., *Plato und Dionys*, Berlin 1968
Moscati, S., *Sulla storia del nome Canaan*, Rome 1959
Moscati, S., *The World of the Phoenicians*, London 1968

Montet, P., *Byblos et l'Egypte*, Paris 1928
Picard, G. C., *Carthage*, London 1964
Plutarch, *Lives*
Polybius, *The Histories*, Cambridge 1964
Quercu, M., *Falsch aus der Feder geflossen*, Munich 1964
Quintus, C., *History of Alexander*, Cambridge 1951
Renan, E., *Mission de Phénicie*, Paris 1864
Siculus, D., *Diodorus of Sicily*, Cambridge 1963
Schneider, W., *Überall ist Babylon*, Düsseldorf 1960
Schneider, W., *Das Buch vom Soldaten*, Düsseldorf 1964
Schopen, E., *Geschichte des Judentums im Orient*, Berne 1960
Sprague de Camp, L., *Ingenieure der Antike*, Düsseldorf 1964
Virgil, *Aeneid*
Warmington, B. H., *Carthage*, London 1960

Index of Names and Places